TELECOURSE STUDY GUIDE FOR

The Examined Life

FIFTH EDITION

author

J. P. White
Chair, Department of Philosophy
Santa Barbara City College

contributing author

Manuel Velasquez
Professor of Philosophy
Santa Clara University

IN·TELE·COM ®
INTELLIGENT TELECOMMUNICATIONS

This *Telecourse Study Guide for The Examined Life* is part of a college-level introduction to philosophy telecourse developed in conjunction with the video series *The Examined Life*, and the text *Philosophy: A Text with Readings,* eleventh edition, by Manuel Velasquez, The Charles Dirksen Professor, Santa Clara University.

The television series *The Examined Life* was designed and produced by INTELECOM Intelligent Telecommunications, Netherlands Educational Broadcasting Corporation (TELEAC/NOT), and Swedish Educational Broadcasting Company (UR)

Contents

Introduction

THE ADVENTURE

At the dawn of a new century, a new millennium, we bring to this moment of our history nearly 10,000 years of thinking and rethinking the nature of our universe, our world, and ourselves. While vast, elaborate, and complex systems of belief litter the path of our history, we presently face our future with a myriad of belief systems scattered around planet Earth. Not one of the belief systems operative today is without paradox and incompleteness. Yet these systems of belief constitute our understanding and serve as the guides for our actions. *The Examined Life* takes you on an unparalleled adventure of philosophical reflection through the fundamental beliefs and presuppositions that variously underlie all of humanity's various systems of belief. In the company of some of the late twentieth century's finest philosophical minds, you are about to explore *The Examined Life*.

Philosophy, a term believed to have been coined by Pythagoras in the sixth century B.C., comes from two Greek words, *philein*, to love, and *sophia*, wisdom. Philosophy thus means a love of wisdom and marks at least 2,500 years of humanity's passionate commitment to seeking wisdom. But what is wisdom? Who might have wisdom?

Essentially, the history of philosophy indicates that wisdom minimally requires knowledge of both what is and what ought to be. *The Examined Life,* through its 26 episodes, will explore significant philosophical ports of call pertaining to knowledge and value. By embarking upon this adventure, you will experience questions, issues, and viewpoints you may never have considered previously.

In conjunction with Professor Manuel Velasquez's text, *Philosophy: A Text with Readings, The Examined Life* introduces you to specific problems and people who have come to define our philosophical heritage as well as those who are presently defining our philosophical future. Significantly, *The Examined Life* is a problem-based series and not simply an historical narrative. The series is very much alive with its contemporary focus upon issues that are sometimes ancient in their origins yet urgent in their modern application. As the twentieth century Oxford philosopher of history, R.G. Collingwood remarked in *The Idea of History*.

> *In part, the problems of Philosophy are unchanging, in part, they vary from age to age and in the best philosophers of every age these two parts are so interwoven that the permanent problems appear sub specie saeculi, and the special problems of the age sub specie aeternitatis.*

This study guide is one part of the total package you will have available to you when you embark upon the 26 half-hour journeys that make up *The Examined Life*. As a telecourse, this series – in conjunction with your campus instructor as your guide – will also be enhanced by the newly revised eleventh edition of Professor Manuel Velasquez's, *Philosophy: A Text With Readings*. Professor Velasquez has significantly tailored his very popular and thorough text to generously complement *The Examined Life*.

In this Study Guide you will find:

A set of **Learning Objectives**, which will serve as benchmarks for your climb from the unexamined to the examined life.

An Overview of each episode, which highlights the significant concepts and points of view contained in each episode.

Text Links will guide you to relevant sections of the Velasquez text, *Philosophy: A Text With Readings,* for a further, and in most cases more detailed, analysis of the problems and theories under discussion. This scholarly, yet accessible, text also provides an opportunity to read original works, either historical or contemporary.

Key Terms will provide definitions of those philosophical terms which now largely define the professional nomenclature of academic philosophy but may yet be foreign to the novice philosopher.

A **Self-Test** proves a series of questions to assist you in understanding the material in each episode and to provide a method of review.

Paradoxical Pursuits will provide succinct statements of the conflicting points of view brought forth in each episode with suggestions for your further philosophical reflections.

Applied Philosophy will conclude each chapter with suggestions on how you can apply the concepts and theories learned in each episode to other aspects of your life – classes you may be taking, conversations you may have with your family around the dinner table, or just about anywhere reflective people concerned with their intellectual integrity might gather.

Net Links will provide you with addresses to access the rich resource of the Internet. Remember that each site provided here is linked to many other sites. Any one of the websites listed throughout this text will provide even the novice web surfer with potential contacts to the entire world of philosophy.

As Socrates claimed, "The unexamined life is not worth living." *The Examined Life* is the telecourse that will introduce you to the examined life in all of its fascinating and rich detail. Welcome to the adventure. Welcome to *The Examined Life.*

Lesson One

What is Philosophy?

LEARNING OBJECTIVES

Upon completing this lesson, you should be familiar with the concepts contained in the lesson and able to critically discuss:

☞ the distinction philosophers draw between the examined life and the unexamined life.

☞ Plato's Myth of the Cave and its relevance to living the examined life.

☞ at least five of the traditional aspects of the process whereby a person moves from an unexamined life to the examined life.

☞ basic elements of the Socratic method and its application.

☞ the essential role that questions play in defining an examined life.

OVERVIEW

Imagine living your whole life in an apartment with no windows or doors; only electric lights for illumination. All of your information comes from television, and all that ever plays are cartoons in endless variety. You have a few friends who live with you in this apartment but no one knows of the sunny outdoors. The refrigerator and pantry are always stocked with nicely wrapped packages of food and the apartment nicely decorated throughout with artificial plants. You have no idea of what the food products actually are or where they come from, not because you can't get any answers but because the questions never occur to you. You never think of going anywhere because this seems to you all that exists.

One day you're standing alone when part of the wall suddenly slides back. You're grabbed from behind and jerked out of your apartment. Startled and frightened, you are relentlessly pulled up a long hallway to a control center where technicians and support staff work to keep your apartment and other similar apartments functioning. Their booth is illuminated by a large skylight whose filtered sunlight is very harsh compared to what you're accustomed to. You are confused, disoriented. You cannot see very well as you are actually suffering from a condition known as rigid pupilary reflex. The pupils of your eyes have not been exercised as they would have been had you grown up in the complex, ever changing real world of variable natural light. Now your pupils must adapt to this more complex and changing environment. These changes will not, according to the standard prognosis, be comfortable for you.

Again, you are dragged. You pass the technicians' booth. Continuing to squint, as the light hurts your eyes, you can hardly make out who is dragging you so relentlessly. You beg to stop just to get oriented, or plead to go back to the familiarity of your apartment, but they continue to pull you along, up toward an opening that is blindingly bright. Finally, you are tossed out. You can't see a thing but you feel a breeze. This breeze is so very different from the breeze your hair dryer would make. This breeze is not constant but changes in intensity, in temperature, even in smell. The ground also feels different. It is uneven, rough, nothing like your smooth, soft, always-level nylon carpet. Slowly your eyesight returns and you are absolutely stunned by the magnificent onslaught of colors and shades that flood in upon you. The lush panorama stretches to the horizon, the distance of which you had never before imagined. Stunned, you start to smile, then laugh uncontrollably, then finally cry and laugh while muttering, "Reality! So this is Reality!"

What you've just read, as you have no doubt realized since viewing Episode 1 of *The Examined Life*, is an updated variation on Plato's parable, known as the Myth of the Cave. Rather than a cave, we have an apartment; rather than shadows, we have cartoons on television. The question arises here again, 2,250 years after Plato first posed it, would anybody, would you, choose to live out your life at the bottom of Plato's cave, or in the above described apartment? Would you choose to live where your beliefs and thoughts were only directed at shadows or cartoons? Ignorance could perhaps keep one blissful under such conditions but to anyone not ignorant of the alternative, the prospect of such a life of cave or apartment dwelling is no doubt terrifying. The thought of living out one's life under such conditions raises profound questions concerning the value of life itself. As Socrates so eloquently and unconditionally expressed, "The unexamined life is not worth living." Socrates, as we know, gave up his life rather than live the unexamined life, rather than live under conditions of pervasive ignorance.

The prospect of being placed in such a cave or apartment of ignorance awakens in one questions about the role of knowledge in terms of the value of life. For life alone is not worth living, as Socrates reminds us; only the good life is worth living. The good life is not one of ignorance but is the examined life. Socrates inevitably brings this issue directly home to each of us. How extensively have you examined the beliefs that have come to define who you are and how you live your daily life? Has the mass media, the shopping mall mentality, suburban homogeneity socialized you so thoroughly that you live in a world of shadows and don't even realize it? Do you actually live an examined or an unexamined life? Have you fallen prey to such glib, popular views that morals are a matter of how you feel or truth is relative to each of us? Are you, say, a Christian who

believes in one God, because that is how you were raised but had you been raised in India, you would have been a Hindu, believing in many gods? Are we simply socialized cave dwellers oblivious to the processes that have caused our beliefs? Are we ignorant of the questions that might deepen our understanding and thereby provide us with an examined life?

Socrates (469 B.C. to 399 B.C.) has come to historically exemplify this quest for an examined life. Socrates' pursuit is philosophical in the oldest and hence broadest sense of the word philosophical. Philosophy begins in wonderment, as Socrates' student, Plato, pointed out. In that wonderment a question arises but, as Socrates made abundantly clear, not just any answer will do. The acceptable answer is not simply one you may feel comfortable with nor one that you really want to believe. An acceptable answer is ultimately one that satisfies some rational or logical criteria. This reliance upon rational criteria as the test of an answer's acceptability is the primary reason all academic disciplines today award a PhD—the Philosophical Doctorate. Questioning, then searching for rationally defensible answers, is the legacy of Socrates.

Because Socrates would not settle for just any answer, his questions often remained without answers. People sometimes criticize philosophy as consisting of only questions and no answers. Socrates would probably be perplexed by such a criticism and might ask, "And so, what's your point?"

Some questions are very personal; they rattle the foundation of one's belief system. These are the questions that Socrates pursued relentlessly—the questions that finally landed him in prison, facing execution. His questions concerned religious beliefs, and whether or not such beliefs are rational. Socrates encouraged youth to look beyond the shadows of convention and acculturation in the cave, and to expose their beliefs to the light of rational inquiry directed at the truth. For such questioning, Socrates was condemned for impiety and corrupting the youth.

The joy of wonderment, the need to question, the discovery that not just any answer will do are the critical activities that Socrates so vividly exemplified over 2,000 years ago. They still motivate humans to philosophize in its broadest sense. For the philosopher, these activities make life itself worth living. To repeat and emphasize Socrates' point, "The unexamined life is not worth living."

Contemporary philosophers, W. V. Quine, John Searle, Hilary Putnam, Stephen Toulmin, Daniel Dennett, and others describe in this opening episode how they came to philosophy through this same process. Some question initially sparked their sense of wonderment. The realization that not just any answer will do motivated them to search—sometimes for a lifetime—below the surface, behind the shadows.

In this sense, all rigorous pursuers of truth are philosophers and in this sense the Myth of the Cave is about the intrinsic value of education, or, as sometimes translated, enlightenment. Without philosophy in this grand sense there would be no systematic questioning nor would there be the pursuit of answers capable of rational support.

Through Plato, we have inherited a picture of Socrates as someone who relentlessly but systematically both raised questions and evaluated purported answers with such integrity that when finally his own life was held in the balance he chose to die rather than live an unexamined life. Socrates' life and legacy haunts every one of us who are concerned about our intellectual integrity and the quality of our life. Now you must decide for yourself the value of the examined life.

TEXT LINKS

 Turn to Velasquez, *Philosophy: A Text with Readings,* eleventh edition, and read Section 1.1 "What is Philosophy?" How does Velasquez relate Plato's Myth of the Cave to the goal of autonomy? What has autonomy to do with the examined life?

 For a look at an extended example of the Socratic method, turn to Velasquez 1.3 "A Philosopher in Action: Socrates." Included here are selections from *Euthyphro, The Apology,* and *Crito.*

 For a brief discussion of some of the earliest philosophers, see Velasquez 1.5 "Historical Showcase: The First Philosophers." Included are Thales, Heraclitus, and Parmenides as well as a selection from the Upanishad philosophers.

KEY TERMS

Ambiguity: Having more than one meaning in a particular context. The word "pen" is ambiguous in the sentence, "The farmer's pen is empty." Ambiguity is sometimes popularly used to mean vague, but in the study of language vagueness and ambiguity are distinct features. Some have argued that while words, phrases, and sentences can be both vague and ambiguous, concepts and propositions can only be vague and are never ambiguous.

Autonomy: The freedom of being able to decide for oneself by using one's own rationality.

Dogmatism: An inflexibly held position that is not open to inquiry or questioning.

Euthanasia: Good death, in ancient Greek. Today, it has come to be associated with mercy killing.

Explanation: Giving an account of why something taken to be true is true. While all explanations may require descriptions, not all descriptions require or even involve explanations.

Ignorance: Not knowing. Ignorance and stupidity are not treated here as synonyms.

Intrinsic value: The inherent value a thing possesses independent of some external or extrinsic value it might have or bring about.

Metaphysical: Concerning the ultimate nature of reality.

Parable: A story meant to teach a moral or give insight.

Philosophy: A modern variation on two Greek words, *philein,* to love, and *sophia,* wisdom. Hence, philosophy has the traditional definition of being a love of wisdom.

Reasoning: To systematically think about some problem. More specifically, the activity of justifying some position.

Synthesis: The bringing together of conflicting views, claims, and the like to create a new view from those conflicting views. The new view being the synthesis of the old.

SELF-TEST

Multiple Choice

1. According to Socrates
   a. if life could become a party, then life is worth living
   b. too many questions can make life not worth living
   c. fortune and fame alone make life worth living
   d. the unexamined life is not worth living

2. In the Myth of the Cave, Plato describes
   a. a group of curiosity seekers getting lost in the cave of ignorance
   b. a group of people existing in ignorance at the bottom of a cave
   c. a group of persecuted scholars hiding out in a cave
   d. an individual finding the secrets of the universe in the bottom of a cave

3. For Plato, the process whereby an individual leaves his or her state of ignorance will occur by
   a. being dragged out reluctantly and forced into the light of reality
   b. individually breaking lose of the chains of ignorance and bravely pursuing the truth on one's own
   c. conforming closely to what one has been raised to believe
   d. seeking a guru who possesses the ultimate answers

4. The Socratic method primarily focuses upon
   a. answers
   b. clever answers
   c. the most complicated answers
   d. questions

5. For Socrates, the greatest thing a person can do is
   a. having a job that pays a decent wage
   b. question oneself and others to discover what makes us good
   c. accept the status-quo, since the world is never perfect
   d. leave society to meditate and purify oneself

6. According to the Myth of the Cave, the process of getting out of the cave is:
   a. disorienting, painful, frightening, gradual
   b. clear, pleasant, fun, quick
   c. something each individual must do completely alone, in isolation
   d. an act that curious humans do quite naturally

7. Socrates was condemned to death for
   a. giving State secrets to the Spartans
   b. desecrating the temple of Athena
   c. dishonesty and cowardice
   d. impiety and corrupting the youth

8. While the Oracle at Delphi claimed Socrates was the wisest of men, Socrates came to accept this as true because he
   a. knew, he knew
   b. knew he knew more than most people
   c. knew, he didn't know
   d. didn't know he knew, he knew

9. Philosophy consists of all of the following except
   a. thinking
   b. reasoning
   c. facts
   d. arguing

10. The primary value of philosophy is
    a. extrinsic
    b. monetary
    c. vocational
    d. intrinsic

True or False

These questions are only from the reading assignment in Velasquez, Sections 1.1 and 1.3. Specific page references are given in the answer key.

11. The female Greek philosopher, Perictione, wrote that while other subjects study a particular aspect of the world, philosophy is concerned with all that exists.

12. *The Republic* shows Socrates at his trial, defending his life-long commitment to philosophy.

13. Socrates asks Euthyphro to identify the characteristic that makes all beautiful things beautiful.

14. In *The Apology*, Socrates argues that the unexamined life is not worth living.

15. In *Crito*, Socrates argues that we should obey the laws of society because they are established by God.

PARADOXICAL PURSUITS

Some people with Down syndrome, while having very limited IQs, tend to be very pleasant, even joyful. If these are cases of ignorance bringing bliss, would you prefer ignorance and blissfulness to knowledge with its additional burdens? Would you choose to have Down syndrome if you could be guaranteed blissfulness?

Socrates states, "I tell you that wealth does not make you good within, but that from inner goodness comes wealth and every other benefit to man." Jesus asked in the Gospels, "What benefits a person to gain the world and lose her soul?" Do you think Socrates and Jesus share a similar view?

Certain of the philosophers in this series report coming to philosophy as a result of discovering that questions arose regarding beliefs they had previously accepted uncritically. Quine describes being skeptical over his family's religious beliefs, Wong discovered the problem of evil, and Toulmin reacted to his father's dogmatism. What questions of this sort are you facing presently? Be very clear in your answer, then ask this question again after viewing the entire *Examined Life* video series. Have your answers and/or questions changed, increased, decreased?

Which is more important to living the examined life, the art of questioning or the skill in finding an acceptable answer? How do questions shape their answers? Can you give examples to illustrate your claims?

If the pursuit of knowledge is as difficult, gradual, disorienting, and painful as Plato describes in the Myth of the Cave, why do it?

Would you describe your present culture, circle of friends or family as one open to critical inquiry and investigation? If not, what are their limits? If yes, how searching or sophisticated is their inquiry? What types of questions are they typically concerned with?

It was claimed that Socrates often asked questions but no satisfactory answers were ever found though many were suggested. Is it possible that Socrates found no answers to his questions because he was asking the wrong kind of questions?

Quietly reflect and honestly answer, where you are personally more comfortable—at the predictable, cozy bottom of the cave or in the arduous attempt to get out? What actions of yours would support this belief you have about yourself?

Are there limits to examining life? When does the pursuit of knowledge undermine the value of life? When does one become a pedantic bore?

APPLIED PHILOSOPHY

Ask your family and friends what they know about Socrates. In talking with your family or other members of your class, how does your understanding of Socrates compare to theirs?

Try having a discussion with someone during which you don't express your own opinion, but discover the depths of their views by only asking questions.

Tell your friends the Myth of the Cave or describe the story of the apartment, then find out if they believe the examined or the unexamined life is worth living.

Tied to the view of the unexamined life not being worth living is the ancient Greek view that ignorance is the root of misfortune. Reading today's newspaper, how many of the day's misfortunes are tied to ignorance? to someone not thinking clearly?

How often do you become annoyed, frustrated, or even angry because of your own or someone else's failure to think clearly? to not think at all? to act stupidly? Are these all marks of the unexamined life and the loss of life's worth or goodness due to ignorance?

NET LINKS

Check out these Internet sites for additional relevant philosophical information. Remember the Internet is a web. Each of these listed sites is linked to other sites. By surfing you will soon be linked to a resource the vastness of which civilization has never previously had available.

Philosophy Resources:

— http://www.earlham.edu/ ~ peters/phil-inks.htm

This site can link you to the world of philosophy. It is regularly maintained and is very user friendly. It could take you years to exhaust this resource.

— http://www.epistemelinks.com

— http://www.refdesk.com/philos.html

— http://www.erraticimpact.com

Encyclopedia of Philosophy:

— http://www.iep.utm.edu

Philosophy Papers:

— http://philosophy.hku.hk/paper/info.php

— http://cogprints.org/view/subjects/phil.html

Eastern and Western Philosophy:

— http://www.uni-giessen.de/ ~ gk1415/philosophy.htm

This site includes rich references to work in both the Eastern and Western traditions of philosophy as well as information and links to the myriad schools within these two vast traditions. It is also a rather colorful site.

Metaphysics:

— http://plato.stanford.edu/entries/aristotle-metaphysics

— http://mally.stanford.edu

— http://en.wikipedia.org/wiki/Metaphysics

Socrates:

— http://socrates.clarke.edu

Julia Annas:

— http://www.u.arizona.edu/ ~ jannas

David Chalmers:

— http://consc.net/chalmers

An outstanding site.

Paul Churchland:

— http://philosophyfaculty.ucsd.edu/faculty/pchurchland/index.php

Daniel Dennett:

— http://www.2think.org/dennett.shtml

— http://mitpress.mit.edu/e-books/Hal/chap16/author.html

Susan Haack:

— http://www.as.miami.edu/phi/haack

Martha Nussbaum:

— http://www.law.uchicago.edu/faculty/nussbaum

Hilary Putnam:

— http://www.webalice.it/af_gazzola/putnam/home.htm

— http://www.philosophers.co.uk/cafe/phil_jun2002.htm

W.V. Quine:

— http://www.wvquine.org

Richard Rorty:

— http://www.seop.leeds.ac.uk/entries/rorty

Michael Sandel:

— http://kevincmurphy.com/sandel.html

John Searle:

— http://en.wikipedia.org/wiki/John_Searle

— http://globetrotter.berkeley.edu/people/Searle/
searle-con0.html

J.J.C. Smart:

— http://en.wikipedia.org/wiki/J._J._C._Smart

Stephen Toulmin:

— http://en.wikipedia.org/wiki/Stephen_Toulmin

Susan Wolf:

— http://www.philosophy.unc.edu/people/fac-
ulty/susan-wolf

Lesson Two

What is Human Nature?

LEARNING OBJECTIVES

Upon completing this lesson, you should be familiar with the concepts contained in this lesson and be able to critically discuss:

☞ the traditional Greek view of human nature.

☞ the Christian view of human nature and how it arose out of and differs from the Greek view.

☞ the implications of Darwin's principle of natural selection on the traditional western view of human nature.

☞ the significance of the existentialists' claim that existence precedes essence.

OVERVIEW

Risen ape or fallen angel? Is there such a thing as human nature? What do such claims as, "I'm only human after all" or "Just act like a human being" come to? Do the words humanely, humanity, inhuman refer to the presence or absence of something distinctively and significantly human; to a human nature?

Throughout most of our recorded history, we have conceived of ourselves as consisting of two parts, a physical body and a non-physical soul. While many other things have bodies, humans came to be regarded as different, distinctive in their having souls. For most of our ancestors, this soul was believed to survive the death of the body. According to many traditions, the soul was also believed to be immortal. The presence of a soul was the mark of the human.

In the fourth century B.C., the Greek philosopher Plato argued that the soul was contained in the body, like the captain within the body of the ship. Borrowing from his predecessor Pythagoras, Plato held a tripartite view of the soul, describing it as having three parts: appetite, spirit, and reason. Appetite refers to desires, such as the desire for air, nourishment, sleep, shelter, and sex. Spirit refers to more aggressive emotions and feelings such as anger, vengeance, jealousy, and hate. Appetite and spirit were distinct for Plato since two people can have the same desire but have very different emotional reactions to it. The rational part, according to Plato, directs the spirit and appetite. Reason, the rational part, directs spirit and appetite, according to Plato, like a charioteer with two steeds.

Plato's student Aristotle agreed with many of his teacher's views, but broadened his theory because of his own research in biology. For Aristotle, rationality became the defining feature of man. Since everything in nature has its own distinct *telos*, or purpose, Aristotle argued that rationality is man's *telos*. It is what distinguishes man from all other creatures.

Judeo-Christian-Islamic tradition claims in Genesis, the first book of their Bible, that man was made in the image of God. Borrowing from the

9

Greek view, early church thinkers made rationality the feature that is in God's image. The Church also gave a central role to the will and choice. For some, the story of the fall of man in Genesis marks not so much Adam and Eve's failure to reason but rather their willful defiance of God's commands.

St. Augustine, an early church father who lived in the fourth century A.D., was strongly influenced by Platonic views. For Augustine, sin is the result of our inability to control our spirit and appetite. Spirit and appetite are what we share with animals. They are of the body; of the earth. Rationality, which can contemplate the eternal, is divine.

By the thirteenth century A.D., Aristotle's writings had resurfaced in Europe and were strongly affecting the writings of St. Thomas Aquinas. For Thomas, Aristotle's *telos* was a reflection of God's will. Man's purpose or nature is to know God. All motion, causality, all design in the world is the working of the Divine Creator.

While this sense of the uniqueness of human beings has persisted for at least the last three and half millennia, surfacing in various forms in most of the world's cultures, it has not fared well over the last couple of centuries in the West. Belief in a unique human nature has come under attack from most of the social sciences, as well as contemporary philosophers. One of the strongest attacks has come from biology, specifically evolutionary biology, and research related to human evolution.

Tracing human evolution back nearly five million years, proponents of evolutionary biology point to the principle of natural selection at work. One form of this principle was articulated by Charles Darwin in the mid-19th century. According to the proponents of natural selection today, humans are not only risen apes, but ultimately peculiar composites of evolved star dust. While some crucial details may still be missing, the mosaic of scientific knowledge, they argue, is now so complex and powerful in its explanatory and predictive powers that the requisite details are assumed to be forthcoming with more research.

According to the theory of evolution, there is no distinctly human nature as Plato, Aristotle, and the early Church Fathers speculated. Rather, there is an apparently seamless continuity between the human animal and the rest of the kingdom of life. Complex causal patterns give rise to individual variations. Rationality is not a single skill but a concept describing a wide variety of skills or intelligences, with many of these skills possessed in varying degrees by many other species and perhaps now, even some machines. Humans are but a strand in the vast, continuous, complex web of nature, according to the naturalistic view.

Not everyone, of course, accepts Darwin's theory of evolution. Some people have claimed that the theory is mistaken in major ways, and many biologists have expressed serious reservations about many of its details. Nevertheless, the theory of evolution shows how important the natural sciences have become for understanding who and what we are or at least might be.

The quest for understanding who we are includes not only the natural, but also the social sciences. Today, the causal forces shaping the human are readily discussed within the context of not only nature but nurture—nurture within the family, the community, the culture, the greater social milieu. Such discussions of cultural influences go back at least to the seventeenth century French philosopher, Blaise Pascal.

While rationality no longer has wide philosophical support as a unique or divine feature in defining human nature, some twentieth Century thinkers have come to see language and choice as significant features of human beings. For existentialists, the claim is that many of us are condemned to choose. First we exist, then we choose our essence. That is, we are self-defining. There is a universal aspect to the human condition for some existentialists that involves life's condition reflecting ". . . the necessities of being in the world, of having to labor and to die." But there is no universal human nature.

Despite these various theories, questions remain. Do our views mark simply a difference over time or is there progress in our understanding? What do you think? Is there such a thing as human nature and if so, would it prove to be at all interesting or helpful to know?

TEXT LINKS

☞ Turn to Velasquez, *Philosophy: A Text with Readings*, eleventh edition, and read Section 2.2: "What Is Human Nature?" focusing upon the topics, "The Traditional Rationalist View," and "Traditional Western Religious Views of Human Nature." Here you will find a more extended and detailed discussion of the Greek view of human nature followed by a discussion of the Judaic-Christian view. In the section, "The Darwinian Challenge," Velasquez details the impact Darwin's theories have had on these traditional views. The section on "The Existentialist Challenge," describes Sartre's existentialist views, while "The Feminist Challenge" summarizes some feminist criticisms of traditional western views of human nature.

☞ For an in depth look at the views of Plato, Aristotle, and Confucius see Velasquez Section 2.6, "Historical Showcase."

☞ In reflecting on views suggesting that humans are unique, you may wish to read Peter Singer's, *All Animals are Equal*, in Velasquez, Section 7.9.

KEY TERMS

A *priori*: Known independent of sensory experience. Necessary or universal.

A *posteriori*: Knowledge dependent upon sensory experience.

Essence: A property or set of properties that define what a thing is.

Existence: To be, actuality.

Existentialism: Primarily a twentieth century philosophical movement in which concerns about the nature and condition of human existence are central. Existentialism tends to deny that there is a human nature, claiming that existence precedes essence.

Free will: The view that at least some human acts are not completely determined.

Human nature: Generally, that which is distinctive, significant, and serves to define what it is to be human.

Metaphysics: The study of the ultimate nature of reality.

Mental: Used to describe the activities of the mind or cognition.

Rationality: The use of reason or the rules and principles of logical thinking

Soul: a distinct non-physical thing or substance that traditionally constitutes the person and is what sur-

vives the death of the body and retains the identity of the self.

Teleology: The view that the universe is permeated with purpose and is contrasted with **Mechanism**.

Telos: (Greek) A thing's purpose, or goal.

Theory of evolution: Traditionally attributed to Charles Darwin as the theory that accounts for the development and survival of living species.

Virtue: For Aristotle, an excellence either in terms of rationality, the intellectual virtues like wisdom or excellence in action, the moral virtues like courage, justice, and the like.

SELF-TEST

Multiple Choice

1. The traditional study of human nature has been an attempt to
   a. account for why humans are the only animals that smile
   b. discover if there is anything distinct and significant about humans
   c. understand how humans have affected nature
   d. account for why humans typically come in two genders

2. According to the traditional Greek view, the soul was
   a. a single, unified thinking thing
   b. pure synthetic unity of apperception
   c. a bundle of perceptions
   d. composed of three parts: aggression, appetite, and reason

3. Plato compared the parts of the soul to
   a. a wine cask leaking at a party
   b. a chariot with a charioteer and two horses
   c. three dancing nymphs at a Bacchus festival
   d. Poseidon's trident

4. According to Aristotle, reality is permeated with
   a. *telos*
   b. agape
   c. *ideotes*
   d. sin

5. For the Greeks, the essence of human nature was
   a. pleasure
   b. emotion
   c. appetite
   d. reason

6. According to the Judaic-Christian-Islamic view of human nature, humans are
   a. created in the image of God
   b. rational animals
   c. creatures whose existence precedes their essence
   d. different only in degree from other animals

7. The Judaic-Christian-Islamic view of human nature differed from the traditional Greek view in that it emphasized our
   a. natural desire for war
   b. capacity to reason
   c. capacity for choice
   d. need for leisure

8. According to the traditional Christian view, as espoused by Aquinas, it is an essential aspect of human nature to
   a. want to know God
   b. want to make money
   c. be a politician
   d. take philosophy classes

9. The theory of natural selection claims that
   a. humans are the most important animals on earth
   b. there is a difference in kind between humans and all other creatures
   c. there is a difference in degree between humans and all other creatures
   d. societies with big bombs are the most superior

10. By the twentieth century the view that there is something significant and distinct about humans
    a. is embraced by most thinkers
    b. is viewed with skepticism
    c. has been proven by social scientists
    d. has been adequately answered by Sigmund Freud

11. For existentialists
    a. humans are self-defining creatures
    b. humans must do good works to attain salvation
    c. the soul, while not immortal, can live for over two centuries
    d. the soul and the mind are the same thing

True or False

These questions are only from the reading assignment in Velasquez, Section 2.2. Specific page references are given in the answer key.

12. Plato believed the self consisted of reason, appetite, and desire.

13. Saint Augustine borrowed Plato's view that humans have an immaterial and immortal soul.

14. According to Darwin, humans are the products of a purposeful plan.

15. Darwin wrote: "Existence precedes essence."

16. According to the existentialist view, humans create their own nature.

PARADOXICAL PURSUITS

Are we risen apes or fallen angels? Could we be both? For the sake of truth, and your intellectual integrity, make your view clear and provide your strongest defense.

❧

In the context of Aristotle's negative views regarding women and his justification of slavery (recall Bernard Williams remarks) what do you think James Rachels meant when he said, "Aristotle was a smart guy. Aristotle was smarter than me and you and anybody who's gonna see this program . . ."?

❧

At one time in our history, our ancestors believed there was something distinctive and significant about humans. They also believed that the earth was at the center of the universe. Today neither of these views is widely accepted. Are these beliefs similar in that each will be relegated to our past?

❧

Could Aristotle have been wrong about the presence of *telos* in nature but correct about *telos* in humans?

⁓

Could humans have traits that are quite distinctive to being human, but insignificant and irrelevant in answering the question of human nature? What would Aristotle say? What is the relationship between something having a purpose or *telos* and its having some defining or distinctive trait(s)?

APPLIED PHILOSOPHY

Ask your friends and family if they believe there is such a thing as human nature. Do they tend to emphasize the spirit, the appetite, rationality, will or . . . ?

⁓

Ask your psychology, biology, or sociology professor if he or she believes in souls. Does he or she have an answer to the question of human nature?

⁓

According to Sartre, we create who we are. Who are you? Are you trustworthy, honest, generous, kind, loving, supportive of others, positive, rational? Must you choose such traits or do they come naturally to you? Who should you be? How would others describe you?

⁓

In the film, *The Elephant Man*, the horribly disfigured John Merrick finally screams out after ruthless torment, "I am not an animal!" What is the significance of that remark to a discussion of human nature?

⁓

Do you believe there is such a thing as human nature? If not, what would you tell Plato, Aristotle, Augustine, Aquinas? If you think there is such a thing as human nature, what would you tell Rorty, Searle, Dennett, Churchland, Sartre? Make your reasons clear.

NET LINKS

Check out these Internet sites for additional relevant philosophical information. Remember the Internet is a web. Each of these listed sites is linked to other sites. By surfing you will soon be linked to a seemingly vast resource.

Philosophy Resources:

— http://www.earlham.edu/ ~ peters/phil-inks.htm

— http://www.epistemelinks.com

— http://www.refdesk.com/philos.html

— http://www.erraticimpact.com

Encyclopedia of Philosophy:

— http://www.iep.utm.edu

Philosophy Papers:

— http://philosophy.hku.hk/paper/info.php

— http://cogprints.org/view/subjects/phil.html

Evolution:

— http://evolution.berkeley.edu

— http://www.pbs.org/wgbh/evolution

Existentialism:

— http://www.dividingline.com/

Greek Philosophy:

— http://www.friesian.com/greek.htm

— http://www.iep.utm.edu/greekphi

St. Thomas Aquinas:

— http://plato.stanford.edu/entries/aquinas

Aristotle:

— http://www.ucmp.berkeley.edu/history/aristotle.html

— http://www.philosophypages.com/ph/aris.htm

Jean Paul Sartre:

— http://www.dividingline.com/private/Philosophy/Philosophers/Sartre/sartre.shtml

Socrates:

— http://socrates.clarke.edu

— http://www.philosophypages.com/ph/socr.htm

Julia Annas:

— http://www.u.arizona.edu/ ~ jannas

Paul Churchland:

— http://philosophyfaculty.ucsd.edu/faculty/pchurchland/index.php

Daniel Dennett:

— http://www.2think.org/kom.shtml

— http://mitpress.mit.edu/e-books/Hal/chap16/author.html

Ian Hacking:

— http://www.en.wikipedia.org/wiki/Ian_Hacking

James Rachels:

— http://www.uab.edu/philosophy/faculty/rachels

— http://www.jamesrachels.org

— http://en.wikipedia.org/wiki/James_Rachels

Richard Rorty:

— http://www.seop.leeds.ac.uk/entries/rorty

John Searle:

— http://globetrotter.berkeley.edu/people/Searle/searle-con0.html

— http://en.wikipedia.org/wiki/John_Searle

Nicholas Smith:

— http://www.phil.mq.edu.au/staff/smith.htm

Lesson Three

Is Mind Distinct from Body?

LEARNING OBJECTIVES

Upon completing this lesson, you should be familiar with the concepts contained in the lesson and be able to critically discuss:

- the nature of Cartesian dualism and the problem of interactionism.

- the traditional view of materialism and a modern refinement in Gilbert Ryle's logical behaviorism.

- the view of artificial intelligence, and the relevance of the Turing Test.

- the Chinese Room problem and the problems of programming common sense for artificial intelligence views.

- the strengths and weaknesses of reductionists' accounts of mental activity.

OVERVIEW

"I'm overweight." "I need to exercise this old body of mine." "You look so beautiful tonight." "I don't care what you think, just get your body out there and hold that line!" Such remarks may have meaning to you; they may even sound familiar. Ordinary language, however, suggests two underlying and ap-parently incompatible views of what we are, and of what reality might ultimately consist of. Are we minds, separate but seemingly related to our bodies/brains, or are we just bodies/brains that simply function in highly complex ways? Did this subtle physical complexity fool our less sophisticated ancestors into believing we were something more than just bodies? Or have we been intellectually seduced by modern science into thinking we can make all of reality fit into the little box of science? Is mind distinct from body?

To say someone is overweight or beautiful seems to suggest the person simply is his or her body. Yet if I say I need to exercise this old dog of mine, all things considered, I don't claim to be my dog, but rather my dog is something that belongs to me. Hence, "I need to exercise this old body of mine" suggests this body is something that belongs to me. If I don't exercise my body, it too, like my dog, will be something I will have to watch journey to Blubberville. But what then am I? Am I actually a thing distinct from my body? Do I, as a thinking person, exist independently of my body? How do I interact with my body?

If I am not a thing distinct from my body, then how is the salvation or damnation of my soul possible? What is there to be reincarnated, if I am simply my body? The question raised in this episode of *The Examined Life* is one that not only carries profound implications for a large number of belief systems, but involves a belief that typically serves as an assumption for most of the world's major religions. There is much at stake here as civilization searches

15

for the truth as to whether or not mind is distinct from body.

In the seventeenth century, René Descartes—the father of modern philosophy and one of the major contributors not only to the Scientific Revolution but to the discipline of mathematics with his formulation of analytic geometry and Cartesian coordinates—argued for the position of metaphysical dualism. Descartes claimed that reality consisted of two kinds of things. There was body, which existed in space and time and whose essence was to be extended. But there was also the self, the mind or soul, which existed in time but not space and whose essence was thinking.

In his first *Meditation*, Descartes presented a number of skeptical arguments, which raised a specter of doubt that lingers to this day. Despite this doubt, Descartes argued further that no skeptic could shake his clear and distinct idea of himself as a thinking person. He could doubt the existence of his body, but it was inconceivable, to him, that he could doubt that he was doubting. Hence, reality consisted of two substances in Descartes' dualistic metaphysics: mind and matter.

What seemed equally clear was that mind and body—body being that clump of matter most closely related to us—interacted. But where and how? Descartes claimed it all took place in the tiny pineal gland at the top of the brainstem. According to Descartes, ". . . it [the pineal gland] thrusts the spirits which surround it toward the pores of the brain. . . ." However, according to some theorists, the thrusting spirits or any other version of causal interaction between a mind and a body, seem to violate certain fundamental laws of nature. For some of Descartes own contemporaries, it also seemed inconceivable that something not spatial—the mind—could be someplace spatial to interact with a body. This problem of interaction between mind and body has haunted dualism over the centuries.

As the new science grew, with its metaphysical materialist assumptions, a contemporary of Descartes', Thomas Hobbes, argued that, like all reality, humans are matter in motion. There is only one kind of thing, matter, and it variously moves in accordance with the laws of nature. Humans are composites of matter, configured by the laws of nature, according Hobbes.

By the twentieth century, metaphysical materialism was gathering strong support not only from the neurosciences, but from the philosophical theory of logical behaviorism, as well as the budding study of artificial intelligence. According to Gilbert Ryle in *The Concept of Mind*, our mental language—the language we use to talk about our minds—when correctly understood, is actually about our behavior or our dispositions to behave. Thus to claim that Sally is jealous or Sally is in love isn't to refer to some private mental experience, to some ghost in a machine, as Ryle characterized Cartesian dualism, but rather, to behaviors or dispositions to behave given specific cues. It's through such behavior that we learn what mental terms mean, Ryle argued. If our mental language was actually about private mental episodes, then, according to Ryle, we could never learn to use such a language.

By the end of the twentieth century, behaviorism seemed unable to account for a certain residue of consciousness which Descartes had emphasized. However, the neurosciences and artificial intelligence continued mounting the materialist offensive. In the 1970s and 1980s, artificial intelligence advocates were claiming that the mind is really just the software that the brain, the hardware, is running. This computational model of the mind has proven intellectually seductive as computers grow in sophistication and their capacity for growth and change seems limitless.

However, like Descartes' clearly articulated model of dualism, some of the clearly articulated models of artificial intelligence are vulnerable to fundamental conceptual flaws. John Searle argues in his Chinese Room example that at most a computer can manipulate symbols and marks, but it is unable to understand their meanings. For humans, it is the meaning in language that is crucial to our mental lives, and not simply following rules for manipulating words and marks in our language. For Hubert Dreyfus, it is conceptually impossible to program mental capacities like common sense or a sense of relevance into a computer.

From the neuroscience point of view there are significant differences in how mind and computer physically organize and distribute information. A computer primarily distributes its computational load over time since it processes information electronically essentially at the speed of light. The brain, an organic entity, is comparatively slow, and thus primarily distributes its load over space and not time. Thus, some agree, it processes information all at once over billions of neural connections. But even here there is no consensus regarding the level at which purported mental activity occurs. Is it at the neuron level, at a sub-neural level, in neural nets or neural columns, or some combination?

While dedicated neuroscientists search for a feasible neural model, there is a growing concern that this entire reductionist attempt to understand all mental activity as physical brain activity may be conceptually impossible. How can any science provide an objective, third-person description of this first-person experience? Is the I, the self, an illusion? Are we at the brink of re-conceptualizing what we are?

TEXT LINKS

Turn to Velasquez, *Philosophy: A Text with Readings*, eleventh edition, and read Section: 2.3, "The Mind-Body Problem: How Do the Mind and Body Relate?" Velasquez discusses Descartes' views on how body and mind relate, as well as Hobbes and various twentieth century materialist views. The section also explains Searle's Chinese Room example.

For arguments for and against substance dualism by contemporary philosophers see Garrett J. DeWeese's and J.P. Moreland's, "The Self and Substance Dualism" and John R. Searle's "The Mind-Body Problem" in Velasquez Section 2.7.

KEY TERMS

Behaviorism: A school of psychology that restricts the study of human nature to what can be observed rather than to states of consciousness.

Common sense: The way of looking at things apart from technical or special training.

Dualism: The metaphysical view that reality ultimately consists of two kinds of things. Within dualism, distinctions are made between substantive and property dualistic views.

Functionalism: A theory that claims humans should be thought of as complicated computers.

Interactionism: The theory that the mind and the body interact, originally associated with Descartes.

Materialism: The metaphysical position that reality is ultimately composed of matter.

Reductionism: The idea that one kind of thing is, or can be defined as, another kind of thing.

Turing Test: A test for judging when a computer has reached the equivalent of a human mind by determining if the outputs a computer generates in response to the inputs it receives are the same as the outputs a human mind would generate in response to the same inputs.

SELF-TEST

Multiple Choice

1. The metaphysical view that claims reality ultimately consists of two kinds of things is
   a. materialism
   b. dualism
   c. pluralism
   d. dadaism

2. The scientific conception of the nature of the mind tends to take the metaphysical view of
   a. dualism
   b. materialism
   c. scepticism
   d. deism

3. The seventeenth century philosopher who gave us analytic geometry and focused much attention upon the theory of dualism was
   a. Thomas Hobbes
   b. René Descartes
   c. David Hume
   d. Hilary Putnam

4. Traditionally, one of the most formidable problems facing any metaphysical theory of dualism is
   a. how mind and body can interact
   b. how a mind can think logically and non-logically
   c. how souls can be immortal
   d. how the body becomes diseased

5. From a scientific point of view, dualism lacks feasibility since it
   a. tends to be defended by religious thinkers
   b. is most strongly associated with the French
   c. apparently violates the First Law of Thermodynamics
   d. claims that bodies are essentially extended.

6. Thomas Hobbes, a contemporary and critic of Descartes, argued that reality ultimately consists of
   a. matter in motion
   b. bodies and disembodied spirits
   c. only ideas and the minds that think them
   d. people, who possess minds and objects, which have no minds.

7. Which of the following contemporary theories of the mind would be considered a version of metaphysical materialism?
   a. behaviorism
   b. dualism
   c. pluralism
   d. idealism

8. A fundamental problem with all forms of behaviorism is
   a. accounting for the subjective feature of all consciousness
   b. developing adequate schedules of reinforcement
   c. accounting for immortality
   d. the theories are complex and not fun

9. The Turing Test for determining artificial intelligence involves
   a. creating organic computers
   b. requiring a computer to have limited visual experience
   c. requiring that information be computed at a speed of at least 200 megahertz
   d. being unable to distinguish between the responses of a computer and those of a human

10. According to John Searle's Chinese Room argument
    a. the Chinese language is much more complex than English
    b. the Chinese Room demonstrates that computer language also has semantics
    c. computers only manipulate formal symbols
    d. syntax and semantics are synonyms

11. A fundamental distinction between a computer processing information and the brain processing information is that
    a. the brain distributes its load over time but a computer distributes over space
    b. the computer distributes is load over time but a brain distributes over space
    c. the brain transmits information at the speed of light
    d. the computer is dependent upon neural transmitters

12. Theories claiming that mental phenomena are really some type of physical phenomena are considered to be
    a. reductionistic theories
    b. synthetic theories
    c. ad hoc hypotheses
    d. dualistic and Cartesian

True or False

These questions are only from the reading assignment in Velasquez, Section 2.3. Specific page references are given in the answer key.

13. Descartes held that thinking is part of the essence of the self.

14. Traditional dualism holds that a human is composed of a material body and an immaterial mind.

15. According to J.J.C. Smart there is a contingent identity between sensations and brain states.

16. Hilary Putnam uses the example of a "superactor" and a "superspartan" to prove behaviorism is true.

17. Functionalism holds that we should explain mental activities and states in terms of inputs and outputs.

PARADOXICAL PURSUITS

If our mental life is a complex activity of brain states, how is it possible for anyone to dream in images? Where would those images be? If they are in your brain, how are they illuminated?

❧

If consciousness is a neural process, does that mean that self-consciousness involves neurons being aware of other neurons?

❧

According to traditional dualism the mind is a non-spatial thinking thing. If one takes that position of dualism, does that then mean that asking where the mind and body interact is analogous to asking if Thursday is taller than purple? That is, it is non-sense to ask where a non-spatial thing is?

❧

Are you a dualist or a materialist, or do you hold some other view? If your answer is another view, is your view free of the difficulties that plague the views of dualism and materialism presented in this episode?

❧

Has the growth of science made every form of dualism untenable?

❧

Must science rest upon a metaphysical view of materialism?

APPLIED PHILOSOPHY

Ask your priest, rabbi, minister, or spiritual leader what his or her metaphysical views are regarding the mind/body relationship. Ask one of your science instructors what his or her views are regarding the mind/body relationship. How adequately does each resolve the traditional philosophical problems found in these positions?

❧

What metaphysical position is most popular among your friends? How articulate are your friends regarding this debate?

❧

If you believe we have life after death—that is that there is a heaven or hell or reincarnation—must you also accept dualism? If you know someone who believes in life after death, is that person a dualist or a materialist?

❧

It may be that both dualism and materialism are false. Can you think of a viable alternative theory that does not face the problems each of them seem to face?

❧

What, metaphysically, are you?

NET LINKS

Check out these Internet sites for additional relevant philosophical information. Remember the Internet is a web. Each of these listed sites is linked to other sites.

Philosophy Resources:

— http://www.earlham.edu/ ~ peters/phil-inks.htm

— http://www.epistemelinks.com

— http://www.refdesk.com/philos.html

— http://www.erraticimpact.com

Encyclopedia of Philosophy:

— http://www.iep.utm.edu

Philosophy Papers:

— http://philosophy.hku.hk/paper/info.php

— http://cogprints.org/view/subjects/phil.html

Cognitive Science:

— http://cns-web.bu.edu

Dualism:

— http://plato.stanford.edu/entries/dualism

Metaphysics:

— http://plato.stanford.edu/entries/aristotle-meta-physics/

— http://mally.stanford.edu

— http://en.wikipedia.org/wiki/Metaphysics

Neuroscience:

— http://plato.stanford.edu/entries/neuroscience

— http://www.moge.org/okabe/lab/index.html.en

— http://www.petemandik.com/philosophy/papers/brookmandik.pdf

David Chalmers:

— http://consc.net/chalmers

Paul Churchland:

— http://philosophyfaculty.ucsd.edu/faculty/pchurchland/index.php

Daniel Dennett:

— http://www.2think.org/kom.shtml

— http://mitpress.mit.edu/e-books/Hal/chap16/author.html

John Searle:

— http://globetrotter.berkeley.edu/people/Searle/searle-con0.html

— http://en.wikipedia.org/wiki/John_Searle

Lesson Four

Is There An Enduring Self?

LEARNING OBJECTIVES

Upon completing this lesson, you should be familiar with the concepts contained in the lesson and be able to critically discuss:

- the philosophical perplexity concerning an enduring self.

- the role that the idea of an enduring self plays in legal, moral, and religious contexts.

- the criterion of memory in accounting for an enduring self.

- the enduring self as illusion.

- contemporary alternative explanations to account for the idea of an enduring self.

OVERVIEW

"Please sweetheart, I have got to finish writing this chapter," I try consoling my daughter.

"But," she pleads, "you have been working on it forever."

Joking, I smile, "I'm not that old. I've only been working on this chapter for two days."

"Don't forget the day before and the day before!" she corrects.

"That was a different chapter."

"I probably won't even be your little girl by the time you get finished!" With guillotine precision, she cuts-off our conversation.

"I probably won't even be your little girl by the time . . ." her remark echoes in my memory. Isn't there something that will endure, that will remain unchanged over time? Won't she in some sense always be herself, a soul, perhaps even immortal? If immortal, then this enduring self will not be changing substantially for eternity. And wasn't it truly I who wrote those other chapters over previous weeks? And isn't it the same you that will watch and study the different episodes of *The Examined Life*? Yet, as a result of this educational experience, you will indeed change. So what is it that remains the same in the midst of so much change?

Philosophers, both Western and Eastern, have searched long and hard, over many centuries, for this enduring self. This self has proven extremely elusive. Nonetheless, our natural languages, our legal, moral, and religious systems, our concepts of responsibility and promises, all seem to support, if not require, some enduring self. Who is punished with eternal damnation, rewarded with heavenly salvation, or reincarnated to work out karma, if not some enduring self? Who stands before the judge for sentencing but the very same person who purportedly committed the crime, perhaps days or in the case of Klaus Barbie, the Nazi war criminal, decades before his sentencing?

Plato on occasion utilized the notion of reincarnation, and Socrates does at least entertain the possibility of life after death. However, it is Socrates

21

who nevertheless raises the central philosophical problem regarding the actual existence of an enduring self. As Socrates asks, what is it that remains unchanged or endures through a lifetime of changes in both our body and soul?

For some philosophers, like René Descartes, knowledge of the self or soul, and its existence, is known with certainty. "I am, I exist. This is certain," Descartes claimed in his *Second Meditation*. The mind itself is a mental substance that endures through time and remains the same through all the changes we undergo. In Descartes' philosophy, then, we are the same person from one day to the next because we continue to have the same mind or soul from one day to the next.

In the late seventeenth century, John Locke, an English philosopher and the father of modern British empiricism, attempted to give an alternative account of the nature of the enduring self. Locke argued that Descartes' mind-substance is not what makes us remain the same person through time. What then is it than holds the various pearls of past experience together, thereby making our life a single necklace as opposed to only a collection of loose pearls? For Locke, memory is the thread that holds the seemingly independent pearls of past events, experiences, and feelings. Memory creates the enduring self.

Forms of dementia or Alzheimer's may, in part, support Locke's claim regarding the role of memory. As these diseases set in and destroy memory we tend to describe such situations as the loss of self. As Patricia Churchland, philosopher and neurologist, points out, the afflicted person slowly ebbs away, slowly ceases to exist. However, Churchland and many others doubt that there actually is such a thing as a distinct, independent self that could also endure over time.

This skeptical attack on the very idea of a self, enduring or not, was powerfully mounted by David Hume, an eighteenth century empiricist. First, Hume doubted that memory could serve the role Locke claimed for it. Don't we, after all, talk as if our identity reaches beyond the lapses, even the termination points in our memories? Second, when Hume looked inward, he did not find any enduring idea of a self. He found only passing experiences, and thus concluded that the idea of an enduring self was psychological fiction.

Patricia Churchland agrees with Hume. In discussing ordinary perception, she points out that when you claim to see someone across a room smiling at you, you arc not having a single perceptual experience. Rather, your perception of the whole is actually a mosaic of smaller perceptions resulting from your eye moving on average three times per second and your brain then integrating these distinct visual messages into what seems to be a single image. The same kind of integration may be carried out by the brain over the course of time, blending distinct experiences to create the illusion of an ongoing, enduring self.

Other thinkers are willing to accept neurology as the complete story regarding our mental life. (See Episode 3 of *The Examined Life,* "Is Mind Distinct from Body?") They are also reluctant to embrace Descartes' notion of a substantive enduring self. For Richard Rorty, the self is just a name for a variety of relationships amongst our beliefs and desires. Since names are parts of language, Rorty argues, an infant who is not taught a language will not have a self.

Other thinkers, like Daniel Dennett, take a view more typical of contemporary philosophy. Dennett compares our concept of an enduring self to a whirlpool with water continuously flowing through it. The self, not being a specific thing, creates a type of unity in the stream of continuous experiences. Just as the whirlpool is dependent upon the continual flow of water, so is this unity of self dependent upon the flow of experiences. Questions arise. Is this unity of self thus to be understood in terms of a space and time? If, for example, there is a drought and the creek dries up, then the rains return and with them a whirlpool in the same spot, would we judge it to be the same whirlpool? It would seem not to be the same whirlpool, but perhaps a similar whirlpool. Now what do we say about the self after a night of sound sleep, a sort of drought of experience? In the morning are we the same self or a similar self? Is the whirlpool a bad analogy, or do we need to reconceptualize what the self actually is?

Some scholars have argued that the philosophical view of the nonexistent self is also found in some Eastern views such as Buddhism. Massao Abe, a Buddhist philosopher, tells the story of a young man who couldn't find his head until he realized he was looking for his head with his head. This Buddhist story illustrates the confusion between not having knowledge of something because it is elusive, and not having knowledge of something because it is an illusion.

In the rock garden at the Ryoan-Ji temple in Kyoto, there are a total of fifteen stones, but no matter where you stand, you can only see fourteen. According to some disciples, the fifteenth is considered to be the self. It illustrates that the self, the fifteenth stone, actually exists, but is ever elusive, never seen.

Is the self an illusion or just ever elusive? Is the self a creation of language, or a kind of whirlpool in the flow of experience? Who are you?

TEXT LINKS

☞ Turn to Velasquez, *Philosophy: A Text with Readings,* eleventh edition, and read Section 2.4, "Is There an Enduring Self?" This section provides an extended discussion of the traditional philosophical problems of personal identity including Plato's view along with a number of thought experiments. A discussion of Descartes' view of the soul as the enduring self is included along with an analysis of the strengths and weaknesses of John Locke's claim for memory as the criterion for identity. Views which claim that there is no enduring self, found in both Buddhism and David Hume's work conclude this section. The section ends with provocative essay questions.

☞ Section 5.6, "Historical Showcase" provides biographical information along with additional descriptions of the philosophical views of David Hume.

KEY TERMS

Alzheimer's Disease: A nonreversible, degenerative disease of the central nervous system typically afflicting the elderly and bringing on dementia. Named after the German physician, Alois Alzheimer who died in 1915.

Attribute: A quality or property belonging to a person or thing.

Consciousness: To be aware. As used by Locke in this episode, an awareness of the operation of a mental faculty. Closer here to one sense of self-consciousness.

Dementia: Deterioration of mental faculties due to organic brain disorders.

Elusive: Difficult to capture, to find, to understand.

Enduring: To persist. In the sense of an enduring self to remain the same self over time while allowing for some changes without thereby losing one's identity or self.

Idea: For David Hume a copy of an impression which is thereby less lively and vivid than an impression.

Identity: That which either individualizes us or marks a person or thing as being the same over time. This episode of *The Examined Life* is concerned with identity in the later sense of re-identification and specifically of re-identifying a self or person.

Illusion: An erroneous perception or sense experience.

Impression: For David Hume our lively, immediate perceptions.

Introspection: Looking inward to the contents of one's own mind or mental experiences.

Imperishable: Indestructible, non perishable

Memory: The mental faculty which enables us to recall past experiences or a recalled past experience.

Self: Who each of us is, our identity.

SELF-TEST

Multiple Choice

1. The belief in an enduring self is a claim that the self
   a. is an illusion
   b. remains the same through change
   c. is an integration created by the brain
   d. is a construction of language

2. Plato raised some skeptical concerns about an enduring self because
   a. all parts of our body and soul change dramatically over time
   b. all knowledge was doubtful
   c. when he introspected he could find no invariable idea of a self
   d. memory too often failed

3. Which of the following belief systems tends to support the view of an enduring self?
   a. legal systems
   b. moral systems
   c. religious systems
   d. all of the above

4. For René Descartes the self was
   a. known for certain
   b. ever elusive
   c. only an illusion
   d. a psychological fiction

5. Some philosophers, including John Locke, have argued that personal identity or sameness of self resides in
   a. having the same body
   b. immortality
   c. continuity of memory
   d. a mystical super-glue

6. According to David Hume, if the self is to be known then it is known through
   a. perception
   b. mystical experience
   c. introspection
   d. experimentation

7. According to David Hume, we have
   a. a vivid and lively idea of an enduring self
   b. a certain and distinct idea of an enduring self
   c. a divinely inspired idea of self
   d. no constant and invariable idea of an enduring self

8. Some modern neurological accounts consider the notion of an enduring self to be
   a. an illusory integration created by the brain
   b. a religious object beyond scientific investigation
   c. a mental substance better studied by metaphysicians
   d. that thing which is channeled over time in different bodies

9. Some contemporary philosophical views have argued that our idea of an enduring self is better understood as
   a. a construction of language
   b. a religious object beyond philosophical reflection
   c. a something; I know not what
   d. an object of psychic research

10. The Japanese rock garden of the Ryoan-Ji temple in Kyoto suggests that the self is
    a. illusory and unreal
    b. elusive but real
    c. real but stone cold
    d. holy and capable of salvation

True or False

These questions are only from the reading assignment in Velasquez, Section 2.4. Specific page references are given in the answer key.

11. A person always remains the same person even when the person has total amnesia.

12. The philosopher Diotima argued that "unlike the gods, a mortal creature cannot remain the same throughout eternity."

13. Descartes wrote that "if I should wholly cease to think . . . I should at the same time altogether cease to be."

14. Locke held that what makes a person at one time the same person he is at a later time, is the fact that he continues to have the same soul.

15. According to the Buddha, the idea of an enduring self is an illusion that produces suffering and egoism.

PARADOXICAL PURSUITS

If the self is elusive and never to be seen, why entertain an idea of its reality? Analogously, suppose your car mechanic told you that your car runs badly because you have gombers in your engine. Confused, you ask, "What's a gomber?" When your mechanic tells you they are invisible things that can never be seen because they are elusive yet they are the cause of your car running badly, would you doubt that gombers existed? Would you doubt the sanity, or at least the competence, of your mechanic? Does this differ from saying you have a "self"?

❧

You are the judge in the following purported sales scam. Mr. Smith always wanted to own a genuine Indy race car that had actually raced in the Indianapolis 500. After the Indy race one year, Mr. Smith sought out the owner of car number 54, the car that won the race that year. He insisted on buying the car for one million dollars from its reluctant owner. However, while changing the car's tires, oil, etc., the owner insisted that Mr. Smith could not have car 54 until the entire racing season was over. Disappointed, Mr. Smith agreed and made a half million dollar down payment. The remaining money would be turned over when the car was delivered at the end of the Formula 1 racing season. In its next race, car 54 hit a wall and had to have its entire front end replaced. In the following race, not only was the driver of 54 seriously injured when he was rear-ended during a practice run, but car 54 was unable to even enter that race. During its final race of the season, though it caught fire during a qualification run and needed extensive body work, car 54 went on to win another title. At the end of the season, the owner went to deliver car 54 to Mr. Smith but instead of collecting the remaining half million dollars, Mr. Smith was suing the owner to regain his half-million dollar down payment. Mr. Smith claimed that the owner was trying to pass off another car. You, as the judge, must decide whether the car 54 delivered to Mr. Smith at the end of the racing season is the same car he originally agreed to purchase at the end of the Indy 500 race. Mr. Smith argues that photos taken over the course of the racing season prove that all the parts of car 54 were replaced, and the car is no longer the car he agreed to buy. The owner insists that such changes are a common occurrence, and that everyone who races would agree that he is delivering the now famous car 54 to Mr. Smith. If it is the same car, what makes it the same? Suppose that someone had gathered up all of the damaged parts and reassembled the car, even the burnt hood with its painted 54. Is this the car Mr. Smith actually agreed to pay one million dollars for? What is your verdict? Is there really an enduring car 54?

Try David Hume's thought experiment and look inward; introspect. Do you find something that continues invariably, that endures throughout all of the changes in experience?

Consider Daniel Dennett's analogy to a whirlpool. If there is a sudden surge of water and the whirlpool suddenly disappears, but a whirlpool suddenly forms just a few feet away from the original location, is that the same whirlpool or a different whirlpool? What if a rock on the river bank rolls in, changes the flow of water, and though the whirlpool continues spinning, it moves three feet further into the stream, is it the same whirlpool? What gives a whirlpool its identity over time? Does this analogy of a whirlpool provide any insight for understanding the idea of a self? Can you think of a better analogy?

Does it make sense to imagine all of your memories being in another body but you remaining in your body? Are you just your memories?

Under what conditions would you not hold someone responsible for a crime committed on the grounds that he or she is not the same person that had committed the crime?

APPLIED PHILOSOPHY

How would you decide the case of Tammy Fisher, who was executed in Texas in 1998 for a brutal murder she committed while high on alcohol and drugs? While in prison she became a born-again Christian. Some made the argument that she had changed so completely, it would be wrong to execute the new Tammy for what the old Tammy had done. What does the notion of born-again imply about the notion of an enduring self?

Get out your baby pictures, grade school pictures, high school pictures, and some recent pictures. Make a list of your likes and dislikes during each of these periods in your life. If you believe in an enduring self, show who that constant, invariable you actually is throughout these different times. Try this with your grandparents.

Speak with the elders in your own family or with friends who are elderly and ask them if they believe there is something that remains the same throughout the length of one's entire life.

Ask your priest, rabbi, minister, mullah, or other spiritual leader what his or her views are on the possibility of an enduring self actually existing. What is it that he or she believes is actually saved, damned, or reincarnated?

❧

As an experiment, borrow a small amount of money from a friend and agree to pay it back in a couple of days. When it is time to pay it back tell your friend that you are not the same person and do not repay the debts of strangers. Does your friend agree with your reasoning or at least think it is funny?

NET LINKS

Check out these Internet sites for additional relevant philosophical information. Remember the Internet is a web. Each of these listed sites is linked to other sites.

Philosophy Resources:

— http://www.earlham.edu/ ~ peters/phil-inks.htm

— http://www.epistemelinks.com

— http://www.refdesk.com/philos.html

— http://www.erraticimpact.com

Encyclopedia of Philosophy:

— http://www.iep.utm.edu

Philosophy Papers:

— http://philosophy.hku.hk/paper/info.php

— http://cogprints.org/view/subjects/phil.html

British Empiricism:

— http://www.fiu.edu/ ~ hauptli/IntroductionTo-BritishEmpiricism

— http://en.wikipedia.org/wiki/empiricism

Cognitive Science:

— http://cns-web.bu.edu

Eastern and Western Philosophy:

— http:/www.uni-giessen.de/ ~ gk1415/philosophy.htm

Neuroscience:

— http://plato.stanford.edu/entries/neuroscience

— http://www.moge.org/okabe/lab/index.html.en

— http://www.petemandik.com/philosophy/papers/brookmandik.pdf

René Descartes:

— http://radicalacademy.com/adiphilrationalism.htm

David Hume:

— http://www.iep.utm.edu/h

Socrates:

— http://socrates.clarke.edu

— http://www.philosophypages.com/ph/socr.htm

David Chalmers:

— http://consc.net/chalmers

Patricia Churchland:

— http://philosophy.ucsd.edu/faculty/pschurchland/index_hires.html

Daniel Dennett:

— http://www.2think.org/kom.shtml

— http://mitpress.mit.edu/e-books/Hal/chap16/author.html

Lesson Five

Are We Social Beings?

LEARNING OBJECTIVES

Upon completing this lesson, you should be familiar with the concepts contained in the lesson and be able to critically discuss:

◈ the atomistic and social views on the forming of self.

◈ influences of the historical-social context on the forming of self.

◈ the experience of self-respect when belonging to a valued culture.

◈ problems of multi-culturalism in retaining minority cultural identity.

OVERVIEW

Have you ever heard someone make remarks such as "I wish I had lived one hundred years ago" (or however long)? "Back then I would have . . ." or "I wish I had lived as a pilgrim" (or just fill in the culture/group you'd prefer). Do such wishes rest upon a fundamentally flawed understanding of who we actually are? If the self is molded by its historical-social context, then there appears to be no self which exists independent of its specific historical-social moment. Self is instead like a rose, each petal the product of a complexity of historical-social forces.

Take away the petals, and nothing remains. Hence, to imagine you could change your culture and still remain yourself may reflect a fundamental misconception as to what your identity, your self, actually is.

René Descartes, the father of modern philosophy, set out on a systematic search for a secure foundation for knowledge. Descartes initially was skeptical about nearly all his own beliefs. But he discovered that skepticism could not touch his knowledge of himself. For Descartes, the self is a thing that thinks, wonders, imagines, desires, and feels. The self is a mental substance that performs various mental activities but is not to be mistaken as simply being those activities. By analogy, I can run, walk, crawl, but I am not the run, or the walk, or the crawl. I am not simply the activities but something in addition. (See Episodes 2, "What is Human Nature?" and Episode 3, "Is Mind Distinct from Body?" for more detailed discussions of the self.) Thus, Descartes would probably disagree with the description of the self as only a product of some historical-social context.

Descartes would claim there is a core self that is independent of the historical-social context in which we live, though Descartes readily accepts that context does have an influence. This view of our identity as consisting of some core self is sometimes referred to as an atomistic view. Such an atomistic view of the self would seem to underlie the wish to live in another historical period. Only if there is such an independent kernel of a self, could such a wish make sense. From the atomistic view point, we are not like roses but more like cherries, with a very specific pit—a specific ego or self—at our core.

Ancient Greek philosophers, like Aristotle, argued that we are social creatures by nature, and can be human only when affiliated with social groups like the family and larger units like a city or state. This Greek view constituted one of the early social views of the self.

By the early nineteenth century, at the outset of the Romantic Era, the self was again said to result from social forces. In fact, Wilhelm Friedrich Hegel, an influential philosopher from this period, maintained that a person cannot have an identity independent of a social context. A similar view of the self can be found in Karl Marx's writings, which are borrowed in part from Hegel. For Marx, however, the specific forces shaping a society are quite different from the forces Hegel claimed to have discovered.

This social view of the self explains many of the experiences of contemporary people whose cultures are being displaced. In the case of the Sami, a distinct culture living in northern Scandinavia and northwestern Russia, there is a shared worry that as their cultural ways disappear, they themselves are being lost. As they lose some of their Sami ways, they describe themselves as getting "flattened out," as "becoming something else." Similar, though less drastic, are the experiences of people who visit another culture. After awhile some people will start longing for "home." It may start with wanting their cultural food. If, by chance, they meet someone from their country, or their hometown, they feel a powerful and spontaneous camaraderie that would likely be absent if they had been at home and met the same person. On the other hand, some people will describe themselves as finally "being themselves" or "feeling really at home" once they've left their culture and entered another. Poignant experiences support the powerful influence of historical-social context for the forming of the self.

However, when one culture comes to dominate another culture—either intentionally or unintentionally—and the dominant culture has a negative attitude toward the dominated culture, members of the dominated culture may experience shame and a loss of self. These feelings can arise out of conditions that have no bearing on the group or what someone actually does or believes. Hegel metaphorically describes this experience of being defined by another in his example of the master and the slave. Since slavery is a relationship in which a person's freedom is lost, and thus the person is not free to choose how to define herself or himself, who that

person is, is largely under the control of the master. Since slavery is conventionally understood as a negative circumstance, the feelings of shame and loss of self-respect may cause the slaves to try to change aspects of themselves that cannot be changed. Although the case of the Sami people is less oppressive than slavery, it is still a case of a dominant culture negatively viewing a subculture. A young Sami girl describes how in high school she was so ashamed at being Sami that at night she would use adhesive tape to try and make her eyes grow in the opposite direction.

When one's identity is so determined by one's historical-social context, the contemporary issues of multi-culturalism become delicate yet very urgent. Can unique cultures continue to exist in a world where global communication is instantaneous, international business the norm, and traveling around the planet more and more typical? In this age of vast and fast change throughout every strata of society, perhaps we are all experiencing some subtle sense of cultural loss, a loss of identity. And what do we do about those cultures that do not seem worthy of saving? Nazi culture, the Khemier Rouge, the KKK and other cultures of hate, discrimination, and violence seem better not to exist. How far should the tolerant tolerate the intolerant? Ironically, as liberal, tolerant societies are fast discovering, it may be their unconditional commitment to tolerance that undermines other communities' cultural identity. If freedom of speech and assembly must be tolerated, how can communities that abhor pornography, for instance, rid themselves of that which is protected by such freedoms? Can a larger, tolerant community tolerate well-defined intolerant smaller communities?

As we continue to discover the forces that shape each of our identities, we will be pulled between contrasting views of self—the atomistic view of Descartes and the social view of Hegel. Will the future of planet Earth be one in which a rich mosaic of different cultures will flourish or will there be the emergence of one pervasive, homogenous culture, shaped by a historical-social context of international technology?

TEXT LINKS

Turn to Velasquez, *Philosophy: A Text with Readings,* eleventh edition, and read Section 2.5, "Are We Independent and Self-Sufficient Individuals?" In this section you will find an extended discussion of the atomistic view of the self from the writings of Walt Whitman to the philosophical views of Descartes and Kant. This view is contrasted with the social view of the self as presented by the contemporary philosopher, Charles Taylor, and the historical views of Aristotle and Georg Wilhelm Friedrich Hegel.

KEY TERMS

Atomistic view: As used in this context, the view that the self is a subsistent thing upon which culture can have some influence.

Culture: As used in this episode, the totality of socially transmitted behavior patterns.

Descartes' *Meditations*: A series of six short articles/meditations that Descartes wrote in the late 1630s to summarize some of his views in epistemology and metaphysics.

Age of Enlightenment: An eighteenth century European intellectual movement in which reason was optimistically assumed capable of answering all intellectual and social questions.

Identity: Those features or properties that define an individual as that particular individual.

Sami: A culture of nomadic people living in areas of northern Scandinavia, Finland, and northwestern Russia.

Multiculturalism: The inclusion of many cultures; tolerance of cultural diversity.

Paradox: Beliefs accepted as true, but which are contrary or contradictory.

Romantic Era: In European history, beginning around the turn of the nineteenth century.

Self: As used in this episode, that part of a person that persists or remains the same through change.

Social-historical forces/context: The totality of forces, excluding physical or biological forces, which act in shaping a person at any particular moment in that person's history.

Social view: As used in this context, the view that the self is the end product of a variety of social-historical forces.

Tolerance: To allow.

Universal: Applies in every context. To be true in all possible worlds.

SELF-TEST

Multiple Choice

1. According to the atomistic view of the self, the self is
   a. formed solely by genetic factors
   b. essentially independent of historical-social forces
   c. essentially a reflection of its historical-social forces
   d. the end product of forces of conditioning

2. According to the social view of the self, the self is
   a. formed solely by genetic factors
   b. essentially independent of historical-social forces
   c. essentially a reflection of its historical-social forces
   d. the end product of forces of conditioning

Which view seems most clearly exemplified by the remarks that follow?

   a. the atomistic view
   b. the social view

_____ 3. To be—to actually come from the people we do come from, and not be flattened out and become something else.

_____ 4. Every human being is an individual in a very absolute sense. All my knowledge is founded on things that I myself experience.

_____ 5. You have a closeness all the time in Sami families that you don't have in Swedish families.

_____ 6. The essential thing in us—our ability to reason, to decide what we shall believe and think—that is common to all human beings.

7. The ancient Greeks primarily took
   a. a social view of the self
   b. an atomistic view of the self
   c. no view of the self as it had not yet been discovered
   d. a view that the self was essentially a rugged individualist

8. According to Hegel, the self is best understood in the
   a. atomistic view
   b. social view
   c. Marxian view
   d. biological view

9. Ironically, one of the strongest forces undermining a culture's identity may be
   a. religion
   b. tolerance
   c. war
   d. hunger

10. Descartes' view of the self is a(an)
    a. atomistic view
    b. social view
    c. Marxian view
    d. biological view

True or False

These questions are only from the reading assignment in Velasquez, Section 2.5. Specific page references are given in the answer key.

11. Descartes turned to the company of others and to conversation with others to discover the truth about himself.

12. For Kant the real me is a being who can choose or will for himself.

13. Descartes wrote "I must acknowledge my belonging before I can understand myself."

14. According to Hegel, the self's struggle for freedom is the basis of the rise of masters and slaves.

15. According to Taylor, we can become full human beings only by withdrawing from others and discovering who we really are by turning within and realizing our independence from others.

PARADOXICAL PURSUITS

If our identity—that is, who we are—is formed solely by the historical-social context in which we live, how is it ever possible to think "outside" of that historical-social context? How could I make these remarks, or how is this episode of *The Examined Life* possible, unless the self is more than some historical-social context?

❧

If cultures now consist of subcultures, and the line between culture-subculture and sub-subcultures is unclear, in what sense are we shaped by some historical-social environment? What is a culture in today's complex, industrialized societies?

❧

Do we tend to describe the forming of our self in terms of the atomistic view, while we describe the forming of other selves in terms of the social view?

❧

Is there a middle path between the atomistic and social views? Clearly articulate that view.

APPLIED PHILOSOPHY

Ask your parents what they believe were the strongest influences in shaping your identity. How does that description compare to their description of the strongest influences in shaping their own identities?

❧

Ask your brothers and sisters what they believe were the strongest influences in shaping their identities. How do these compare to your parents' descriptions? Ask your friends the same questions.

❧

Ask someone the questions in the opening sentence of the Overview, so as to elicit his or her view of our identities. Is the respondent's view, assuming it is consistent, most similar to the analogy of the rose or the cherry? Give philosophical descriptions of the rose and the cherry analogies.

NET LINKS

Check out these Internet sites for additional relevant philosophical information. Remember the Internet is a web. Each of these listed sites is linked to other sites.

Philosophy Resources:

— http://www.earlham.edu/ ~ peters/phil-inks.htm

— http://www.epistemelinks.com

— http://www.refdesk.com/philos.html

— http://www.erraticimpact.com

Encyclopedia of Philosophy:

— http://www.iep.utm.edu

Philosophy Papers:

— http://philosophy.hku.hk/paper/info.php

— http://cogprints.org/view/subjects/phil.html

Culture Studies:

— http://hirsch.cosy.sbg.ac.at/www-virtual-library_culture.html

Greek Philosophy:

— http://www.friesian.com/greek.htm

Aristotle:

— http://www.ucmp.berkeley.edu/history/aristotle.html

— http://www.philosophypages.com/ph/aris.htm

René Descartes:

— http://radicalacademy.com/adiphilrationalism.htm

Georg Wilhelm Friedrich Hegel:

— http://www.hegel.org

Lesson Six

What is Real?

LEARNING OBJECTIVES

Upon completing this lesson, you should be familiar with the concepts contained in the lesson and be able to critically discuss:

☞ the metaphysical problem of the ultimate nature of reality.

☞ the metaphysical views of both materialism and idealism.

☞ the view that language is the source of metaphysical confusion.

☞ the distinction between realists and antirealists.

☞ the claim that reality is a social construct.

OVERVIEW

In the middle of the night, I comfort my son, "Don't be afraid. It was only a dream." While many of us discovered early in life that Santa Claus is not real, we are also aware of the tremendous variety of beliefs concerning spirit worlds and dimensions of reality that different cultures hold. Nonetheless, we believe that there is a significant distinction between what is real and what is not real. It may even seem obvious. However, when we begin to systematically and critically search for the line between the two

when we begin to itemize what we would consider to be real (physical objects, events, numbers, concepts, relationships), we discover that sharp, clean categories are a bit elusive.

Metaphysics is the branch of philosophy that rationally pursues the basic or ultimate nature of reality. Thus far in our journey into *The Examined Life*, we have encountered views that claim the mind and its ideas are metaphysically distinct from physical or material things. Thinkers who argue that there are two types of real things are called dualists. Monists claim that only one type of thing is real. If that one real thing is matter, the monist would also be termed a materialist; if only mind is real, an idealist. A pluralist claims that what is real includes more than what a dualist would be willing to accept. So, what is real?

By the fifth century B.C., human beings were beginning to think philosophically, and specifically, metaphysically. Democritus, who defended the monist position of materialism, believed that all of reality is constructed out of atoms. The word "atom" is Greek for uncuttable. Atoms are the smallest existing things and are what, in various combinations, make up everything else including earth, air, fire, humans.

Materialism was not the dominant metaphysical view during the Middle Ages. It is incompatible with religious assumptions about reality that tend to be dualistic. (See Episode 3, "Is Mind Distinct from Body?" for a closer look at dualism.) Materialism, nonetheless, returned to prominence after the Renaissance, which marked the rebirth of classical

33

thinking. Its prominence grew during the century alongside the rise of modern science. One of modern materialism's earliest and most able spokespersons was the English philosopher, Thomas Hobbes.

According to Hobbes, only matter exists, and it is in motion. Hence, all that is real can be accounted for in terms of matter or matter in motion. The human body, for example, is a machine moved by the subtle movements of other bits of matter in motion. If a person uses words like soul, mind, or thought to refer to nonmaterial things, Hobbes claimed, then that person does not know what she or he is talking about. For Hobbes, such words can only refer to the brain and its motions.

Yet there remains a kind of residue of the mental. What does one say about dreams, memories, intentions? If I describe my dream last night of flying over jagged, snowy peaks against a mountain panorama, a materialist like Hobbes would have to explain how matter in motion (neurons firing, to use a more contemporary description) constitutes or creates these dream images. Or, if we are sometimes self-conscious, how can one neuron or neural network know another neuron or neural network? The notion of neurons or any sort of matter accounting for these mental phenomena seems impossible to imagine. As David Chalmers remarks in this episode, "to generate consciousness, you have to go beyond the fundamental ingredients of physics."

Now if we start with consciousness—or our ideas, to use an older expression—then, as George Berkeley argued, it's difficult to imagine material or physical reality existing. Interestingly, George Berkeley, an Anglican Bishop and a scientist who studied optics, argued that only minds and their ideas really exist. For Berkeley, that we have ideas is not in dispute. But how do we know that there are things independent of our ideas? How could an idea, a mental thing, be caused by a material or physical object, which is not itself an idea but exists in a completely different metaphysical realm? Berkeley considered the entire idea of material or physical objects muddle-headed and unwarranted. According to Berkeley's famous summation of his idealism, "To be is to be perceived." This may be true of dreams, hallucinations, and illusions, but is it reasonable to believe that all that is real exists only when it is perceived?

Perhaps materialism, idealism, and all such metaphysical talk is nonsense. That is, it has no real meaning. Rather, perhaps such talk is the result of linguistic confusion. That is what some twentieth century philosophers, like A.J. Ayer, have argued. What we think is meaningful talk about ultimate reality is really disguised, subtle nonsense that expresses a variety of emotions. A.J. Ayer claimed that "No statement which refers to a 'reality' transcending the limits of all possible sense-experience can possibly have any literal significance. [Such talk] is devoted to the production of nonsense." For Ayer, all such metaphysical talk may be similar to asking if your dream last night weighed two pounds or ten pounds.

If language is a significant component in determining what is real and what is not real, Darwin's theory of evolution seems to present a picture of language that plays a crucial role in our adaptation and survival. It is this picture of language that was picked up by a school of philosophers known as pragmatists. According to this view, language is a tool for survival. Language is an adaptive behavior in one's arsenal for survival and not an abstract way of representing reality. For many pragmatists, any question concerning the warrant of a belief about reality must to be understood in terms of the practical consequences of holding such a belief or having such a language. Does language describe a real, existent world, independent of our awareness, or is reality a reflection of the particular language we speak? These seem to be questions that not only go beyond the particular pragmatist standard presented, but seem to be at the heart of the question, what is real?

Realists like John Searle argue that what is real is external to us. It exists whether or not we have experience of it, which is to say that it is not dependent upon our consciousness. Antirealists like Goodman, Putnam, and Rorty have contend that we construct all reality. All reality is dependent on us and our consciousness. While there may be something "out there" that is external to us, whatever it is, it is essentially shaped by our concepts or ideas. It is, metaphysically, nothing to us until we name it or conceive of it. Hence, we know what is real only through our descriptions, our language.

Perhaps you are a realist or a materialist who argues that when we discuss an issue, what we are really talking about is our brains being variously configured in terms of synaptic weights. Or perhaps you are an antirealist who argues that all such are just conceptual models. Both realists and antirealists believe that much of what we take to be reality is social construction. For some thinkers, like John Searle, there are many social or institutional facts that are social constructs. But for Searle, who is a realist, there are also objects that exist independent of our experience. Others, from the feminist camp, along with a number of disenfranchised minorities, might want to add concepts like gender or racial superiority and inferiority to the list of socially constructed "facts."

Is there something real beyond such social constructs? Don't all social constructs occur in a three dimensional world of physical objects, or is space a conceptual construct along with physical object? What is real?

TEXT LINKS

☞ Turn to Velasquez, *Philosophy: A Text with Readings,* eleventh edition, and read Chapter 3, Section 3.1 for an introduction to the general issues of what constitutes ultimate reality.

☞ For a more complete discussion of the issues involved in the debate between materialism and the non-materialists see Section 3.2 of Velasquez.

☞ Read about the pragmatists' view of reality in Section 3.3 of Velasquez.

☞ While this episode only briefly mentions the views of A.J. Ayer, he was a representative of logical positivism, a powerful philosophical force during the mid-twentieth century. Their views of metaphysics as involving linguistic nonsense are given an extended introduction in Velasquez Section 3.4, "Reality and Logical Positivism."

☞ Velasquez Section 3.5 brings the discussion of ultimate reality up to the present with an overview of contemporary antirealist positions.

☞ For a more detailed discussion of Thomas Hobbes and George Berkeley, which includes extended passages of their work, see Velasquez, Section 3.9.

KEY TERMS

Antirealism: A metaphysical view that the objects of experience do not exist independently of our experience.

Atomism: A materialist view first attributed to a school of thought in Ancient Greece which argued that all of reality is reducible to elementary things called atoms, which means uncuttable, since they are the ultimate building blocks.

Idealism: The metaphysical view that reality ultimately consists of ideas and the minds that have them. Again, there are variant views of idealism such as transcendental idealism.

Monism: Metaphysical view that reality ultimately consists of one thing.

Neuron: A nerve cell.

Pragmatism: A philosophical school of thought, which epistemologically tests truth in terms of "usefulness" or "workability." Tends to be metaphysically pluralistic.

Realism: The metaphysical view that the objects of experience exist independently of their being experienced.

Synapse: The gap between the dendrite of one neuron and the axon of another neuron.

Synaptic weight: A metaphorical reference to the changes that occur within the brain, specifically the number and locations of synapses, as living experiences "shape" the brain's neural anatomy.

SELF-TEST

Multiple Choice

1. Metaphysics, as a branch of philosophy, is
   a. the theory or study of knowledge
   b. the study of good and bad reasoning
   c. the study of the ultimate or basic nature of reality
   d. another term for theoretical physics

2. The idea that reality is composed not of matter, but of minds and their ideas, was espoused by
   a. Thomas Hobbes
   b. George Berkeley
   c. John Dewey
   d. Democritus

3. Pragmatists reject the significance of the debate between metaphysical materialism and idealism because
   a. it has no experiential consequences
   b. it arises out of a misuse of language
   c. it is focused on abstractions that have little to do with reality as it is revealed to human consciousness
   d. there are many realities

4. According to some critics of materialism, the fatal flaw of materialism is that reality seems to contain
   a. some unpredictable sub-atomic particles
   b. only matter in motion
   c. objects that may not be causally related
   d. a mental residue beyond physics

5. One of the earliest materialist views was expressed in the
   a. twentieth century by Albert Einstein
   b. nineteenth century by J.J. Thompson
   c. seventeenth century by Thomas Hobbes
   d. fifth century BCE by Democritus

6. According to early materialists,
   a. only matter in motion is real
   b. only minds and their ideas are real
   c. only minds and the bodies they inhabit are real
   d. nothing is real

7. For George Berkeley, to exist—that is, to be—is to
   a. endure as a physical object
   b. be an event involving physical objects
   c. be described by a language
   d. be perceived

8. In the history of philosophy, an outstanding defender of metaphysical idealism was
   a. A.J. Ayer
   b. George Berkeley
   c. René Descartes
   d. Thomas Hobbes

9. According to a pragmatist like William James, metaphysical disputes can be resolved by
   a. scrupulously analyzing the nature of an idea
   b. leaving all such issues to scientific investigation
   c. studying closely the sacred literature of many cultures
   d. tracing each view's practical consequences to see if they make any real difference

10. Much of the debate between realists and anti-realists about the nature of reality turns on the claim that
    a. reality is external and independent of our consciousness of it
    b. language is shared by non-human animals
    c. metaphysical pluralism must be true
    d. language is only a label for our thoughts

True or False

These questions are only from the reading assignment in Velasquez, Sections 3.1, 3.2, 3.3, 3.4, and 3.5. Specific page references are given in the answer key.

11. As Robert Nozick has said, to say something is real is to say it has "value, meaning, importance, and weight."

12. Idealism is the view that matter is ideally the ultimate constituent of reality.

13. According to subjective idealism, the world consists of my own mind and things that are dependent on it.

14. In his work on pragmatism, William James agrees that the dispute between materialism and idealism has important practical consequences.

15. Logical positivists like A. J. Ayer view metaphysical statements as meaningless because they are neither tautologies nor statements of fact that can be verified by observation.

PARADOXICAL PURSUITS

If you are a materialist and if you believe that the functioning brain is all that we are in terms of our experience, then who are you? How can a neuron or a bunch of neurons cause the tongue to say, "To be or not to be? That is the question." This remark is very different from just a tape recording. Who says it and how is such a sense of self, and reality, possible?

If there are conscious states that are different from the things they are supposedly about—tables, chairs, classes, family—how can they be about things that are so different?

❧

Professor Gerald Jacobs of the Neuroscience Research Institute at the University of California, Santa Barbara has remarked, "We live in a world of color, but color is only a useful illusion created in the brain. It is an interpretation of wavelengths of light . . ." If color (your experience of yellow, red, blue) is not *in* the world but is an illusion, how and where does it occur in the brain? No neurologist examining your brain, in whatever detail, will ever *see* you experience of a blue sky. Are colors real?

APPLIED PHILOSOPHY

Take a philosophical field trip and do some sidewalk metaphysics. Ideally, take a video camera and interview people on the street asking if they are monists (probably materialists), dualists, or pluralists. If they don't know what they are, explain the different positions then ask if it is important to know the metaphysical assumptions inherent in one's system of belief?

❧

Make a list of all the things you believe are real. Can you place them all in some neat, comprehensive categories like material or physical object, mental or spiritual object, or abstract objects? How many categories do you need? Which do you honestly believe are real and which are only fictional?

❧

Invite your friends over and take a metaphysical census to see what each believes makes up the stuff of reality.

NET LINKS

Check out these Internet sites for additional relevant philosophical information. Remember the Internet is a web. Each of these listed sites is linked to other sites.

Philosophy Resources:

— http://www.earlham.edu/ ~ peters/phil-inks.htm

— http://www.epistemelinks.com

— http://www.refdesk.com/philos.html

— http://www.erraticimpact.com

Encyclopedia of Philosophy:

— http://www.iep.utm.edu

Philosophy Papers:

— http://philosophy.hku.hk/paper/info.php

— http://cogprints.org/view/subjects/phil.html

Metaphysics:

— http://plato.stanford.edu/entries/aristotle-metaphysics

— http://mally.stanford.edu

— http://en.wikipedia.org/wiki/Metaphysics

David Chalmers:

— http://consc.net/chalmers

Paul Churchland:

— http://philosophyfaculty.ucsd.edu/faculty/pchurchland/index.php

Nelson Goodman:

— http://www.aesthetics-online.org/memorials/index.php?memorials_id = 6

Hilary Putnam:

— http://www.webalice.it/af_gazzola/putnam/home.htm

Richard Rorty:

— http://www.seop.leeds.ac.uk/entries/rorty

John Searle:

— http://en.wikipedia.org/wiki/John_Searle

— http://globetrotter.berkeley.edu/people/Searle/searle-con0.html

Lesson Seven

How Do We Encounter the World?

LEARNING OBJECTIVES

Upon completing this lesson, you should be familiar with the concepts contained in the lesson and be able to critically discuss:

☞ Edmund Husserl's development of phenomenology.

☞ the role of phenomenon and the significance of human subjectivity.

☞ the role of intention in consciousness.

☞ the significance of *noema* and *lebenswelt* as well as their relationship.

☞ Heidegger's view of human double nature, inauthenticity and determination.

OVERVIEW

"Let's go and watch the sun set. It promises to be quite beautiful this evening," you might remark. "The colors, with all of their subtle hues, are magnificent." "Look how they reflect off of the clouds and slowly change as the sun goes down." According to the accepted scientific account of a sunset, not only does the sun not go down but the colors themselves are not objective features of the world. Rather they are subjective parts of our experience. The various wave-lengths and frequencies of electromagnetic radiation, it is theorized, cause us to experience colors. What about other properties that only appear to be features of our consciousness? Quite naturally the question presents itself, "How do we encounter reality?"

In the history of philosophy the seeming gap between appearance and reality has generated many theories that attempt to bridge this gap. Some theories attempt to show that there really is no gap. However, with the philosophical movement of phenomenology, whose founding is often attributed to Edmund Husserl, there is an attempt to avoid such theorizing and deal only with consciousness itself. *Phainomenon* is the Greek word for appearance. Thus, Husserl starts with human subjectivity, the subjective consciousness.

In Husserl's phenomenology the first question is, "What does it mean to be aware of something?" This deceptively simple question belies the deceptively simple understanding most of us have about the nature of our awareness or consciousness, regardless of its relationship to the world. The first thing to realize, according to Husserl, is the large number of assumptions, particularly cultural assumptions that we bring to every experience. An analogy is sometimes drawn to the training of a painter or photographer who must relearn how to see in order to appreciate the subtle role our learned perspective plays in effecting how we ordinarily see.

To illustrate the role of assumption in perception, consider any of the cases of ambiguous figures. The duck-rabbit ambiguous figure shown in the episode illustrates that the figure itself presents a single bit of visual information, yet this singular information can be experienced in more than one way. How does such a shift in perspective occur? If someone had no conception of a duck, then they might see only a rabbit and vice-versa. The assumptions we bring to experience seem to play a very significant role in what we actually experience.

For phenomenologists, all consciousness involves an intentional act. What this means is that every act of conscious awareness is directed toward an object. We always seem to see, feel, hear, smell, desire, believe *something*. We may believe *that* the president is the commander in chief or desire *that* we be able to eat sooner rather than later. Consciousness is never simply pure belief or pure desire or pure feeling but always an intentional believing *that*, or desiring *that* or feeling *that*. The object of our beliefs need not be real, as in the case of a child who believes that a monster lives under the bed. For Husserl the distinction between what is real and what is unreal or fictional is not important. Rather, we must *put the world in parentheses* and simply describe subjective consciousness.

In describing subjective consciousness, Husserl introduces the notion of *noema*. *Noema* is a part of the intentional act inherent in consciousness. While all consciousness is intentional, directed toward an object, *noema* refers to the structural aspect of consciousness in which the object of consciousness is determined to be the object that it is. Using again the duck/rabbit ambiguous figure as an illustration, the *noema* is the structure of the anticipations or assumptions that determine whether we see a duck or a rabbit at any one time.

The subjectively-experienced world that results from our *noema* is our *lebenswelt*, our life-world, according to Husserl. It reflects the world that we live in from our childhood experiences onward. In an important sense, there are unique, individual aspects to each *lebenswelt*. A large part of the phenomenological method is to uncover and reveal the complicated pattern of anticipations and assumptions. Yet if each *lebenswelt* is structured by some *noema*, then isn't Husserl's entire phenomeno-

logical method itself simply another *lebenswelt* or life-world?

For Martin Heidegger, one of Husserl's most famous pupils, the phenomenological method was not focused on consciousness itself, but upon the object of consciousness. Heidegger searched for a phenomenological insight into what it means to be anything at all—into the very meaning of being itself.

The being of man is marked by a double nature. We are physical objects and thus exist like rocks, dirt, trees, and fire, but we also have a mind, a consciousness, and hence a conscious relationship to the world. Heidegger's major work, *Being and Time* (1927), is a systematic attempt to describe the ways that this conscious relationship to the world differs from the relationship a non-conscious being has in the world. In short, while other beings are, we exist. We are not merely *in the world*, we *have a world*. And to have a world means to live a life that is marked by *sorge*, a caring relationship.

For Heidegger, we do not, for the most part, live simply as spectators of our lives. To understand is not simply a pure intellectual act. Rather, life is practical. A person has projects, possibilities. These projects and possibilities only reveal themselves through a mood. Thus, for Heidegger, the world reveals itself very differently to those gripped by a mood of paranoia, than to those influenced by a mood of happiness or gloom. For Heidegger, if we had no moods, the world would not reveal itself at all.

When we care not just for a variety of beings but for being itself, we act most authentically, according to Heidegger. To act inauthentically is to fall into the world of others. We cease to be ourselves, and become what others expect or demand of us. The authentic individual lives from personal choice, not from some cultural stereotype. *Sorge*—for the future, for the past, for other beings and the community—gives reality to our lives as well.

People also escape inauthenticity through the experience of angst. Angst or anxiety is experienced in our recognition of death. Anxiety, in this sense, is not the same as fear according to Heidegger, because it has a cognitive aspect. This cognition results in a discovery of our freedom as well as knowledge of our eventual termination. In view of our inevitable death, we must choose a life that justifies itself, makes itself worthy. Thus for Heidegger, reality reveals itself through *sorge* or care, but to live authentically the *sorge* that guides us must be our own and not that of others. The authentic individual cares for others but does not live to conform to their care or demands.

TEXT LINKS

☞ For a more detailed discussion of phenomenology and its relationship to existentialism see Velasquez, *Philosophy: A Text with Readings*, eleventh edition, Section 3.6, "Encountering Reality: Phenomenology and Existentialism."

☞ The issues of consciousness and subjectivity recall were also central concerns of metaphysical idealists such as George Berkeley. For an extended discussion of Berkeley, along with extended excerpts from Berkeley's writing, see Section 3.9, "The Historical Showcase."

KEY TERMS

Authentic: To be, to act, to feel as one genuinely is. To live one's individuality.

Consciousness: Awareness of a world, experience of the world. Consciousness is sometimes distinguished from unconsciousness, in which there is no awareness or experience of a world. Consciousness is not the world, but of the world. For Husserl, consciousness could be bracketed and simply studied in itself and significantly independently of the world or its relationship to the world.

Gestalt psychology: A German school of psychological study founded in the early twentieth century by Max Werthheimer. Gestalt psychologists claimed that perception or sensory consciousness goes beyond the basic physical data provided by the senses.

Intentional: As used by phenomenologists, an essential aspect of the structure of consciousness in which consciousness is always directed toward an object or objectivity. Thus, it is not possible to simply believe, but one must believe that something is the case. One cannot simply feel, but one must feel pain, or joy, or pleasure.

Lebenswelt: In Husserl's phenomenology, it is the life-world or that structured world that we live in and that reflects our past experience from our childhood onward.

Noema: Those expectations or assumptions within consciousness that are involved in structuring the content of our consciousness. In the case of ambiguous figures, such as the duck-rabbit example, the *noema* is that aspect of consciousness which determines that we see the figure as a duck as opposed to a rabbit and vice-versa.

Phenomenology: A twentieth century school of philosophy whose founding is traditionally attributed to Edmund Husserl. In phenomenology, philosophical study starts with our subjectivity or consciousness; consciousness being ultimately real and hence the ground of being itself.

Phenomenon: Within the school of phenomenology, the phenomenon is that which appears, the immediate contents of consciousness.

Sorge: A German word used by Martin Heidegger and usually translated to mean care. Care or *sorge* is used to characterize the different ways in which our consciousness relates to the world.

Subjectivity: The starting point for phenomenologists, which concerns the structure and content of consciousness and nothing that exists apart from it.

SELF-TEST

Multiple Choice

1. According to Heidegger, reality reveals itself to us through
   a. ideas
   b. material or physical objects
   c. moods
   d. prayers and grace

2. For phenomenologists, the starting point of philosophical study is/are
   a. atoms and the void
   b. consciousness
   c. the subconscious
   d. sociology and anthropology

3. Phenomenon, in phenomenology, is
   a. that which appears or shows itself
   b. a hypothesis of ontology
   c. *noema*
   d. *noumena*

4. To claim that consciousness is essentially intentional is to claim that
   a. all conscious acts are about physical objects
   b. fictional objects are composites of actual objects
   c. all mental activities are directed at *something*
   d. unconsciousness is always accidental

5. Ambiguous figures, like the duck/rabbit, illustrate Husserl's view of the role of
   a. intentional objects
   b. *noema*
   c. authenticity
   d. angst

6. Taking the phenomenological point of view, for Husserl, required that we put the world within
   a. brackets
   b. the scientific method
   c. some *lebenswelt*
   d. *sorge*

7. *Noema* is Husserl's term for how
   a. consciousness, in part, determines its object
   b. an existentialist confronts absurdity
   c. consciousness grasps material objects
   d. consciousness gives words meaning

8. For Husserl, a *lebenswelt* or life-world is the
   a. structured world of our experience
   b. structure of the world itself
   c. laws which govern nature
   d. customs or mores of a society

True or False

These questions are only from the reading assignment in Velasquez, Section 3.6. Specific page references are given in the answer key.

9. Husserl, the founder of phenomenology, asks that we "bracket" the "natural standpoint."

10. Soren Kierkegaard wrote "What I really lack is to be clear in my mind what I am to do, not what I am to know."

11. According to Heidegger traditional thinking is confused over the question of being.

12. Edmund Husserl divides reality into being-for-itself and being-in-itself.

13. According to Sartre, psychology has proven that a man cheats and robs because of the conditions under which he grew up.

PARADOXICAL PURSUITS

According to phenomenology, *we* must start with subjectivity, with consciousness. How do *we* start with subjectivity? Isn't the claim of *we*, already to place us in an objective world beyond subjectivity?

When a phenomenologist distinguishes in consciousness the object of consciousness, then describes this as objectivity or being, itself, in what sense is the object of one's own consciousness objective? Is this the ordinary sense of objectivity you are familiar with?

If, as phenomenologists direct, we should start with subjectivity, can we ever get out of subjectivity? (Recall Descartes problems from Episode 3, "Is Mind Distinct from Body?" along with those and other problems arising again for Descartes as well as for George Berkeley in Episode 6, "What is Real?")

APPLIED PHILOSOPHY

Consider Heidegger's view that if we had no moods, the world would not reveal itself to us. How do you see other people when you are in a bad mood as opposed to a good mood? How do your family members and friends differ in moods, how does this affect how they "see" the world?

Find someone who is a painter and discuss with that person what is involved in relearning how to "see." Is this what Husserl had in mind?

Discuss Heidegger's angst or anxiety about death with your family or friends. Do you and they agree that such angst is a source of authenticity and the discovery of freedom and life's worth?

Do you live authentically or inauthentically? Are you more authentic around some people than others? Why? Is it easier to live authentically as an adult than as a child or adolescent? Why? Do you sometimes feel you are simply the product of your culture or the expectations of others? Look at your nails. Are they painted? How is your hair cut? What do your clothes look like? Must you own a particular style of car or house to be "cool"?

NET LINKS

Check out these Internet sites for additional relevant philosophical information. Remember the Internet is a web. Each of these listed sites is linked to other sites.

Philosophy Resources:

— http://www.earlham.edu/ ~ peters/phil-inks.htm

— http://www.epistemelinks.com

— http://www.refdesk.com/philos.html

— http://www.erraticimpact.com

Encyclopedia of Philosophy:

— http://www.iep.utm.edu

Existentialism:

— http://www.dividingline.com/

Phenomenology

— http://www.phenomenologycenter.org/phenom.htm

— http://www.phenomenologyonline.com/

— http://plato.stanford.edu/entries/phenomenology/

Martin Heidegger:

— http://en.wikipedia.org/wiki/Martin_Heidegger

— http://www.iep.utm.edu/heidegger

Edmund Husserl:

— http://www.husserlpage.com

Jean Paul Sartre:

— http://www.dividingline.com/private/Philosophy/Philosophers/Sartre/sartre.shtml

Richard Rorty:

— http://www.seop.leeds.ac.uk/entries/rorty

Lesson Eight

Do We Have Free Will?

LEARNING OBJECTIVES

Upon completing this lesson, you should be familiar with the concepts contained in the lesson and be able to critically discuss:

- the philosophical perplexity regarding the problem of determinism and freedom of the will.

- the position of libertarianism in the free will/determinism debate.

- compatibilism and incompatibilism in the free will/determinism debate.

- the relationship between responsibility and freedom of the will.

OVERVIEW

Most everyone reading this overview will have passed through puberty. This event in your life was causally determined by your genetic make-up. The time of onset, the duration of this passage from childhood to adulthood was largely, if not totally, beyond your choice.

Still others of us have watched our hair turn gray. Hair turning gray marks another causally determined event. However, with hair color we may also believe we can choose to change our natural gray. We believe we can choose to give our hair, even ourselves, a younger look.

Then we realize we live in a culture peculiarly obsessed with youthfulness and sexual attractiveness urged on by mass media. It becomes apparent that our desire to color our hair, to have a certain look, to even feel a certain way, has been causally implanted within us, the result of the subtle power of socialization.

So some desires are biologically determined, and others appear to be socially determined. Where does free will fit into this pattern of causality? After all, nature seems a seamless web of complex causal relationships and homo-sapiens are a part of nature. How can we be an exception to this causal determinism? Is free will an illusion? Do we have free will?

Today, there is a cynical attitude among people in the United States regarding legal responsibility. Some social critics use the phrase, "culture of victims" to refer to what they believe to be a failure on the part of people to take responsibility. Individuals found guilty of committing horrendous crimes are excused because they were victims of "bad" upbringing, "bad" social environment, or in the case of Clarence Darrow's defense of Nathan Leopold and Richard Loeb, victims of "good" upbringing and a "good" social environment. There has been a "junk food" defense for a murderer, and a high on drugs defense for rapists, torturers, and murders. What is the role of free will and moral responsibility in a world in which both our natural and social sciences increasingly direct us to look for the cause?

Our ideas regarding legal responsibility, and the whole of morality, seem to require that we rise above fate, act autonomously, and exercise a genuinely free will. Among various philosophical positions, libertarians claim that we do have genuine alternatives to select from, and that we are free to choose our actions. As one commented, "The future is a garden of forking paths. We have alternative possibilities at least some of the time." Traditionally, going back to at least Plato, we exercise free will when our rational faculty governs our desires and tempers our emotions. (See Episode 2, "What is Human Nature?" for a more complete description and discussion of Plato's views.) However, can libertarianism be reconciled with the ever growing and powerful deterministic model of the universe that science presents us?

Determinists take the view that human beings are but a small part of a vast system of cause and effect. For a determinist, it is naive to consider humans outside this vast web of causality which defines the law-like behavior of the universe. Human beings, like all other physical things, are collections of matter that move according to a variety of natural laws. Some of these laws are well understood, some not so well understood, and others are yet to be discovered. But the fact that nature operates according to causality is not in doubt from the scientific point of view.

Some have argued that an area of theoretical physics—quantum physics, which deals with the very small—has shown that the behavior of at least some things, such as an electron, is indeterministic. That is, it is not always possible to predict the behavior of an electron. Yet unpredictability is not freedom. Free will seems to be more than mere chance.

The position of compatibilism, a position taken by the great sixteenth century materialist Thomas Hobbes, accepts determinism but claims there is still room for our notions of free will, choice, and responsibility. As Hobbes argued, what is central to having choice or free will is that our actions not be blocked—that we not be physically stopped from doing that which we desire to do. Our desires are, as a part of our natural fabric, determined. But as long as there are no external impediments to satisfying those desires, we are said to be free.

With the rise of modern psychology, and the work of Sigmund Freud, the idea of unconscious motivations, of compulsions and phobias, gained prominence. These unconscious desires and needs so effectively determined behavior that the person caught in their invisible web lacked a free will. So while there may be no external forces preventing or forcing a person to eat or gamble, it appears that internal, perhaps unconscious, needs and desires influence behavior with as much effectiveness as external forces.

Contemporary compatibilists qualify the presence of these more subtle psychological forces by describing free agents as people who act on or express their "true" desires and values. Such distinctions are unpersuasive to the determinist, who takes seriously the idea of universal causality in nature. They wish to rule out any meaningful role for free will; all things in nature are causally determined. Because human beings are things in nature, they are causally determined. But perhaps nature only covers part of reality.

Immanuel Kant argued that nature, which consists of a vast network of causal relationships, is in the realm of phenomena. There is another realm in reality, the realm of *noumena*, in which we exist as free agents and as moral agents. In the realm of phenomena, we are causally determined along with the rest of the world of phenomena. If one understands these as two distinct realms, then one faces problems of interactionism. (See Episode 3, "Is Mind Distinct from Body?" for a more complete discussion of the problems of dualism and interactionism.) On the other hand, perhaps Kant's distinction is a distinction between two different ways of looking at our world. If so, then we seem to be back where we started. Is the world of *noumena* only an illusion since the world of phenomena and science seems so persistent?

If we accept determinism, then it appears that we have to rethink our ideas about responsibility. We do not hold people responsible for being a certain race, going through puberty, or suffering from nightmares. How is someone held responsible if he or she could not have acted otherwise? As some have argued, perhaps punishment should be replaced by re-education and retraining. We may have to change our punitive practices, our prison system and our jails, if we accept determinism as the most reasonable view.

Rethink as we may, we are still stuck with having to choose in actual, concrete situations. Our capacity to reason allows us to assign values to different courses of action in our daily lives. As the existentialist writer, Jean Paul Sartre, claimed, humans are ". . . condemned [determined] to be free, each of us is responsible for the world and for ourselves as a way of being." Yet, how is this conceivable? How can we be such an exception to all of nature?

TEXT LINKS

🖎 Read Velasquez, *Philosophy: A Text with Readings*, eleventh edition, Section 3.7, "Is Freedom Real?" Velasquez discusses the three key positions of determinism, libertarianism, and compatibilism.

🖎 See also Velasquez, Section 7.7, "Ethics and Moral Responsibility" for a discussion of moral responsibility and its relationship to the primary positions in the free will/determinism debate.

KEY TERMS

Consistency: Following logically without contradiction

Compatibilism: In the free will/determinism debate, the position that determinism does not rule out what is meant by free will.

Determinism: In the free will/determinism debate, the position that all things are determined by antecedent conditions. That everything occurs according to some pattern or law.

Fate: The inevitable unfolding of events beyond anyone's control.

Free will: In the free will/determinism debate the position that at least some humans have a genuine capacity for self-determined choice.

Incompatibilism: In the free will/determinism debate, the position that given that all things are caused, there is no genuine free choice.

Intentional: To act deliberately; to act with or for a purpose.

Libertarianism: In the free will/determinism debate, the position that humans do make genuinely free choices, that humans do have free will.

Matter: Physical stuff which exists independent of anyone thinking about it.

Necessity: In referring to the relationship between events, the claim that certain events must occur in the sequence in which they present themselves.

Neurotic: A person who may suffer from any of a number of functional disorders of the mind or emotions. Generic for emotional dysfunction.

Phobia: An irrational fear, such as hydrophobia, which is an irrational fear of water.

Quantum mechanics (physics): An area of theoretical physics that studies the very small, quanta.

Responsibility: Being held accountable for what one does. To be the author of some event that result from one's choice.

Theory of determinism: As used in this episode, the view that all events are caused.

SELF-TEST

Multiple Choice

1. In the free will debate, libertarians claim
   a. genuine free will is an illusion
   b. having a free will is to be without external and/or internal obstacles
   c. we are free to choose our actions
   d. government should be at an absolute minimum

2. In the free will debate, compatibilists claim
   a. genuine free will is an illusion
   b. having a free will is to be without external and/or internal obstacles
   c. we are free to choose our actions
   d. government should be at an absolute minimum

3. In the free will debate, determinists claim
   a. genuine free will is an illusion
   b. having a free will is to be without external and/or internal obstacles
   c. we are free to choose our actions
   d. government should be at an absolute minimum

4. The scientific point of view rests upon the assumption that
   a. all events and things in nature are caused
   b. creatures other than humans have a free will
   c. only God has a free will
   d. only humans escape the laws of cause and effect

5. In western civilization, the classic or traditional view of human beings is that they are
   a. matter in motion like everything else
   b. slaves to their passions
   c. creatures living in both the noumenal and phenomenal realms
   d. reasoning, free moral agents

6. To hold someone responsible for his or her action seems to require that
   a. the person could have chosen another course of action.
   b. the person's act was simply reflex behavior
   c. the person had no idea why he or she did the act
   d. all events are causally determined

7. Existentialists tend to be
   a. determinists
   b. compatibilists
   c. libertarians
   d. Freudians

8. Traditional compatibilists failed to account for
   a. cases of external obstacles to freedom or liberty
   b. cases of internal obstacles to freedom or liberty
   c. the role of science in providing natural explanations
   d. the role of value in choice

Use the categories below to identify the statements that follow. (Be ready to defend your answers.)

a. determined
b. free will

_____9. Being a member of a particular race

_____10. Being a drug addict

_____11. Being a member of a particular religious group

_____12. Brushing your teeth in the morning

_____13. Wanting a particular candy bar, car, piece of clothing

_____14. Having a particular sexual preference

True or False

These questions are only from the reading assignment in Velasquez, Section 3.7. Specific page references are given in the answer key.

15. The determinist view of reality claims that determinism does not rule out personal responsibility.

16. Sigmund Freud wrote that "the unconscious is the master of every fate and the captain of every soul."

17. The libertarian view of reality holds that human freedom and causal determinism are both true.

18. The compatibilist holds that a couple must be compatible if their marriage is to succeed.

19. Thomas Hobbes was a libertarian.

PARADOXICAL PURSUITS

In view of the theory of determinism, as presented in this episode, all events, including the thoughts you are now having, are caused. The chain of causes that brought about these thoughts stretches into the distant past. Hence, you could not have had any other thoughts than those you are now having, have had, and will have. If this is so, whatever position you take on this debate, you were caused to take. Thus, if determinism is true, no one could know it is true since all positions are determined. Do you agree with this analysis?

A profound shift is presently underway in how Americans view drug addiction. For most of our history, drug addiction has been considered a weakness of the will, an inability to control one's desires. But now there is a growing consensus in the medical and treatment communities that addiction is a disease. What is the relevance of the free will/determinism debate for this shift in thinking about drug addiction?

Causal determination is the more well-known form of determination but others would argue that there is also logical determination. Once the logic or justification of some belief is understood, a rational person is compelled to accept the belief. Since most of us have abandoned our childhood belief in Santa Claus, could you choose to actually believe in Santa again? Do we ever choose our beliefs?

APPLIED PHILOSOPHY

Professor Van Inwagen claims that if we ever have choice, it is about the "great decisions in life." Professor Searle claims that if, "You go into a restaurant, they confront you with a menu. . . . You have to make up your mind (choose)." If you were having dinner with these two fellows, what would you say? Who would you side with? Are they in disagreement?

≈

Watch a show that you find funny. When you laugh, did you choose to laugh at the moment you laughed or was it simply the effect of a cause? What caused you to laugh? Does broad comedy, physical antics, farce, or more subtle comedy like plays on words and innuendo make you laugh? Do you share your sense of humor with some members of your family but not others? Is sense of humor determined or chosen?

≈

Make a list of your most prominent physical and personality traits, then trace them causally through your family. Who gave you your eye color, hair texture, sense of humor, your smile? Draw up a list of those things over which you believe you clearly have a choice. Why are these things on this list and not the causal list?

≈

Consider the music most repulsive to you—punk rock, opera, rap, polka, new age, techno, whatever. Could you choose to like it? Could you not choose to play it but choose to genuinely appreciate it, like you do the music that is "your music"? Most would argue that you do not choose your appreciation of music. What does your musical taste tell you about your cultural conditioning, about how you've been socialized? What choices are you capable of in this domain?

NET LINKS

Check out these Internet sites for additional relevant philosophical information. Remember the Internet is a web. Each of these listed sites is linked to other sites.

Philosophy Resources:

— http://www.earlham.edu/ ~ peters/phil-inks.htm

— http://www.epistemelinks.com

— http://www.refdesk.com/philos.html

— http://www.erraticimpact.com

Encyclopedia of Philosophy:

— http://www.iep.utm.edu

Philosophy Papers:

— http://philosophy.hku.hk/paper/info.php

— http://cogprints.org/view/subjects/phil.html

Existentialism:

— http://www.dividingline.com/

Metaphysics:

— http://plato.stanford.edu/entries/aristotle-metaphysics

— http://mally.stanford.edu

— http://en.wikipedia.org/wiki/Metaphysics

Jean Paul Sartre:

— http://www.dividingline.com/private/Philosophy/Philosophers/Sartre/sartre.shtml

Daniel Dennett:

— http://www.2think.org/kom.shtml

— http://mitpress.mit.edu/e-books/Hal/chap16/author.html

Larry Hinman:

— http://ethics.sandiego.edu/about/editor/index.asp

Nicholas Jolley:

— http://lib.uci.edu/libraries/pubs/scctr/Philosophy/jolley.html

Gary Watson:

— http://lib.uci.edu/libraries/pubs/scctr/Philosophy/watson.html

Susan Wolf:

— http://www.philosophy.unc.edu/people/faculty/susan-wolf

Lesson Nine

Is Time Real?

LEARNING OBJECTIVES

Upon completing this lesson, you should be familiar with the concepts contained in the lesson and be able to critically discuss:

- the difference between felt time and objective time.

- paradoxes regarding the nature of time.

- the passage or flow view of time.

- absolute versus relational theories of time.

- the view of time in the theory of special relativity.

OVERVIEW

A student of mine once remarked, rather nobly it seemed, "If I could travel back in time, I would have assassinated Adolf Hitler and stopped World War II." Despite what may be a naive view about how such assassinations actually occur, how complex historical events unfold, or even the morality of killing someone before he or she does something wrong, there is perhaps the more basic question as to whether time travel is even possible. We do readily travel through space to different locations, why not through time to different times? Is it simply because

we lack the technology, as we do in sending humans to other planets? Or is time travel logically, or as some might say, conceptually impossible? You really can't imagine time travel any more than you can imagine Thursday beating the sun in gymnastic floor exercises. What is time? Is it a thing that exists in reality alongside other stuff? Is it part of the very fabric of reality? Is it only part of our experience of reality? Is time real?

Is there a difference between how we measure the movement of time by our feelings versus how time itself really moves? Our feelings tell us that the flow of time is not smooth or continuous. It seems to speed up or slow to a crawl. Children invariably report that time moves very slowly while people in late adulthood describe weeks becoming like a day, a month like a week, a year, a month. Even decades seem to speed by. The beginning of a new millennium appears to mark quite a significant moment for large numbers of people. But it is only significant, it only exists, given our calendar. This sense or feeling of time, felt time, we distinguish from what we sometimes describe as objective time, or cosmic or world time. External objective time we describe as being continuous and independent of our felt time. Our finest clocks measure the external objective time. But what is time exactly?

If you measure my office, your act of measuring is one thing. The tape measure, or whatever instrument you use to measure, is another thing. And then there's my office itself, existing whether or not it is measured. But what is time such that it is independent of all instruments of measurement?

51

Time is not seen, smelled, touched, heard, nor tasted, but seemingly felt. But it is not felt through our nervous system like the heat of a fire or the coarseness of sandpaper. We seem to have no literal sense or contact with something that is time independent of our individual fickle feelings. So what is time?

St. Augustine seemed to know what time was as long as no one asked him the question, "What is time?" He commented that if he had to give an account of time, he wouldn't know what time was. Is this only an autobiographical remark by a wise man who knows the limits of his own understanding? I would give a similar response if asked questions about gene splicing by molecular biologists. While I may not be able to give an account of gene splicing, I know someone can. Is it just that St. Augustine is not particularly informed or knowledgeable about time, or is his remark a profound statement about time itself?

Aristotle claimed that time is paradoxical. If you take any segment of time like the present, whatever its length, it exists between the past which is no-longer, and the future which is not-yet. How is it possible for the present, a seemingly existing thing, to be so intimately related or connected to things that have no existence? Since the future and the past are so much greater in length than the present, it would seem that so much non-existence would mean that the present is nothing as well.

At the turn of the twentieth century, the Cambridge philosopher J.M.E. McTaggart argued that time is unreal. McTaggart's work has been the focus of much of the philosophical debate over the nature of time during this century. McTaggart claimed that since past, present, and future are incompatible properties—that is one and the same thing—an event cannot have all of these properties. Analogously, if you were holding a block of wood behind your back and asked someone to guess its shape and that person said it is both square and circular, you would probably be confused and ask the person which shape he or she meant. A piece of wood cannot be both circular and square because these are incompatible properties. The wood could be square and blue, since color and shape are not incompatible. If time were real, McTaggart argued, events would have the properties of being future, being present, and being past. Thus, since actual things cannot have incompatible properties, like the piece of wood, we know that time does not exist.

If one were to suggest to McTaggert, "But no event has those incompatible properties simultaneously, hence the properties are not actually incompatible. If the block of wood can be circular now but square later, then square and circular are not incompatible." However, McTaggert argued that one had to introduce the ideas of simultaneity and succession, both temporal concepts, in order to resolve a problem about time. Using time to resolve a paradox about time leads one into an infinite regress.

While it may appear that our idea of time is filled with riddles and paradoxes, perhaps such problems are only true of our idea of time and not the reality of time in itself. Immanuel Kant claimed that time in itself does not exist. Time is completely mind-dependent as is space, according to Kant. (See Episode 14, "Does the Mind Shape the World?" for a more detailed look at Kant's epistemological and metaphysical theories.) Time, Kant argued, is an intuition of our sensory understanding. It forms a part of our experience of an external world. Without creatures having the kind of experience of the world that we have, time would not exist.

On the other hand, when science studies the universe, it largely assumes that time is in some sense a feature or a part of reality, independent of our thinking. Time exists on its own and has certain features or qualities that we can objectively describe. We even discover some new things about time as we discover new things about our solar system—which exists, we assume, independent of our thinking about it. For Isaac Newton, one of the founders of modern physics, time was absolute. Time exists as duration and would exist even if other objects and things did not exist. Time, like space, is a sort of container with its own, objective existence. Everything in the universe exists in the present, in the now, though it has had a long history, its past, and has a future which appears to stretch far in the distance, or so at least it seems at this time.

In 1905, Albert Einstein published his theory of special relativity, which generated what has come to be known as the twin paradox. Contrary to Newton, Einstein argued that the present is not a simultaneous event occurring throughout the universe. Not all things share our now. Rather, as things approach the speed of light, which is a constant throughout the universe, time and space change. Now moves. As one approaches the speed of light, time slows. Thus, if twins were born on earth and one twin grew up to be an astronaut and took a trip traveling through space at a very high rate of speed, he would age more slowly than his twin on earth. If the astronaut twin had started his travels on their 25th birthday, and traveled for one year as he marked off the days *on the calendar in his spaceship,* upon returning to earth he would be 26 years of age. But the twin who had remained on earth, in a different reference frame, would now be 35 years of age since ten years would have passed in earth's frame of reference compared to the astronaut twin's frame of reference.

According to Einstein, as your frame of reference approaches the speed of light, time slows. So the question naturally arises, what does now mean? Does now refer to a specific moment in time? As Einstein remarks, "You have to accept the idea that subjective time with its emphasis on the now has no objective meaning. The distinction between past, present, and future is only an illusion, however persistent." Neurologists, like Paul Churchland, have taken a similar position viewing our notion of the passing or flow of time as an illusion, which our brains are wired to think in terms of. Some have argued that our notion of time flowing or moving is analogous to our ancestor's belief that the sun moves from east to west. Now we know that the sun's apparent motion is an illusion and that its actual motion cannot be detected by our senses.

However, philosophers like William Lane Craig insist that the passage or flow of time cannot be some universal and gigantic illusion. To doubt that time moves pushes us to the edge of absurdity analogous to your being able to genuinely doubt that you are presently reading this sentence.

So what is time? It is intimately with us every moment of our existence but remains mysterious. Neither history nor thought would be possible without it. But is time real, and if time is real, what precisely is it and how precisely does it exist?

Text Links

⤳ Turn to Velasquez, *Philosophy: A Text with Readings*, eleventh edition, and read Section 3.8, "Is Time Real?" This discussion gives you a much more in-depth look at St. Augustine's view of time from the human and from God's point of view in addition to a more extensive look at problems within the passage or flow view of time. There is also included an extended discussion of the view of Henri Bergson, which is not presented in this episode.

Key Terms

Absolute theories of time: The view that time exists independently of things and that time would pass or occur even if nothing was happening in the universe.

Einstein's relativity theories:

— **Special theory of relativity**: Concerns space/ time and the claim that all of the laws of physics are equally valid in all nonaccelerated frames of reference; light has a constant speed and these have the consequences that the mass of an object increases as it approaches the speed of light and time slows in reference to other frames of reference.

— **General theory of relativity**: An extension of the special theory of relativity to a geometric theory of gravitation with the principle that gravitational and inertial forces are equivalent.

Flow theory of time: The view that time is in motion. That moments of time, like water in a river, flow from the varyingly distant future into the present then recede into the more and more distant past.

Incompatible: Two claims are said to be incompatible when it is not possible for both of them to be simultaneously true though they could both be simultaneously false. For example, if I say today is Tuesday and you say it is Thursday, we cannot both be correct though we could both be wrong. Hence our two claims are incompatible.

Newtonian physics: Typically having to do with the theories of motion and universal gravitation described by Isaac Newton.

Paradox: When two apparently justified beliefs are seen to be incompatible or inconsistent.

Relational theories of time: The view that time could not exist independently of the existence of changing things and thus time should be conceived of as a kind of dimension of changing things.

Twin paradox: Generated from the special theory of relativity in which twins are no longer the same age. The different ages of twins results from one twin traveling away from earth at a highly accelerated speed. Since this accelerated and thus different reference frame, according to theory, will have time slow in relationship to the reference frame of earth, the traveling twin will age slower than the earth twin.

SELF-TEST

Multiple Choice

1. According to this episode, the Earth's 24 time zones resulted from
   a. a need for uniform global time by airlines
   b. a need for uniform global time by steamship lines
   c. a need for uniform global time by military planners
   d. a need for uniform global time by railroads

2. Aristotle found the existence of the present difficult since the present
   a. is always changing
   b. never changes, it always remains the present
   c. is a part of the future and the past which do not exist
   d. seems to speed up and slow down

3. According to J.M.E. McTaggert, time is
   a. unreal
   b. absolute and real
   c. real but only an idea
   d. intimately related to space, hence there is space time

4. McTaggert argued that no event could be said to be past, present, and future since these properties are
   a. incompatible
   b. of different durations
   c. imbalanced regarding their extent
   d. intrinsic to the flow of time

5. The view that time is a mind-dependent intuition was held by
   a. Aristotle
   b. Plato
   c. Kant
   d. Einstein

6. According to the subjective view of time,
   a. time actually has motion or movement
   b. there is only the present, and time motion is

an illusion
   c. time is a primitive concept and cannot be defined
   d. time is only in the mind of the beholder

7. St. Augustine's understanding of the nature of time is best summed by the quote
   a. "time does not exist independent of the space-time continuum"
   b. "time is part of the structure of our experience of the world"
   c. "time has both psychological, subjective and objectively reality"
   d. "I don't know"

8. The twin paradox was the result of
   a. Einstein's special theory of relativity
   b. Newton's theory of absolute time
   c. McTaggert's paradoxes of time
   d. Aristotle's paradox of time

9. Einstein seemed to prove that as one approaches the speed of light
   a. time slows relative to another, slower, frame of reference
   b. time speeds up relative to another, slower, frame of reference
   c. time is time and speed is only relevant to space
   d. time converts from seconds to nanoseconds

True or False

These questions are only from the reading assignment in Velasquez, Section 3.8. Specific page references are given in the answer key.

10. Immanuel Kant said "If no one asks me, I know what time is; if someone asks and I want to explain it, I do not know."

11. Saint Augustine argues that the present instant is the only part of time that is real.

12. The Australian philosopher J. J. C. Smart argues that our experience of time as passing is valid.

13. Real time for Henri Bergson is the time flow that I experience as moving from future, through present, and into the past.

14. According to Einstein, "the distinction between past, present, and future is only an illusion."

PARADOXICAL PURSUITS

If motion is a relational concept that is, something can be said to move only in relation to something else, which itself may or may not be moving. What is it that time moves in relation to, if we want to believe that time does in fact move or flow?

❧

You decide to travel back in time to kill Hitler and save the world from the horrors of World War II. You arrive in Berlin and it is 1929. Fortunately, you remember the stories your grandfather told you about these times and you brought a very old postcard with his boyhood Berlin address on it. You search out and find your grandfather. He is about your age, a bit younger. You befriend him, then together you find an old rifle at his home. It is a powerful weapon. As you examine it, it accidentally goes off and kills your grandfather. Do you cry in horror or do you do suddenly vanish since you couldn't exist because now your grandfather never had children, hence you never had parents, so you never existed.

❧

Is it possible to get into a capsule and travel slower than the earth is presently traveling, so that the twin paradox works in reverse? The returning astronaut is now older than her twin.

❧

Since we do not believe that fictional characters like Mickey Mouse or Hamlet could actually and literally do anything in the real world—after all, they don't really exist—how is it that the present is actually anything since it does seem to be affected by what doesn't actually exist, namely the future and the past?

❧

If you believe that time is real and moves or flows, do you believe that its motion is uniform and constant or does its flow vary? What keeps it constant, if you believe that it is constant? If you believe it flows evenly or at a constant speed, why is our experience of time so strewn with illusions? What is the cause of such an illusion?

APPLIED PHILOSOPHY

Ask a physics professor or a physicist why time is affected by speed. Then ask him or her if he or she thinks time is objectively real. Do they agree with Einstein that the word now has no objective meaning?

❧

Ask your grandparents or some other senior citizens if they think time speeds up as one gets older. Ask children if time seems to speed along.

❧

Given the twin paradox, if you were the traveling twin what would be the psychological effects upon you when you returned to Earth now that everyone you left behind is so much older?

❧

Do you think that St. Augustine's claiming not to know what time is, is simply an autobiographical remark about his ignorance or is there something to be learned about the very nature of time?

NET LINKS

Check out these Internet sites for additional relevant philosophical information. Remember the Internet is a web. Each of these listed sites is linked to other sites.

Philosophy Resources:

— http://www.earlham.edu/~peters/phil-inks.htm

— http://www.epistemelinks.com

— http://www.refdesk.com/philos.html

— http://www.erraticimpact.com

Encyclopedia of Philosophy:

— http://www.iep.utm.edu

Philosophy Papers:

— http://philosophy.hku.hk/paper/info.php

— http://cogprints.org/view/subjects/phil.html

— http://ndpr.nd.edu/review.cfm?id = 2201

Philosophy of Science:

— http://philsci-archive.pitt.edu

— http://www.friesian.com/science.htm

Aristotle:

— http://www.ucmp.berkeley.edu/history/aristo-tle.html

— http://www.philosophypages.com/ph/aris.htm

Albert Einstein:

— http://www.westegg.com/einstein/

Immanuel Kant:

— http://www.friesian.com/kant.htm

— http://www.hkbu.edu.hk/ ~ ppp/Kant.html

J.M.E. McTaggart:

— http://en.wikipedia.org/wiki/ J._M._E._McTaggart

Paul Churchland:

— http://philosophyfaculty.ucsd.edu/faculty/pchurchland/index.php

William Lane Craig:

— http://www.leaderu.com/offices/billcraig/index.html

Dagfinn Follesdal:

— http://lib.uci.edu/libraries/pubs/scctr/philoso-phy/follesdal.html

Hugh Mellor:

— http://people.pwf.cam.ac.uk/dhm11/

Paul Ricoeur:

— http://en.wikipedia.org/wiki/Paul_Ricoeur

— http://plato.stanford.edu/entries/ricoeur/

Quentin Smith:

— http://www.infidels.org/library/modern/quentin_smith

Lesson Ten

Does God Exist?

LEARNING OBJECTIVES

Upon completing this lesson, you should be familiar with the concepts contained in the lesson and be able to critically discuss:

- St. Anselm's ontological proof of God's existence.

- St. Thomas Aquinas's cosmological proof for God's existence.

- William Paley and the argument from design.

- the relevance of the big bang theory to God's existence.

- the problem of evil and God's existence.

- a sense of the sacred—secular or divine.

OVERVIEW

Across the midwest and southern part of the United States of America stretches what has come to be known as the Bible Belt. While its boundaries are not sharp, the Bible Belt refers to the deep cultural presence of Christianity. Christians, as most of us know, and Jews and Muslims as well, structure their lives around the belief in a single God. This belief in their God gives both meaning and purpose to all as-pects of their lives, from personal and family values to social and political values. While Christianity, Judaism, and Islam are some of the world's major religions, there are other world religions that do not include a belief in one God or even in any God or gods. Thus the question naturally presents itself, Does God exist?

For some who do believe in the existence of such a God, the evidence supporting this particular belief seems to be either obvious or unnecessary. For those who find evidence for the existence of a God inadequate or unpersuasive, the belief in a God seems to be motivated by some psychological need or socialization process rather than logical persuasion. Since belief in a God is not only an ancient belief, but also a claim about the nature of reality, about what actually exists, the debate among believers and nonbelievers over God's existence has had a long and varied history.

In the eleventh century A.D., a European theologian, St. Anselm, argued that God's existence could be deduced from the nature of God's being. Anselm's argument is known as the ontological argument or the ontological proof of God's existence. God, Anselm reasoned, is "that than which none greater can be conceived." Now, what if God were just an idea? If so, we could easily conceive of something greater—a God who actually existed. Therefore, Anselm concluded, if God is "that than which none greater can be conceived," then God must exist.

Over the centuries there have been many adherents and many critics of St. Anselm's ontologi-

57

cal argument. To many people today the argument seems wrong, in part because of the gap between thinking and reality. Having an idea about something that exists in reality seems in need of something more than its just being an idea. This concern is also reflected in other proofs or arguments for God's existence. Many of the more popular arguments for God's existence start not with an idea, but with our actual experience of the world.

In the thirteenth century A.D., another European theologian, St. Thomas Aquinas, gave five proofs for God's existence called The Five Ways. These arguments, he said, would persuade any rational person of the existence of God. Many people today still accept one or more of these arguments.

Aquinas' first argument relates to why things are in motion. The medieval physics of Aquinas' day considered rest as the only natural state; the law of inertia had not yet been formulated. Aquinas says whatever is moved is moved by another. If in a simultaneous series of motions A moves B, which moves C, which moves D, there must be a "first mover." That first unmoved mover, Aquinas claimed, is God.

According to Aquinas's second proof, God is the "uncaused cause." There are a number of versions of this argument but the one discussed in this episode concerns God as the Creator. For many scientifically-minded thinkers, evidence for the big bang, or some other naturalistic beginning for the universe, seems overwhelming. However, defenders of the existence of God claim that some reason must yet be given for the big bang, and this sort of reason science cannot provide.

Appealing to the principle of sufficient reason (or as this principle is referred to in this episode, the principle of universal explanation), believers argue that some explanation must be given for every fact of reality. The fact that there is a reality, that there is something, rather than nothing, marks a reason for God's existence. After all, what could be the cause of the universe as a whole but something that is regarded as being outside of the whole of nature, said to be timeless, nonspatial, changeless, and enormously powerful? Such a cause sounds a lot like the traditional view of God, according to a number of theologians such as William Lane Craig. Nonetheless, that argument alone does not demonstrate that this creator-God still actually exists, nor that it has the traditional features of an all knowing, all powerful, and all supreme being.

Others, while not focusing upon the origins of the universe, claim that the detailed intricacy and functioning of nature are sufficient to prove the existence of the traditional God. This type of argument is traditionally referred to as the teleological or design argument. While Aquinas's fifth proof was similar to the teleological argument, it was the nineteenth century European theologian, William Paley, who gave one of the most compelling design arguments. Paley used the example of someone finding a watch while crossing a heath. One could as easily apply Paley's example to finding a watch at the beach or while hiking through a forest. Upon finding a watch and observing the intricacy of its design, no one would hesitate to infer that it had been constructed intentionally by some intelligence. For Paley, if one examines closely the intricacy of nature, which is by far greater than that of a watch, the conclusion one should draw is that there is a divine designer—God.

However, not all organization and order is the result of intentional design. In his *Origin of the Species*, published in 1859, Charles Darwin described mechanisms of evolution, such that the order of nature, in particular that of all biological species, could be readily accounted for without an appeal to anything supernatural or beyond nature. (The second episode of *The Examined Life*, "What is Human Nature?" discusses how Darwin's views attacked the idea that nature exhibits design and purpose.) While some claim that the theory of evolution is just that, a theory, the ever-expanding fields of molecular biology, genetics, and organic chemistry have served to intensify the present debate between creationists and advocates of a naturalistic evolutionary view.

However, if the universe were designed by God, some thinkers are troubled by the presence of evil. The existence of evil seems to counter the idea of a God who is all knowing, all powerful, and all good. However, according to believers, evil is either the result of human choice and thus not really God's, or is a mystery woven into the fabric of reality in the form of natural disasters, diseases, and congenital deformities. Finite humans, the believer will argue, cannot fathom the wisdom of God in drawing good out of such evil.

Those who think the presence of evil is incompatible with the possible existence of God are simply too sentimental. This claim that God is not so sentimental as to eliminate all evil or that it is a mistake to hold God directly responsible for everything that happens fails, according to some critics, to account for such absolute horrors as Hitler, famines, or the crushing despair of disease. These sorts of cases cannot be accounted for by a vague appeal to mystery or our ignorance. And so the debate continues. Does God exist?

Perhaps the belief in the existence of God is not based upon argument or reason but is rather a personal, existential response to one's experience of the world. Some believers will accept all of the various problems concerning the purported evidence for and against God's existence, but evidence is not the source of their belief. For them, God's existence is a given. God's existence may or may not be within the realm of reason, and the difficulties surrounding issues of evidence may or may not be settled. But, for these believers, belief in God's existence is simply the best way for them to make sense of the world.

Social theorists, like the late nineteenth century psychologist Sigmund Freud, have argued that such commitments to a belief outside of all reasoning or evidence indicate psychological need. According to Freud, there is in all of us a sense of helplessness, or fear of death. Humans have created the idea of a God to soothe these fears. Still earlier thinkers, like the great late-eighteenth century philosopher, Immanuel Kant, argued that our moral understanding could not function without our also postulating the existence of God. While Kant also argued that no metaphysical proofs could rationally establish the existence of God, he did claim that God's existence was necessary for our belief that morally good people will be rewarded while evil people will be punished.

Some of us will look up at the vast night sky at a beautiful sunset or into the eyes of a baby and see evidence of God's existence. Others of us look upon the same sky, the same sunset, and the same baby and, while sharing a sense of awe and wonderment, never relate the experience to a God. In both cases the sense of awe is shared but one finds something sacred while the other remains secular. And so the question persists. Does God exist?

TEXT LINKS

☞ Turn to Velasquez, *Philosophy: A Text with Readings,* eleventh edition, and read Chapter 4, Section 4.1, "The Significance of Religion" for an introduction to the general issues of what constitutes religion.

☞ Section 4.2 of Velasquez, "Does God Exist?" places this ongoing philosophical debate in its rich historical context with detailed discussions of Aquinas, Anselm, and Paley.

☞ In Section 4.3, "Atheism, Agnosticism and the Problem of Evil" Velasquez provides extended descriptions and analyses of the positions of atheism and agnosticism along with a discussion of the problem of evil. This section also discusses the views of Freud and Kant on God.

KEY TERMS

Agnosticism: The view that sufficient or persuasive evidence has not been given to atheism.

Atheism: The view that sufficient or persuasive evidence has been given to believe that God does not exist.

Law of inertia: An object in motion will remain in motion unless acted upon by an external force and a body at rest will remain at rest unless acted upon by an external force.

Ontology: Area of study within metaphysics focused primarily upon the nature of being and existence.

Ontological argument: An argument that appears to prove God's existence based upon our idea of God.

Principle of sufficient: See principle of universal explanation.

Principle of universal explanation: The claim that for every positive fact of existence there is some, at least one, explanation for its existence.

Theism: The belief in a God (monotheism) or many gods (polytheism) or that God is everything (pantheism).

Theologian: A systematic study of the nature and existence of God or gods.

SELF-TEST

Multiple Choice

1. According to Saint Anselm, God's existence could be proven by starting with the
   a. Bible and Scripture
   b. miracles of Jesus
   c. need for a creator
   d. idea of God

2. According to the ontological proof of God's existence
   a. God is the greatest conceivable or the most perfect being
   b. evil is necessary for free will
   c. God is the unmoved mover
   d. God is the uncaused cause

3. The principle of universal explanation states that
   a. every positive fact of reality has an explanation
   b. God is the uncaused cause
   c. acceptable explanations are always scientifically testable
   d. some explanations are universally accepted

4. For Saint Thomas Aquinas, God was
   a. an enigma wrapped in a mystery
   b. an object of mystical intuition
   c. an uncaused cause
   d. a something; I know not what

5. To prove God's role as a designer of the universe, William Paley draws an analogy to finding a
   a. Bible
   b. butterfly
   c. moths adapting to changing environments
   d. watch

6. According to someone like Sigmund Freud, God is
   a. a creation of man to soothe his fear
   b. the greatest conceivable being
   c. the uncaused cause
   d. the unmoved mover

7. As discussed in this episode, the reality of the big bang theory as an account of the origin of the universe
   a. proves God does not exist
   b. proves God must exist
   c. neither supports nor undermines the possibility of God's existence
   d. proves God once existed but does not now exist

8. Darwin's theory of evolution raised problems for the traditional argument from design since
   a. according to Darwin there is no design or order
   b. design and order could be accounted for naturalistically
   c. with so much intricate design and order there must be more than one God
   d. evil in the design raises questions about God's goodness

9. The problem of evil initially claims that if God is all good, all knowing, all powerful, and there is in fact evil, then
   a. God cannot be all of those things or God doesn't exist
   b. God has abandoned Earth
   c. mysticism is the only solution
   d. polytheism is true

True or False

These questions are only from the reading assignment in Velasquez, Sections 4.1, 4.2, and 4.3. Specific page references are given in the answer key.

10. Monotheism is the belief that there is only one God.

11. The ontological argument is an argument for the existence of God deduced from the nature of God's being.

12. One version of the argument from design argues that "it is necessary to admit that there is a first efficient cause."

13. Spinoza supported pantheism, the belief that everything is God and God is everything.

14. The agnostic holds that the existence of evil proves conclusively that there is no God.

PARADOXICAL PURSUITS

According to the problem of evil, no God can be all good, all powerful, and all knowing if evil exists. If you claim that evil is necessary for choice, does such necessity limit God's power thus forcing you to give up the idea of God being all powerful?

❧

According to a popular form of the paradox of all powerfulness (omnipotence), an all powerful God should be able to create something so large that it cannot be moved, but if God creates something so large that it cannot be moved, then God is not all powerful. If God can't create something that large, then God is not all powerful. Hence nothing can be all powerful, as nothing can—in a similar context—be a married bachelor. How would you solve this paradox?

❧

Can it be true that there is one God, as some world religions claim, and that there are many gods, as other world religions claim? Can both positions be correct? Could both positions be mistaken?

❧

Is faith an alternative to reasoning for discovering the truth? Can you give a clear example of using faith outside of a religious context to discover truth?

❧

Can an atheist have faith that there is no God?

APPLIED PHILOSOPHY

Interview your friends and family about their belief in the existence of God. Does everyone agree on what God is like? Do they tend to offer arguments about creation and the way the world is, like Aquinas, or do they appeal simply to ideas like Anselm?

❧

Often on college campuses there are religious crusaders doing missionary work. Ask them why they hold the beliefs they hold. Do they offer evidence? Is the evidence like Aquinas's or Anselm's? Are you persuaded?

❧

Have a discussion about God, but do not use any references to the Bible.

❧

Attend a religious service, preferably one you are not very familiar with. Does this congregation understand God as you do? What are the differences? What are the similarities?

NET LINKS

Check out these Internet sites for additional relevant philosophical information. Remember the Internet is a web. Each of these listed sites is linked to other sites.

Philosophy Resources:

— http://www.earlham.edu/ ~ peters/phil-inks.htm

— http://www.epistemelinks.com

— http://www.refdesk.com/philos.html

— http://www.erraticimpact.com

Encyclopedia of Philosophy:

— http://www.iep.utm.edu

Philosophy Papers:

— http://philosophy.hku.hk/paper/info.php

— http://cogprints.org/view/subjects/phil.html

Philosophy of Religion:

— http://www.philosophyofreligion.info

— http://www.friesian.com/religion.htm

Philosophers discuss God's existence:

— http://www.infidels.org/library/modern

Atheist/Agnostic:

— http://www.infidels.org/library/modern/
nontheism/atheism/

Christian Connections:

— http://www.christiancadre.org/Philosophy.html

Evolution:

— http://evolution.berkeley.edu

— http://www.pbs.org/wgbh/evolution

Metaphysics:

— http://plato.stanford.edu/entries/aristotle-meta-
physics/

— http://mally.stanford.edu

— http://en.wikipedia.org/wiki/Metaphysics

St. Thomas Aquinas:

— http://plato.stanford.edu/entries/aquinas

Lesson Eleven

Can We Know God Through Experience?

LEARNING OBJECTIVES

Upon completing this lesson, you should be familiar with the concepts contained in the lesson and be able to critically discuss:

➣ varieties of religious experience.

➣ recurrent features of mystical experience.

➣ introvertive and extrovertive mystical experiences.

➣ the role of culture in interpreting mystical experience.

➣ hyper-religiosity and temporal lobe stimulation.

➣ the principle of credulity, the will to believe and the role of rationality and evidence in religious experience.

OVERVIEW

"Can we know God through experience?" is a rather simple and easy question for millions of people. Is an experience of God much like an experience of the ta-

ble in front of me or the chair I am sitting on? In most reported cases, such experiences are not described as ordinary perceptual experiences similar to perceiving the furniture around me. Nonetheless, all of the world's religions have reported, and continue to report, cases of individuals who have seen a God, or an angel or some divine reality by means of ordinary perceptual experience.

At Fatima, at Lourdes, children reported seeing the Virgin Mary. Mohammed describes seeing the angel Gabriel. The Buddha is reported to have seen all his past lives like a spinning wheel of fire. In 1981 in Medjugorje, in present day Bosnia-Herzegovinia, six teenagers described a vision of the Virgin Mary. In 1995, two women reported seeing the Virgin Mary on a hilltop near Santa Maria, California. These sorts of perceptual experiences are unusual. For those hearing of these sightings second hand there is typically skepticism, as there is in the case of the hierarchy of the Roman Catholic church.

For most religious people, having a religious experience seems instead to involve a deep sense of gratitude, guidance and order, and mystery or awe. Although there is often a sense that what is happening can't be identified with nature, a religious type of experience may also result from ordinary devotional practices. These sorts of religious experiences are not considered to be ordinary perceptual experiences, which are our typical means of discovering the

63

world around us. Rather they are closer to what William James described as involving that "feeling [which] is the deeper source of religion."

Another type of experience, traditionally regarded as also being religious, is a mystical experience. Mystical experiences have been reported among all of the world's major religions—Judaism, Christianity, Islam, Hinduism, Buddhism. They appear to be not only cross cultural, but also trans-historical, having been reported by individuals for over two thousand. Are such mystical experiences actual encounters with the divine as an objective reality, or are mystical encounters powerful but private experiences generating an illusion of contact beyond oneself? Western Christian mystics inevitably described their experience as bringing them into contact, or union, with God. Eastern mystics do not have such a God in their religious system of belief. Their encounter is typically with nothingness. These widespread differences in the content or interpretation of reported mystical experiences appear to be, in part, culturally relative.

Further distinctions are drawn between kinds of mystical experiences. Some are described as being extrovertive while others are described as introvertive. In the case of the extrovertive mystical experience, there is a sense of the world being transfigured or transformed; all distinctions and differences seem to dissolve or disappear. Such distinctions are only a reflection of our rational minds; in the mystical experience, all is one. In the case of the introvertive mystical experience, one enters into "the deepest and darkest part of oneself, detaching oneself from one's ordinary state of consciousness."

In the mystical experience there appears to be a breaking down of ordinary consciousness, which has been described by some philosophers as intentional in its structure. Intentional consciousness draws a distinction between the subject of experience and that which is experienced by the subject. (See Episode 7, "How Do We Encounter the World?" of *The Examined Life* for a discussion of the intentional structure of consciousness according to phenomenology.) The mystic reports a state of consciousness that is empty of the ordinary contents of consciousness yet is not a state of unconsciousness. The mystic is fully conscious though no longer separate from the world but one with reality. While mystical experiences do not last for long periods of time, they are often extremely powerful in their transformative effects upon the individual.

The mystical experience is also described in terms of feeling an overwhelming loving presence, an experience some call blessedness. St. Teresa of

Jesus, reported that the experience took "away my vices and made me virtuous and strong; for it was quite clear to me that these [mystical] experiences had immediately made me a different person." Some people refer to this transformative feature of a mystical experience as an ethical test of mysticism. To them, it demonstrates that such experiences are not just personal, subjective mental states, but are rather unique, profoundly transformative experiences of divine reality.

Since the mystical experience is one in which rationality and ordinary understandings of the world dissolve, mystics do not argue for nor try to prove their claims. Rather, they state with a seemingly unshakable conviction that the mystical experience is self-authenticating. Anyone who has had such a powerful experience finds it impossible to doubt that he or she was not in touch with something ultimately beyond one's self.

Advances in science have allowed researchers to monitor the brain at very subtle levels. Studies of brain functioning in relation to mystical experiences have yielded fascinating results. Brain scans reveal that someone in a mystical state has neural activity significantly distinct from neural activity when a person is awake, in a deep sleep, or unconscious because of injury or trauma. Thus the mystic appears to be conscious without being conscious of anything, as is consistently reported by mystics.

Since mystical experiences are rare could they be the result of some peculiar neurophysiological event or are they indeed unique encounters that are self-authenticating? According to Richard Swinburne's principle of credulity, such mystical experiences "ought to be taken at their face value in the absence of some positive reason for challenge." For Swinburne, the burden of proof is not the responsibility of the mystic, but of the person who doubts the mystic's claim. On the other hand, if the mystic's claim is about the nature of reality and the relationship between oneself and the world, then questions about the nature of the self and the relationship between self/mind and body do arise. Thus, the burden of proof may actually shift back to the mystic. (For a detailed discussion of the possible nature of the self see Episode 2, "What is Human Nature" and for a detailed discussion of the mind/body issues See Episode 3, "Is Mind Distinct from Body?" of *The Examined Life*.)

Perhaps proof, rationality, scientific investigation are not the appropriate or relevant methods for deciding issues raised by mysticism. William James, in "The Will to Believe," argues that some issues, particularly metaphysical issues must be decided by our passional nature. While not denying the importance of reasoning and evidence for many of our beliefs, James claims that in certain cases we are faced with a choice that is

a) a forced option—one in which we have no alternative;

b) a vital option—a choice that will make a significant difference in our lives; and

c) a living option—a choice that is not theoretical but actual in that it presents itself to us in the concreteness of our daily existence.

Given these conditions, we must choose according to our emotional predilections, that is our passional nature.

Whether emotional predilections provide some psychological comfort, or whether the mystical experience is so powerful that it relegates issues of truth and knowledge to a secondary role, the ongoing occurrence of mystical experiences remains a fascinating means by which people claim to know God.

TEXT LINKS

☞ Turn to Velasquez, *Philosophy: A Text With Readings*, eleventh edition, Section 4.4, "Traditional Religious Belief and Experience" for a detailed discussion of the views of William James along with descriptions of different mystics.

☞ Section 4.5 of Velasquez, "Nontraditional Religious Experience," focuses upon the contributions to religious thought that Soren Kierkegaard, Paul Tillich, and contemporary feminist theologians have made to the discussion of knowing God. This section concludes with discussions of Eastern religious traditions including Hinduism and Buddhism.

KEY TERMS

Epilepsy: A disorder of the nervous system characterized either by mild episodic loss of attention or sleepiness or by severe convulsions with loss of consciousness.

Ethical test in mysticism: A test that determines the validity of a person's mystical experiences by whether they make the person a morally better person.

Extrovertive mystical experiences: A sense of the world around one being transfigured and transformed giving the individual the experience of all distinctions becoming one.

Introvertive mystical experiences: A sense of one entering into "the deepest and darkest part of oneself, detaching oneself from one's ordinary state of consciousness."

Mystical experience: An enraptured and indescribable state of union with a higher reality or with God.

Mysticism: A tradition which focuses upon the study of and/or the having of a unique experience called a mystical experience.

Principle of credulity: The view that mystical experiences should be taken at their face value when we have no positive reason to doubt them.

SELF-TEST

Multiple Choice

1. Religious experiences are
   a. always mystical experiences
   b. always visions of saints and angels
   c. not of one kind but varied
   d. not had by children

2. The content or interpretation of mystical experience is said to be
   a. universal and constant
   b. only of God
   c. only of Vishnu
   d. culturally relative

3. According to Rudolf Otto, the essential element in religious experience is an awareness of another as holy and divine, and this awareness is characterized by
   a. awe and dread
   b. joy and fun
   c. pleasure and playfulness
   d. fear and giddiness

4. A universal feature of all mystical experiences is
   a. unity or union
   b. insight into the basic structure of the universe
   c. a profound separation from that which is not human
   d. a terror as one approaches the existential abyss

5. Mystical experiences are found in
   a. only Eastern religious traditions
   b. Eastern and some Native American Indian religious traditions
   c. Eastern and Middle Eastern (Islamic) religious traditions
   d. all of the world's major religions

6. According to the extrovertive mystical experience
   a. one enters into "the deepest and darkest part of oneself, detaching oneself from one's ordinary state of consciousness"
   b. the world around one is transfigured and transformed, giving one the experience of all distinctions and categories of individuals
   c. the world around one is transfigured and transformed, giving one the experience of all distinctions becoming one
   d. one enters into "the deepest and darkest part of oneself, attaching oneself to one's ordinary state of consciousness."

7. A central philosophical question regarding mystical experience is
   a. whether or not such experiences ever really happen
   b. whether or not drugs can induce mystical states
   c. whether or not the mystical state is a powerful but essentially personal, subjective experience
   d. why do more women than men have mystical experiences

8. The ethical test of mystical experience concerns the power of such experiences to
   a. make criminals turn themselves in
   b. profoundly change one to be better
   c. demonstrate to those who have not had such an experience just how good the experience is
   d. allow the individual to gaze directly upon God's goodness

9. According to the principle of credulity
   a. the younger a person is the more credulous that person's beliefs will be
   b. experiences ought never to be taken at their face value
   c. experiences ought to be taken at their face value even in the face of some positive reason for challenge
   d. experiences ought to be taken at their face value in the absence of some positive reason for challenge

10. For William James, a person should choose a belief when there is insufficient evidence for the belief, if the options presented are
    a. very appealing, comfortable, and fun
    b. forced, living, and monumental
    c. isolated, clear, and popular
    d. profound, theoretical, and abstract

11. The syndrome of hyper-religiosity is associated with
    a. anemics
    b. diabetics
    c. epileptics
    d. sinusitis

True or False

These questions are only from the reading assignment in Velasquez, Sections 4.4 and 4.5. Specific page references are given in the answer key.

12. William James in "The Will to Believe" wrote: "'Do not decide, but leave the question open,' is itself a decision."

13. A numinous experience is often characterized by feelings of terror, mystery, and bliss.

14. According to Kierkegaard, God is not subject to rational, objective analysis.

15. Paul Tillich claimed that "Depth is what the word God means, the source of your being, of your ultimate concern, of what you take seriously without any reservation."

16. According to feminist theologian Mary Daly, the male conception of God has had a profoundly oppressive impact on women.

PARADOXICAL PURSUITS

Within the mystical tradition, the mystical experience is described as ultimately ineffable, meaning it cannot be adequately described with language. If so, why is there so much talk by mystics about mysticism? Can you think of other ordinary aspects of your experience which are ineffable? What about colors, tastes, temperatures, pleasures, and pains?

In this episode Professor Patricia Churchland suggests that mystical experiences may be "ways that the brain is just doing things, perhaps not even very healthy ways of doing things." How would the possibility of these "unhealthy ways" relate to the ethical test of mystical experience?

If God is an infinite, all-powerful deity, how could a finite, relatively powerless creature come into union with such a being, as mystics describe? Is this similar to trying to imagine yourself being carried along, balanced with both feet on the back of a spider?

APPLIED PHILOSOPHY

Have you ever had a mystical experience? Be sure not to confuse it with popular "weird" experiences people report like out of body experiences, or seeing UFO's. Be sure you understand the essential marks of the mystical.

Have any of your family or friends had mystical experiences? What do they believe such experiences are? Do they agree or disagree with the descriptions presented in this episode?

Ask your priest, rabbi, mullah, or preacher what he or she thinks of mysticism. Do they agree or disagree with the descriptions presented in this episode?

NET LINKS

Check out these Internet websites for additional relevant philosophical information. Remember the Internet is a web. Each of these listed sites is linked to other sites.

Philosophy Resources:

— http://www.earlham.edu/ ~ peters/phil-inks.htm

— http://www.epistemelinks.com

— http://www.refdesk.com/philos.html

— http://www.erraticimpact.com

Encyclopedia of Philosophy:

— http://www.iep.utm.edu

Philosophy Papers:

— http://philosophy.hku.hk/paper/info.php

— http://cogprints.org/view/subjects/phil.html

Buddhism:

— http://www.buddha101.com

— http://webspace.ship.edu/cgboer/buddha-intro.html

Christianity:

— http://www.mcgill.ca/phwr/

Eastern and Western Philosophy:

— http:/www.uni-giessen.de/ ~ gk1415/philosophy.htm

Islam:

— http://www.muslimphilosophy.com

Metaphysics:

— http://plato.stanford.edu/entries/aristotle-metaphysics/

— http://en.wikipedia.org/wiki/Metaphysics

Mysticism:

— http://plato.stanford.edu/entries/mysticism/

Marilyn Adams:

— http://en.wikipedia.org/wiki/
Marilyn_McCord_Adams

William Alston:

— http://www.homestead.com/philofreligion/
Alston.html

Patricia Churchland:

— http://philosophy.ucsd.edu/faculty/pschurch-
land/index_hires.html

William Lane Craig:

— http://www.leaderu.com/offices/billcraig/
index.html

William James:

— http://www.des.emory.edu/mfp/james.html

Lesson Twelve

Is Reason the Source of Knowledge?

LEARNING OBJECTIVES?

Upon completing this lesson, you should be familiar with the concepts contained in the lesson and able to critically discuss:

- the difference between rationalism and empiricism.

- the significance of mathematics, particularly geometry, for rationalism.

- the significance of innate ideas for rationalism.

- Plato's Dialogue, *The Meno*, and its significance for the theory of innate ideas.

- rationalism's difficulty with experimental science/empiricism.

OVERVIEW

You overhear someone remark that he is a proud, new uncle. Without listening further, you think about the idea of being an uncle and you reason that this fellow must have either a niece or a nephew. Your reasoning does not necessarily commit you to either one of these possibilities but you do know for certain, from reasoning alone, that this is true. With pure reasoning about an idea, you have discovered a truth about the world.

On the other hand, suppose an evil sociology professor had assigned you the task of taking an informal poll to determine the average income of married bachelors. You would not undertake this poll. Rather, through reasoning alone, you could infer that the world does not contain a single married bachelor. These may be trivial examples of what the great philosophical school of thought known as rationalism claims on a grander scale. However, for a rationalist, the answer to the question, "Is reason alone the source of knowledge?" would be a straightforward, "Certainly."

By the seventeenth century, central tenets within the traditional European system of belief were in upheaval. For centuries, most people had believed that the earth was at the center of the universe and the sun daily moved from east to west. Thanks to Nicolas Copernicus, the earth was no longer believed to be at the center. The sun's motion was actually an illusion generated by the spinning motion of Earth as it orbited the sun. While some members of the church attempted to suppress such views, the work of Johannes Kepler in northern Europe, and Galileo Galilei in southern Europe, seemingly outflanked traditional views.

During this tumultuous time, the prevailing system of belief seemed infested with doubt. René Descartes, the father of modern philosophy, was not only keenly aware of this upheaval, but claimed to have discovered the solution to humanity's deep-seated doubts and confusion. Being one of history's great mathematicians, Descartes was fully convinced that by fixing upon at least one idea that he could know with certainty, he could build anew the foundations of a solid system of knowledge. Following the method of geometry, in which one starts with apparently obvious assumptions (axioms) in order to deduce not so obvious conclusions (theorems), Descartes believed he could set all of human knowledge on a secure foundation.

Descartes claimed that his knowledge of himself, as a thinking thing, could not be doubted. This gave him a starting to point to build upon. (See Episode 2, "What is Human Nature?" and Episode 3, "Is Mind Distinct from Body?") As Descartes built on this foundation, he discovered that even his idea of material or physical objects did not come from experience or through his senses, but was innate to his mind. As he pondered a piece of wax, he first noted all of its physical properties—its color, taste, temperature, shape, smell, the sound it made when tapped. But when he brought the wax close to a flame all of these physical properties changed. Yet, as Descartes noted, we still judge the wax to be the same piece of wax. The idea of a physical or material object—the idea of a thing that endures through all of these perceived changes—is, for Descartes, an innate idea.

Innate ideas have served as a defining characteristic of the philosophical school known as rationalism. Rationalists not only argue that many, if not most or all, ideas do not and could not arise from experience. Opposing the rationalists, and pitted in an intellectual battle over the source of ideas were the empiricists. Where the rationalists viewed perception as a confused way of thinking, empiricists claimed that the mind is a blank tablet, a *tabula rasa,* at birth. We obtain our ideas only through perception and experience.

Some of history's great rationalists—Plato, Descartes, Spinoza, and Leibniz—were extraordinarily gifted mathematicians. Descartes developed analytic geometry and cartesian coordinates. Leibniz developed the calculus which may have predated Newton's work in the field. What mathematical and logical systems seem to provide are necessary truths—truths, according to Leibniz, that hold in all possible worlds.

Experience and the experimental sciences provide contingent truths, which are sometimes characterized as being true in at least this world and possibly some other worlds, but are not true in all possible worlds. While in this world, gravity may make it possible for you to get up from where you are at this moment and walk across the floor to a wall. Gravity makes it impossible for you to walk up the wall to the ceiling then across the ceiling. In the world of your imagination, you might imagine yourself violating the restraints of gravity. Hence the truths of science regarding gravity seem to be contingent truths—truths that are true in this world but not in the world of your imagination. On the other hand, no matter what world you are in or imagine, a rationalist would claim, a triangle will have three sides and two plus three will equal five. These are the necessary truths of mathematics and logic known only through pure reasoning, a rationalist would claim.

If experience is not the source of innate ideas and necessary truths, what is their source? Plato argued that our soul had come into contact with these ideas in a previous life. Due to the trauma of our soul entering the body we forgot them. For Plato, learning about these ideas is actually a case of remembering. In his dialogue, *The Meno,* Socrates demonstrates to Meno how such innate ideas can be elicited even from a slave boy's memory by means of questioning.

The necessity of mathematics and logic suggested to the rationalists that all knowledge should be accounted for through reason alone. For Descartes, and Galileo, reality ultimately consisted of corpuscles; what the ancient Greeks had called atoms. These, the smallest bits of matter, have only mathematical properties such as spatial location, motion, shape, figure, and size. Other properties like color, taste, or sound were not considered objective but subjective properties. For Descartes, these subjective properties were located in the mind. For rationalists, only mathematical or quantifiable properties were objective. Hence, one could know about reality from pure reasoning, since reality was ultimately mathematical in nature.

According to many rationalists, this view of reality as "ultimately mathematical" was consistent with their religious view that reality had been created by God with an underlying, eternal order. Since the human mind is made in the image of God, as claimed in Genesis, man through his capacity to reason could know the will of God. By exercising this divine capacity, humans became god-like. (See Episode 2, "What is Human Nature?" for a more complete treatment of the religious view of human reason as unique and its relationship to the divine.) The empiricist view of the human mind as a blank tablet seemed undignified to many a rationalist.

As the experimental sciences grew, the rationalist view of innate ideas underwent much criticism and change. After John Locke attacked Descartes' doctrine of innate ideas, Gottfried Wilhelm Leibniz described innate ideas as tendencies, inclinations, or natural potentials. For Leibniz, innate ideas are not the full fledged, content-filled ideas of Plato or Descartes. Instead, innate ideas need experience to shape. Leibniz's comparison of innate ideas to a block of marble with veins running through it, which mark out the shape of Hercules, is intended to illustrate how Hercules is innate to the marble. According to Leibniz such a marble block would be more "determined" to take the shape of Hercules than some other figure. So we are more disposed to think of reality one way as opposed to another because of the innate ideas within us.

While Leibniz's analogy has not been universally accepted, the rationalists' view that mathematics and logic yield truths, and that the language of reality is mathematical, seems to support what William James called our "sentiment of rationality." According to James, we have a deep desire for explanation, a conviction that whatever our inquiry, there should be a reason to explain it. And what better explanations than those that appear necessary and eternal—the so called laws of nature, mathematics and logic.

Text Links

➣ Turn to Velasquez, *Philosophy: A Text with Readings*, eleventh edition, and read Section 5.1, "Why is Knowledge a Problem?" for an interesting discussion of why we need to understand knowledge.

➣ Read 5.2, "Is Reason the Source of Our Knowledge?" where Velasquez discusses the rationalists, focusing on Descartes, Plato, and innate ideas.

➣ Check Velasquez, Section 5.7, "A Defense of Skepticism" by Peter Unger and "How Do We Know Anything?" by Thomas Nagel for nicely written, accessible contemporary discussions of the sorts of skeptical doubts raised by Descartes.

Key Terms

Axioms: A proposition or truth claim held to be self-evidently true and so neither requiring nor capable of proof. (See the definitions of theorem and proof below.)

Contingent Truths: Truth claims that are described by some philosophers as being true in a particular context or dependent upon at least one world but not all worlds. Thus, if it is a contingent truth that there is an apple on my desk, it is contingent since there are other circumstances or worlds where it is false that there is an apple on my desk. (See the definition of necessary truth below.)

Empiricism: The view that all of our ideas come from experience and that no belief about any matter of fact can be known independently of experience.

Geometry: The mathematical study of the properties and relationships of points, lines, angles, surfaces, and solids.

Innate ideas: The actual having or the disposition to acquire ideas or concepts such as being, substance, duration, and even God in some cases.

Law of inertia: According to Galileo and Newton, a natural law describing the fact that an object at rest will remain at rest, while an object in motion will remain in motion.

Necessary truths: Truth claims that are described by some philosophers as being universally true, or true in all possible worlds. Thus, if it is a necessary truth that three is a prime number, then three is a prime number in all possible worlds or is universally true.

Proof: A belief or set of beliefs or propositions that are offered in support of the truth of the claim of another belief or proposition. The proof that this U.S. president is a U.S. citizen is that all U.S. presidents are U.S. citizens. Also the act of giving reasons to believe.

Properties: A quality or attribute of a thing or substance that cannot exist independent of some substance. Color and beauty are properties. While a bicycle can exist without being blue, blue can only exist as part of a bicycle or substance.

Pure reasoning: As used in this episode, it means to think or understand independent of sensory experience.

Rationalism: The view that the mind has "innate" ideas or powers and that by means of this knowledge, matters of fact or reality can be had independent of sensory input.

Tabula rasa: Literally, the blank tablet; philosophically, a description most often associated with empiricists' views of the "empty" or "blank" mind prior to experience furnishing the mind with impressions or ideas.

Theorems: Propositions or truth claims that are typically deduced using logical rules from a set of axioms or first principles.

Theory: A general and/or abstract proposition used to explain a set of phenomena or to give an account of a confirmed hypothesis.

SELF-TEST

Multiple Choice

1. Rationalism is the view that
   a. our knowledge of the universe comes through our senses
   b. we can discover basic laws of the universe through pure reason.
   c. a rigid experimental method is needed to acquire knowledge of the universe
   d. knowledge of the universe ultimately rests upon authority

2. Empiricism is the view that
   a. our knowledge of the universe comes through our senses
   b. we can discover basic laws of the universe through pure reason
   c. a rigid experimental method is needed to acquire knowledge of the universe.
   d. knowledge of the universe ultimately rests upon authority

3. European thought during the seventeenth century A.D., like that of fourth century B.C. Greece, was marked by
   a. stability and widespread social acceptance
   b. simplicity and lack of imagination
   c. staleness and stagnation
   d. change, uncertainty, and perilousness

4. Geometry proved an ideal model for rationalistic thought since it
   a. yielded truths that appeared indisputable and certain
   b. was only known by a select few researchers
   c. relied only upon experience for its axioms
   d. was discovered by a Greek

5. Descartes uses the example of the wax to demonstrate that
   a. ideas ultimately arise within experience
   b. some innate ideas are acquired from experience
   c. he could not be certain he was awake or dreaming
   d. we know physical or material objects through an intuition of the mind

6. Rationalists prefer mathematics and logic since these yield
   a. contingent truths
   b. personal truths
   c. necessary truths
   d. historical truths

7. Most _____ believe that that basic principles of logic and math are innate.
   a. rationalists
   b. empiricists
   c. philosophers
   d. mathematicians

8. Truths based upon experience are said to be
   a. contingent truths
   b. personal truths
   c. necessary truths
   d. historical truths

9. According to many rationalists, the only properties of an object that are objective are its
   a. mathematical properties
   b. visual properties
   c. acquired properties
   d. cultural properties

10. Innate ideas are traditionally regarded as those ideas that we
    a. acquire through experience
    b. have independent of experience
    c. acquire on legitimate authority
    d. acquire through our culture and upbringing

11. According to Plato, learning is best understood as
    a. being filled with ideas
    b. rote memorization of new ideas
    c. remembering ideas one already possesses
    d. acquiring new ideas through the work of others

12. In Plato's dialogue, *The Meno*, Socrates has a slave boy solve
    a. a puzzle about the nature of justice
    b. a mathematical problem
    c. a dispute over the nature of a fair wage
    d. the problem of freedom and slavery

13. Leibniz's example of veins in a block of marble marking out the figure of Hercules was an attempt to illustrate the nature of
    a. Greek mythology in modern European culture
    b. the evolution of sculpture in European history
    c. the nature of innate ideas
    d. the power of empiricism

True or False

These questions are only from the reading assignment in Velasquez, Section 5.2. Specific page references are given in the answer key.

14. Plato and Descartes were rationalists.

15. Descartes's assumed that "some evil genius not less powerful than deceitful, has employed his whole energies in deceiving me."

16. Most of the rationalists felt that the basic principles of logic and math could not be innate ideas in us.

17. In the *Meno*, Socrates claims that ideas about geometry are remembered and must have been acquired at some time before we were born.

18. Leibniz completely rejected the theory of innate ideas.

PARADOXICAL PURSUITS

Can there be any laws of nature or mathematics if you believe you get all of your ideas from experience? Remember that experience only gives us contingent truths.

❧

Does it tend to be true that 2 + 2 = 4 or is it always and forever true that 2 + 2 = 4? Do you think that perhaps in China or Italy you could meet someone who was an uncle but had neither niece nor nephew? How about in an alien culture on another planet?

❧

If an idea, like the ideas of chair, book, ice cream, and having fun, are general in nature—that is, they can apply to a number of different, particular things—how do such ideas come to pick out the particular things they seem to obviously pick out? Can you avoid answering this question by simply listing more ideas (probably giving a definition of what an idea means by using other ideas in your definition) and hence only putting the question off and not really answering it at all?

APPLIED PHILOSOPHY

Ask a math teacher if he or she is an empiricist or a rationalist regarding mathematics. Does he or she regard mathematics as a system of contingent truths or necessary truths? How would you describe the views of empiricism and rationalism if this teacher is unfamiliar with them?

❧

Ask a science teacher if he or she is an empiricist or a rationalist regarding science. Does he or she regard the laws of nature as a system of contingent truths or necessary truths? How would you describe the views of empiricism and rationalism if this teacher is unfamiliar with them?

❧

Try out Descartes' wax example on some of your friends or family. Are they persuaded that the idea of a material object is innate? Do they think the wax has remained the same wax through all of its perceptual changes?

NET LINKS

Check out these Internet websites for additional relevant philosophical information. Remember the Internet is a web. Each of these listed sites is linked to other sites.

Philosophy Resources:

— http://www.earlham.edu/ ~ peters/phil-inks.htm

— http://www.epistemelinks.com

— http://www.refdesk.com/philos.html

— http://www.erraticimpact.com

Encyclopedia of Philosophy:

— http://www.iep.utm.edu

Philosophy Papers:

— http://philosophy.hku.hk/paper/info.php

— http://cogprints.org/view/subjects/phil.html

Rationalism vs. Empiricism:

— http://plato.stanford.edu/entries/rationalism-empiricism

René Descartes:

— http://radicalacademy.com/adiphilrational-ism.htm

William James:

— http://plato.stanford.edu/entries/james

— http://www.des.emory.edu/mfp/james.html

Gottfried Wilhelm Leibniz:

— http://plato.stanford.edu/entries/leibniz-mind

— http://mally.stanford.edu/leibniz.html

Plato:

— http://www.philosohypages.com/ph/plat.htm

— http://classics.mit.edu/plato/meno.html

— http://plato-dialogues.org/plato.htm

Lesson Thirteen

Does Knowledge Depend on Experience?

LEARNING OBJECTIVES

Upon completing this lesson, you should be familiar with the concepts contained in the lesson and be able to critically discuss:

☞ the general characteristics of the philosophical position of empiricism.

☞ John Locke's empiricism and its troublesome "gap" between mental experience and the material world.

☞ George Berkeley's solution to Locke's "gap" and David Hume's skepticism regarding any rational solution to Locke's "gap."

☞ David Hume's skepticism regarding our knowledge of the uniformity of nature.

☞ empiricism, naturalism, and science.

☞ W.V. Quine's view of contemporary empiricism and language.

OVERVIEW

Are you male or female? Are you now standing, sitting, or walking? Are you now reading this Overview? Questions such as these, which seem to have easy and ready answers, appeal to our sensory experience or perception of the world. We seem to see, hear, taste, smell, and feel our way through a three dimensional world of objects. If you claim or believe that sensory experience or perception is the means by which we come to know the world or, perhaps a bit stronger, that through sensory experience or perception our minds come to have the ideas we have, then you are an empiricist. A true empiricist would claim that all of our knowledge comes from experience.

The tenets of empiricism seem to be some of the strongest of our philosophical presuppositions. Our fascination with technology and the historical relationship between science and empiricism may have nurtured our strong empiricist beliefs.

Among the great British empiricists—John Locke, George Berkeley, and David Hume—it was John Locke and David Hume who were particularly impressed by the accomplishments of Sir Isaac Newton. Newton described his theories as having been "inferred from the phenomena." As a physicist, he was not concerned with understanding how our

75

knowledge or experience of the world was possible. But for John Locke, the philosophical problem of how the mind is furnished with the materials of knowledge dominated his philosophical reflection.

In his *Essay Concerning Human Understanding*, published in 1690, John Locke argued that all knowledge is founded in experience. "Let us suppose the mind to be, as we say, white paper, void of all characters, without any ideas," Locke began. First, the mind becomes aware of simple ideas such as color, taste, sound, and smell. Given the mind's power of understanding, these simple ideas are repeated, compared, and united into complex ideas. Some complex ideas are already united in experience when they are perceived and these we judge to be material objects. But it is not in the power of anyone, Locke maintained, to frame or invent one simple new idea.

According to Locke, our ideas represent to us the way the material or physical world exists. To draw an analogy, our mind is like a mirror reflecting the external world. The immediate object we know is the reflected image in the mind rather than the things that cause the reflection.

One of the key questions to arise out of Locke's view concerning the relationship between ideas and external material objects is how exactly do mental things—ideas—copy material things? (For a related discussion concerning the relationship between mind and body and their purported interaction see Episode 3, "Is Mind Distinct From Body?") Locke was acutely aware of this gap between an idea of a physical object and the object itself. Though he built no theoretical bridge across the "gap," he did claim that no one in earnest could be so skeptical as to doubt the existence of an external material world. In short order, both of Locke's successors—George Berkeley and David Hume—would doubt our knowledge of a material or physical world.

For Bishop George Berkeley, there were not two distinct realms to be bridged but only one—the realm of ideas. Objects are just collections of ideas. "Thus, for example, a certain color, taste, smell, figure, and consistence, having been observed to go together, are accounted one distinct thing, signified by the name apple. Other collections of ideas constitute a stone, a book, a tree, and the like," argued Berkeley. However, some ideas seem to come to us involuntarily and persist independent of our individual experiences. For Berkeley, such ideas could only be accounted for by something that could perceive or think ideas constantly, and the only mind capable of such a feat was God.

David Hume viewed God as yet another thing external to our own experience. Thus God's existence, like material objects, could not simply be postulated but must be proven. Not only could David Hume not find satisfactory proof for the existence of God, Hume found all proofs of an external, material world impossible as well. Hume fully understood the apparent impossibility of moving beyond the realm of one's own experience to another realm that is independent and outside of all experience.

According to David Hume, we have no way of proving that the future will resemble the past or the present. For Hume, causality is a matter of the constant conjunction between experiences. We come to say that cause C brings about effect E because we always experience C before E; that is, they are constantly conjoined. Hume argued that no one has experienced the constant conjunction between a material world and our experiences independent of one's experiences. Thus, no one could claim that our experiences are caused by an external, material world.

It was Hume's keen analytic mind that took Locke's empiricist principles to their apparent logical conclusion—skepticism—an idea that is intellectually formidable even to this day. But Hume admitted that when he left his study and was among friends, perhaps playing one of his favorite games—backgammon, these skeptical doubts were forgotten.

Among contemporary philosophers—like John Searle of UC Berkeley and Hilary Putnam of Harvard University—the empiricism of seventeenth and eighteenth century philosophers Locke, Berkeley, and Hume is the result of a false start. The basic problem is in postulating that sensation occurs in some "inner theatre," or that we are only indirectly aware of material objects by means of ideas in our mind caused by external objects. For both Searle and Putnam, we directly see books, hands, and bicycles.

For much of the history of philosophy, the view of our minds as some private, inner world that can only be known indirectly by others if we choose to communicate through language, was the dominant model. However, some contemporary philosophers have claimed that this "inner theatre" view, which results in skepticism, is itself the result of a false view of language. Language is not a way of labeling inner thoughts but, as W.V. Quine remarked, "The child learns language from his elders, not by seeing what's going on inside of the mind of the person who's using the words and then relating the thoughts to the words. [Rather] language is learned only from one another's behavior. And all the meanings that we gather and grasp are learned finally by observing other people's behavior in situations, observing under what circumstances they utter the words."

Some have described Quine as the twentieth century's David Hume. According to Quine, we as children learn cognitive language (that part of our language used to make statements of fact or belief), through learning to assent or dissent to *occasion sentences*. Occasion sentences, like "It is windy" or "I am sitting" are true or false at particular moments and places when uttered in the presence of appropriate stimulations. Occasion sentences are not the sorts of sentences that are true or false once and for all. For Quine, occasion sentences elicit a response that is immediate, unthinking, and unreflective. These are the types of sentences a child first learns.

Occasion sentences are a form of observation sentences. Observation sentences are sentences about the world that are fundamental to science. Observation sentences are the evidence for scientific theories, according to Quine.

While both Hume and Quine are empiricists and naturalists, Quine does not share the traditional view of the mind as some "inner theatre." Additionally, Hume has been described as taking a "narrow inductive" view of the relationship between our experience and scientific theories whereas Quine talks about our "web of belief." Quine's views have been described as holistic compared to Hume's more piecemeal approach. While Hume argued that our scientific beliefs are individually drawn from experience, Quine argues that our scientific beliefs form a complex, elaborate web and that experience only impinges along the web's periphery. Theories tell us what observable conditions should occur given some prior set of observable conditions. If the second set of observable conditions fails to occur given the first set of conditions, then our theory does not pass its test.

While empiricists tend to be naturalists, searching for rational accounts of natural phenomena within the sphere of nature as opposed to the supernatural, the progress of science supports neither empiricism nor rationalism to the exclusion of the other. For in science we seem to find an ever so subtle wedding of reason and experience. It may be that a complete understanding of our experience of the world requires some synthesis or combination of rationalism and empiricism.

TEXT LINKS

- Turn to Velasquez, *Philosophy: A Text with Readings,* eleventh edition, and read Section 5.3, "Can the Senses Account for All of Our Knowledge?" for an extended overview of empiricism.

- Read Section 5.6, "Historical Showcase: Hume." These showcases contain not only extended excerpts from original works by the figures who are being showcased, but also fascinating biographical information placing each in the context of his historical period. There is also a set of questions which follow. These are excellent essay questions, which will further test your understanding.

KEY TERMS

Cognitive language: The use of language to make claims which have truth value or to express beliefs.

Ideas: As used by empiricists, basically the contents of the mind which have been acquired, ultimately, through sensory experience.

Inductive: Either an act of the understanding in which a generalization is made from some particulars, or a probable inference is claimed to hold between two or more statements.

Naturalism: Seeking natural explanations for empirical phenomena or experience as opposed to supernatural explanations for the same phenomena or experience.

Observation sentences: For W.V. Quine, those sentences which report observable situations.

Occasion sentences: Observation sentences that are true on a particular occasion but may not be true on another occasion. For example, "It's raining" or "I'm wearing a coat."

Skepticism: To doubt the truth of some claim or the adequacy of the justification for some claim.

Sensory experience: That experience which results from our senses such as sight, smell, hearing, touch, and taste.

SELF-TEST

Multiple Choice

1. Empiricism is the view that
   a. the mind has certain ideas innately
   b. innate ideas are abstract entities
   c. all legitimate ideas come from authority
   d. sense experience is the source of ideas

2. According to John Locke, which of the following is a simple idea?
   a. a chair
   b. a color
   c. a blade of grass
   d. a single apple

3. According to John Locke, which of the following is a complex idea?
   a. intense heat
   b. powerful pleasure
   c. a single desk
   d. the color yellow

4. According to Locke's empiricism, there is a gap between
   a. simple ideas and complex ideas
   b. ideas and the material objects they are supposed copies of
   c. causes and their effects
   d. religion and justice

5. For George Berkeley, material objects
   a. are what science studies
   b. can only be known indirectly
   c. are rare and difficult to know
   d. do not exist

6. George Berkeley argued that an object is
   a. a something; I know not what
   b. a material thing
   c. always an illusion
   d. a collection of ideas

7. According to David Hume, ideas are distinguished from impressions by
   a. ideas being real while impressions are not
   b. impressions having more force and vivacity
   c. impressions being copies of ideas
   d. ideas being one and all complex

8. David Hume argued that causality was
   a. the constant conjunction between distinct events
   b. the necessary relationship between a cause and its effect
   c. the universal and eternal relationship between natural events
   d. the mortar between events, as divinely designed

9. Our belief in an external, material world is, for Hume, the result of
   a. a rational analysis of the nature of a sense impression
   b. a rational analysis of the nature of an idea
   c. a very likely cause given its effect, which is our experience
   d. custom and habit

10. According to some contemporary philosophers, traditional empiricism resulted in skepticism because it treated experience or sensation as
    a. only being about the external world and not our internal world
    b. being "inside us," or occurring in some "inner theatre" of our mind
    c. a confused form of thinking
    d. requiring innate ideas

11. According to a contemporary empiricist like W.V. Quine, we learn the meanings of a language by
    a. correctly labeling ideas in our mind
    b. getting the correct label on specific objects in the world
    c. observing people's behaviors in specific situations while specific words are uttered
    d. studying dictionaries early in life

Use either a or b to indicate how Quine would label each of the following sentences.

a. occasion sentence
b. not an occasion sentence

_____12. I am answering a question in this booklet.

_____13. Force equals mass times acceleration.

_____14. My pen is out of ink.

_____15. The sum of the interior angles of a triangle equals 180 degrees.

_____16. This page is rectangular.

True or False

These questions are only from the reading assignment in Velasquez, Section 5.3. Specific page references are given in the answer key.

17 Empiricism is the belief that all knowledge about the world comes from or is based on the senses.

18. The British empiricists were Locke, Berkeley, and Hume.

19. Locke's primary qualities include color and smell, and his secondary qualities include size and shape.

20. Berkeley denied that there are houses, books, trees, and cats.

21. Contemporary philosopher Barry Stroud argues that we have no way of checking to see what the real world might be like.

PARADOXICAL PURSUITS

"Thus, for example, a certain color, taste, smell, figure, and consistence, having been observed to go together, are accounted one distinct thing, signified by the name apple. Other collections of ideas constitute a stone, a book, a tree, and the like," argued Berkeley. If you believe there are material or physical objects, how would you answer Berkeley?

❦

For David Hume the belief in an external, material world cannot be rationally justified but can be accounted for in terms of habit and custom regarding our psychology. What is the relationship between the psychology of beliefs and the logic of beliefs? Do you agree with Hume as to which category the belief in an external world belongs?

❦

Did David Hume use the essentially public and objective activity of language to prove that public, objective activities cannot be known?

❦

Since the word "chair" is meaningful and is not only used as a complex idea but as a general idea (general in the sense that it apparently applies to a type of object), do we actually have general ideas or do we only have simple and complex ideas? Remember, the general idea or concept "chair" is not a synonym for the plural "chairs." Can you think of the general idea or concept chair without the word "chair"?

❦

If, as some contemporary philosophers claim, our sensory experience does not occur in some "inner theatre," where do such experiences as dreams and hallucinations occur? What would Quine say about the sentences we use to report such experiences?

APPLIED PHILOSOPHY

Recall, according to Locke's theory of ideas, that simple ideas, as opposed to complex ideas, are those that cannot be broken down into other ideas. For example, colors are simple ideas. According to Locke, in order to have or understand a simple idea you must have an experience of it. In this regard consider describing colors to a blind person or sounds to a deaf person.

❦

According to recent studies a large percentage of men are color deficient, which is sometimes misleadingly described as "color blind." Are any of your fellow students color deficient? If so, how does the world appear to them?

❦

John Locke makes the following claim, "It is not in the power of the most exalted wit, or enlarged understanding, by any quickness or variety of thought, to invent or frame one, new, simple idea in the mind." Do you believe Locke is correct? Can you think of a case that would count against Locke's claim? Can you imagine a type of sensory experience beyond or in addition to your present senses? (Note: Bats are said to have a sonar capability which is so sophisticated that a bat can locate, at some distance, an insect in flight, then catch it. What is a sonar experience? What is it like to be a bat?)

Ask your family and friends Locke's question, "How do our minds come to be furnished?" Are their responses primarily empiricist or rationalist? If one is a Lockean empiricist, can you lead them down Hume's logical path to skepticism?

Go to a park or volunteer at a day-care center and observe how very young children linguistically relate with adults. Is Quine's description of the use of occasion sentences with children assenting and dissenting to the sentences accurate?

Net Links

Check out these Internet websites for additional relevant philosophical information. Remember the Internet is a web. Each of these listed sites is linked to other sites.

Philosophy Resources:

— http://www.earlham.edu/ ~ peters/phil-inks.htm

— http://www.epistemelinks.com

— http://www.refdesk.com/philos.html

— http://www.erraticimpact.com

Encyclopedia of Philosophy:

— http://www.iep.utm.edu

Philosophy Papers:

— http://philosophy.hku.hk/paper/info.php

— http://cogprints.org/view/subjects/phil.html

Metaphysics:

— http://plato.stanford.edu/entries/aristotle-metaphysics/

— http://mally.stanford.edu

— http://en.wikipedia.org/wiki/Metaphysics

George Berkeley:

— http://www.iep.utm.edu/berkeley

David Hume:

— http://www.iep.utm.edu/h

John Locke:

— http://www.iep.utm.edu/locke

Paul Churchland:

— http://philosophyfaculty.ucsd.edu/faculty/pchurchland/index.php

Hilary Putnam:

— http://www.webalice.it/af_gazzola/putnam/home.htm

W.V. Quine:

— http://www.wvquine.org

John Searle:

— http://globetrotter.berkeley.edu/people/Searle/searle-con0.html

— http://en.wikipedia.org/wiki/John_Searle

Lesson Fourteen

Does the Mind Shape the World?

LEARNING OBJECTIVES

Upon completing this lesson, you should be familiar with the concepts contained in the lesson and be able to critically discuss:

☞ philosophy's scandal and Immanuel Kant's synthesis solution of empiricism and rationalism.

☞ the *a priori* and *a posteriori* in experience.

☞ the Age of Enlightenment giving way to Romanticism.

☞ the relativized *a priori* and the linguistic version of Kant.

☞ Wilhelm von Humbolt's linguistic *weltanschaung*.

☞ whether reality is the shadow cast by language or language is the shadow cast by reality.

OVERVIEW

What a scandal, Immanuel Kant claimed, philosophy had fallen into just beyond the midpoint of the eighteenth century. He wrote ". . . it still remains a scandal in philosophy and to human reason in general that the existence of things outside us . . . must be accepted on faith, and if anyone thinks good to doubt their existence, we are unable to counter these doubts by any satisfactory proof." The scandal: if experience gives us our ideas and these ideas exist in our minds as mental pictures or copies of the objects as the early empiricists had argued, then we seem unable to have any genuine knowledge of those objects which we initially claimed caused our ideas. Empiricism thus seems to end up in David Hume's skepticism. (See Episode 13, "Does Knowledge Depend on Experience?") If, on the other hand, sensory experience is only a confused way of thinking and we start instead with the certainty of some of our ideas, as the rationalists argued, then we seem unable to relate the realm of ideas and thinking to the world of material objects. (See Episode 12, "Is Reason the Source of Knowledge?") Descartes' dualism seemed unable to bring these two realms, the mental and the material, back together again. Kant's resolution to this scandal, since he took it as quite obvious that we do have knowledge of an external, objective world, was to find what he considered the middle ground between the extremes of empiricism and rationalism. Kant's solution was to synthesize these two great traditions.

Originally schooled in rationalism, Immanuel Kant was educated in and lectured initially on the philosophy of Liebniz. Kant's life as a professor took place entirely in Konigsberg, his home town, where he lived all his life. He is said to have never ventured more than fifty miles from his home. However, intellectually Professor Kant had an international reputation as people came from all over Europe to Konigsberg to meet the great philosopher.

Kant's synthesis of rationalism and empiricism began by pointing out that ". . . it has been assumed that all of our knowledge must conform to objects. But all of our attempts to extend our knowledge to objects have ended in failure. We must therefore make trial whether we may not have more success if we suppose that the objects must conform to our knowledge." Kant's key idea is that we do not passively receive our knowledge of objects. Instead, the mind somehow takes the sensations it receives and actively puts them together into the objects we know. The world of objects that we see around us is a world that our own mind constructs. Our knowledge of the world, then, comes from two sources. First, our senses passively receive sensations of color, sound, touch, taste, smell, etc. This is where empiricism was right: all our knowledge begins with the senses. But, second, the mind then actively puts these sensations together into the orderly world of objects we experience around us. This is where rationalism was right: the *order* we see in the world has its source in our own reason, and so reason also contributes to our knowledge of objects. For example, Kant argued that every object we know is connected to other objects through cause-and-effect relationships. That is, every object is caused to be what it is by other objects. But these causal relationships, Kant claimed, are put there by the mind itself. The mind takes the sensations it receives and organizes them into objects that are causally related to each other.

For Kant, all our daily, ordinary experience contains elements that are necessary and found in every object we know. Kant referred to these elements as the *a priori* elements. By *a-priori* Kant means prior to, or independent of, our sense of experience. For Kant, for example, causality is *a priori*. It is *a priori* because it is a relationship that is put there by the mind, and not a relationship that our senses perceive. Hume failed to realize this because he did not understand the structuring role that the mind

plays when we know the world around us. Hume had objected that our senses do not *see* causality. So he was led to skepticism about causality. Kant agreed that we do not have sensations of causality. Nevertheless, he argued, all objects are causally related because the mind itself organizes objects into causally related objects. Causality is part of what our mind contributes when it shapes our world.

According to Kant, the *a priori* contributions the mind makes to the world it knows include more than causality. Kant claimed that space, time, unity, plurality, substance, properties, and all other such relationships are also *a priori*. Altogether, he argued, there are twelve basic relationships or categories, that the mind uses to organize its sensations into related objects.

But where do our sensations come from? Kant claimed that our sensations had their source in the *ding an sich* or thing-in-itself. The *ding an sich* is whatever it is that produces the sensations we experience. We cannot ever hope to know what this *ding an sich* is in itself, though, because we can know something only after it has been organized by the mind. We cannot know what there is "out there" in "external" reality apart from the mind's ordering activity. Some have argued that this reduces Kant's own views into a form of skepticism regarding our ability to know the external world as it "really" is. But Kant would answer that for us the only "reality" is the reality our minds organize for us. So that is the way the world "really" is for us.

Kant's writings were very much a part of a general cultural or historical period now known as the Age of Enlightenment. The Age of Enlightenment marked a period in European history when the power of reasoning was considered paramount, not only in relation to discovering truth, but also in shaping society. The Age of Enlightenment gave way to the Romantic Age in which feeling, emotion, a fascination with the exotic and the conditioning effects of culture and history were highlighted. During this transition, Kant's seemingly universal, fixed, finite categories of the understanding came to be seen as more a reflection of his own time. Kant's insight into the mind as a shaper of experience was not abandoned, but his notion of the *a priori* as universal and necessary came to be relativized—relativized to a historical period or a language.

A critic of Kant, Wilhelm von Humbolt was a philosopher and a linguist with a specialty in non-Indo-European languages. Von Humbolt argued that different languages create different worlds for us to live in. The world-view, or the *weltanschaung*, created by Kant's *a priori* concepts may not be the same as those created by another language group. A simple example cited in this episode concerns the Chinese word *chuenlee*, which is used in translations for our word right, but is very close in sound to the Chinese word for power. It is suggested by Professor Harbsmeier that since the Chinese tend to translate *chuenlee* as power, because their language does not have a word for right, they seem not to understand the political world in terms of rights but rather in terms of power.

Some contemporary philosophers such as Professor Richard Rorty treat the notion of *a priori*, not with Kant's view of universality or necessity, but rather as a way some philosophers, within a particular language, pay compliments to concepts they consider central to their particular views. The question thus arises as to whether views like Kant's are only reflections of distinctions found in grammar. Could our experience of enduring objects in a three-dimensional space be a kind of shadow cast by the universal conceptual structure, as Kant would argue? Or is our reality of three-dimensional objects but the shadow cast by a particular language, as von Humbolt argues? Or do you think that our thoughts and language are a reflection or shadow cast by the world, as Locke would argue? Do you believe the mind shapes reality, or does reality shape the mind?

TEXT LINKS

For a more detailed and highly readable discussion of Immanuel Kant's metaphysics and epistemology see Velasquez,: *Philosophy: A Text with Readings*, eleventh edition, Section 5.4, "Kant: Does the Knowing Mind Shape the World?" This section not only provides rich explanations of Kant's and von Humbolt's views but also offers a brief description of gestalt psychology's research into structured perception and a brief discussion of the Hopi Indian *weltanschaung*.

See also the "Historical Showcase," Section 6.5, which features Immanuel Kant.

KEY TERMS

Age of Enlightenment: A period in European history, usually identified with the late seventeenth century and the eighteenth century, in which there was a shared optimism regarding the power of reason to know all of reality and to solve all social and personal problems.

A posteriori: Dependent upon or originating in sensory experience.

A priori: Independent of experience or, as suggested in this episode, prior to experience.

Conceptual schemes: The integrated system of concepts and beliefs which constitute our understanding.

Ding an sich: Kant's term for the thing-in-itself or the unconceptualized source of our sensory intuitions.

Necessary: A claim that is always and everywhere true or a concept that applies always and in every case.

Noumena: Kant's terms for the *ding an sich* (see above definition).

Rationalism: The philosophical view that experience is not the sole source of our ideas but that certain ideas and principles are innate, or *a priori*.

Relativism: The theory that beliefs or conceptual schemes not only vary, perhaps from culture to culture—cultural relativity—but are fundamentally rationally indeterminate or incommensurate.

Romanticism: A viewpoint that accentuates feeling and emotion over reason.

Synthesis: The bringing together or unifying into a new viewpoint of two or more diverse viewpoints.

Universal: Applies always, everywhere.

Weltanschaung: World-view, conceptual scheme.

SELF-TEST

Multiple Choice

1. Immanuel Kant attempted to philosophically prove that
   a. empiricism was more tenable than rationalism
   b. rationalism was more tenable than empiricism
   c. a synthesis between Greek and Medieval thought was necessary
   d. a synthesis between empiricism and rationalism was necessary

2. According to Kant
   a. our mind shapes the world
   b. the world shapes our mind
   c. our culture shapes our mind
   d. our personalities give each of us our own special world

3. In Kant's view our mind provides
   a. structure
   b. content
   c. structure and content
   d. neither structure nor content

4. Kant argued that a criterion for discovering the formal structuring components of experience is
   a. a culture's religious concepts
   b. the *a priori* nature of some concepts
   c. the *a posteriori* nature of some concepts
   d. the personal importance of some concepts to an individual

5. To solve David Hume's skepticism regarding anyone ever proving that our experience of objects actually conforms to the nature of the objects themselves outside or beyond experience, Kant made
   a. it apparent that all of Hume's skeptical arguments were written when Hume was only in his twenties
   b. all of our ideas innate
   c. the mind more of a *tabula rasa* than Locke
   d. objects conform to our experience

6. In Kant's view, the senses provide us with
   a. the content but not the structure of experience
   b. the structure but not the content of experience
   c. insight into the nature of the thing-in-itself
   d. only confused thinking and should not be trusted at all

7. According to Kant, what remains beyond our understanding is
   a. the moral law
   b. an answer to Hume's scepticism regarding causality
   c. the *ding an sich*, or the thing-in-itself
   d. the formal structure of ordinary experience

8. A part of the traditional meaning of *a priori* is being
   a. necessary
   b. skeptical
   c. contingent
   d. sacred

9. According to some critics of Kant's views, his *a priori* concepts are actually relativized to
   a. age
   b. gender
   c. race
   d. language

10. Kant's philosophy is most closely identified with the
    a. Romantic Age
    b. Age of Enlighenment
    c. Age of Uncertainty
    d. Age of Anxiety

11. For Wilhelm von Humboldt, a language embodies a
    a. means for labeling our ideas
    b. strictly *a priori* universal structure
    c. *weltanschaung*
    d. Koyannisqatsi

True or False

These questions are only from the reading assignment in Velasquez, Section 5.4. Specific page references are given in the answer key.

12. Kant rejected the view of knowledge now called transcendental idealism.

13. According to Kant, we need only reason, and not the senses, to know anything about the world around us.

14. Kant's revolutionary claim that the world must conform to the mind is often referred to as the Copernican revolution in knowledge.

15. The romantic philosopher Wilhelm von Humboldt vehemently denied that we construct the world according to the categories of our language that we happen to use.

16. The Sapir-Whorf hypothesis says that the structure of a language determines how a speaker of that language thinks.

PARADOXICAL PURSUITS

In western culture, during the thirteenth century when the bubonic plague hit Europe killing some estimated one-third of the population, the dominant language for understanding reality was religious. Thus, the plague was understood as either the punishment of God or God's abandonment of mankind. In today's world, the dominant language for understanding reality is scientific and so the plague is now understood as caused by a particular bacterium. If this is an example of what von Humbolt had in mind, would Kant find it a criticism of his view?

❧

Many Native American Indian cultures are said to have not had a concept of private property. Thus when the European settlers arrived and laid claim to open land, the Native Americans found this initially rather amusing since it was inconceivable that anyone could own the land. How does this case relate to the Kant, von Humbolt views of the mind shaping reality? What is the role of *weltanschaung*?

❧

According to Kant's view of *dang an sich*, the thing-in-itself is beyond our understanding. How can something be categorized as a thing and beyond our understanding, and not at least be understood to that extent? Can Kant consistently claim the *dang an sich* to exist?

❧

Can you think conceptually without a language? If not, what implication does this have for von Humbolt's view?

APPLIED PHILOSOPHY

Ask some non-philosopher instructors, particularly the natural scientists, if they believe the mind shapes reality, not simply in terms of values, which is a popular view, but in terms of objects and causality? How do they account for the *a priori* nature of causality? What would they say in response to Hume's skeptical arguments?

❧

Survey the philosophy faculty at your school and find out if they are empiricists, rationalists, or Kantians. Ask them how they would answer some of the many questions raised in these last three episodes of *The Examined Life*.

NET LINKS

Check out these Internet websites for additional relevant philosophical information. Remember the Internet is a web. Each of these listed sites is linked to other sites.

Philosophy Resources:

— http://www.earlham.edu/ ~ peters/phil-inks.htm

— http://www.epistemelinks.com

— http://www.refdesk.com/philos.html

— http://www.erraticimpact.com

Encyclopedia of Philosophy:

— http://www.iep.utm.edu

Philosophy Papers:

— http://philosophy.hku.hk/paper/info.php

— http://cogprints.org/view/subjects/phil.html

Metaphysics:

— http://plato.stanford.edu/entries/aristotle-meta-physics/

— http://mally.stanford.edu

— http://en.wikipedia.org/wiki/Metaphysics

David Hume:

— http://www.iep.utm.edu/h

Immanuel Kant:

— http://www.friesian.com/kant.htm

— http://www.hkbu.edu.hk/ ~ ppp/Kant.html

Paul Churchland:

— http://philosophyfaculty.ucsd.edu/faculty/pchurchland/index.php

Richard Rorty:

— http://www.seop.leeds.ac.uk/entries/rorty

Stephen Toulmin:

— http://en.wikipedia.org/wiki/Stephen_Toulmin

— http://www.willamette.edu/cla/Rhetoric/courses/argumentation/Toulmin.htm

Lesson Fifteen

How Does Science Add to Knowledge?

LEARNING OBJECTIVES

Upon completing this lesson, you should be familiar with the concepts contained in the lesson and be able to critically discuss:

👁 Francis Bacon's method of induction.

👁 Immanuel Kant's view of a scientist as pupil or judge.

👁 Karl Popper's criterion of falsifiability.

👁 Thomas Kuhn's paradigms and scientific revolutions.

👁 whether science has a method or methods.

OVERVIEW

So you've watched another episode of *The Examined Life*. Watched it on broadcast television or via a DVD? Technology, or applied science, has not only made this episode and its viewing possible for you, but the entire *Examined Life* series, in addition to my typing this text on a computer and exchanging e-mail with everyone involved in this series. As you glance around, you'll see how much of our present environment reflects our deep dependence upon science and its technology. Modern human existence seems to need science and technology like our bodies need air.

Surprisingly, science is a relatively new way for humans to gain knowledge of the world. Some people would claim that the rise of modern science is as recent as the fifteenth or sixteenth century. Yet, in this short period, modern science has substantially changed our lives. Science has made it possible for members of our species to leave the planet, traveling to the moon and back. Most of us living in the industrialized world live, on average, twice as long as our great grandparents did at the turn of the twentieth century. While most of us know that science has something to do with experiments and observation, such information tells us very little about how science actually works. When one turns to these specifics, not surprisingly there seem to be a number of differing views. So, how does science give us knowledge?

Philosophy of science attempts to give a systematic account of the methods and the concepts which have come to constitute the practice(s) of science. In the modern age, Francis Bacon was one of the first philosophers to give an account of what he believed the scientific method to be. Rather than simply doing science, which he did do, Bacon was also concerned with describing the method scientists follow, or should follow. Bacon's method came to be known as the method of induction.

Bacon's method of induction consisted of a series of activities. First, there was the crucial requirement of making extensive observations. At the outset, the scientist makes a list or table of all the known instances of the phenomenon under study. If one were studying heat, one would list all of the known cases of heat or hot things. Second, one looks for general patterns, in part by noting cases similar to those listed previously but where the phenomenon is lacking. Third, one tests the patterns and fourth, one grasps the underlying laws of nature. Thus, in the end, Bacon believed a scientist would arrive at a warranted generalization from the many particular cases collected and examined.

Essentially, Bacon emphasized the empirical significance of the new science and the need to test all claims in experience or, as he noted, in the book of nature. This emphasis on empirical observation and testing was a radical departure from the Medieval Age, which relied significantly on authority and tradition. By the middle of the seventeenth century, Bacon's method of induction had become the official creed of the Royal Society of London. However, despite its emphasis upon observation, Bacon's method found many critics who disagreed with his description of how science works.

Seeing the mind as a mirror that reflects the world around it, Bacon seemed to accept the traditional empiricists' view that the mind is passive in its confrontation with reality. (As we have already seen in Episode 13, "Does Knowledge Depend on Experience?" the traditional empiricists' model of the mind representing the world through experience culminated in David Hume's skepticism. In Episode 14, "Does the Mind Shape the World?" we discovered that Immanuel Kant brought this entire empiricist's view of the mind as a passive receptacle into question.) He viewed a scientist as a student or pupil of nature who gathers observations, waiting patiently for nature to reveal herself.

Immanuel Kant saw the scientist as a judge, an active pursuer who brings specific questions to nature, then goes about testing for specific answers to the questions he or she compels nature to answer. This view of the scientist as the active pursuer who puts nature to some specifically designed test, is also echoed in this episode by W.V. Quine. He describes the practice of science as "setting a trap as best we can to get one of her [Nature's] secrets . . . a trap in which we're hoping to get nature to express herself." Thus the scientist does not wait for nature to suggest or pose questions and answers, but rather actively constructs hypotheses and puts them to the test. But what sort of test?

According to Karl Popper, when a hypothesis or a conjecture is put forward, the scientist sets out to discover if the hypothesis is right by trying to prove that it is wrong. In contrast to the Baconian inductivist method, a test is not an attempt to find confirming evidence; this is what astrologers and other pseudo-scientists do. Rather, genuine science attempts to *falsify* a hypothesis. If a hypothesis is not falsified by the test, then the hypothesis has some probability of being true. On the other hand, if a hypothesis is not falsifiable—that is, there is no test imaginable that would falsify the hypothesis—then the hypothesis is not a genuine scientific hypothesis but rather a pseudo-scientific hypothesis. Popper would argue that because astrologers always, in principle, have a way to explain away false predictions, their hypotheses are in principle unfalsifiable and hence pseudo-scientific.

While Bacon's methods of induction seem to describe what some scientists have done—for example, Galileo's study of terrestrial motion or Boyle's study of gases—it would appear that Popper's view is closer to describing what Isaac Newton or Charles Darwin appeared to be doing as scientists. However, physicist, philosopher of science, and historian of science Thomas Kuhn believes Popper has only described what scientists tend to do in the midst of "scientific revolutions." According to Kuhn, Popper did not quite capture what scientists actually do during periods of "normal science."

A period of normal science is dominated by a paradigm, according to Kuhn. A paradigm provides a powerful model for explaining the facts we observe. In astronomy, Aristotle's geocentric model of the sun and the planets revolving around the earth provided a paradigm for understanding the order displayed by the apparent motion of the sun, the planets, and the so-called fixed stars. However, there were planetary motions that did not readily fit Aristotle's model because the model was so strongly held that these facts, which appeared to falsify it, instead spurred on revisions introduced by Ptolemy. From the time of Aristotle to Copernicus, roughly 1,800 years, Aristotle's geocentric paradigm was dominant. Then, in the fourteenth century, a paradigm shift occurred when Copernicus introduced his heliocentric model. This paradigm shift constituted a scientific revolution, according to Kuhn. Like political revolutions, there are typically conservative factions in a scientific revolution which insist upon revising the old rather than accepting the new. These conservative factions can make even scientific revolutions violent. For example, Copernicus did not want to let his work be published until after his death, and Galileo spent the last years of his life under house arrest for supporting Copernicus's heliocentric view.

Once a paradigm shift has occurred and the new paradigm is in place, a period of normal science begins once again. Kuhn describes the vast majority of scientific work, as "mopping up." An accepted paradigm doesn't readily yield to one or two false predictions. Rather, anomalies or facts that do not fit the paradigm are typically treated with no serious concern. The paradigm remains undisturbed.

Neither Popper nor Kuhn view themselves as inductivists like Bacon. Neither believes that theories or hypotheses are arrived at inductively by studying some set of facts, then generalizing to some explanatory statement. Rather, a theory or hypothesis first arises from a scientist's imagination and is then tested against some set of facts. However, one point of disagreement between Popper and Kuhn seems to involve the nature of progress in science. Do new theories mark growth in science? Is one theory, in some sense, an improvement over the other, or are different theories simply different models for understanding some set of facts? While Popper finds linear progress in the history of science in which ensuing theories bring greater explanatory power than their predecessors, Kuhn, at times, talks of different theories being incommensurable. Yet he also allows that simplicity and scope or explanatory power may serve as standards of progress.

As philosophers of science have attempted to articulate how science works, perhaps they have only demonstrated that science does not work in just one way. The scientific "method" should perhaps be replaced with the "methods" of science. Rather than viewing science as giving humanity the essential, eternal truth regarding the workings of nature, science is instead a many-faceted undertaking—a historical work in the making.

Text Links

Turn to Velasquez, *Philosophy: A Text with Readings*, eleventh edition, and read Section 5.5, "Does Science Give us Knowledge?" This section of Velasquez will provide a more detailed discussion of Bacon's methods along with examples supporting and countering his inductivists method. Additionally, there are similar extended critical discussions of both Karl Popper's principle of falsifiability and Thomas Kuhn's views of scientific paradigms and scientific revolutions. The section concludes by contrasting these various views about scientific method with pseudo-sciences and their purported methods.

See Velasquez, Section 5.7, "Readings." This section opens with a story by Ambrose Bierce, *An Occurrence at Owl Creek Bridge*, in which the protagonist is deceived by his own psychology. This section of Velasquez also includes two excellent philosophy papers discussing the more general issue of knowledge and scepticism: Peter Unger's, "A Defense of Skepticism" and Thomas Nagel's, "How Do We Know Anything?"

Key Terms

Anomaly: A deviation from what is normal or expected. In this episode, an anomaly is a fact which is not consistent with accepted theory.

Confirmation: Finding a state of affairs or a fact which supports or verifies some claim.

Falsification (to falsify, falsifiable): As used by Karl Popper, a criterion for testing the warrant of a scientific claim. A scientist tests a hypothesis by trying to prove it false rather than trying to confirm or verify.

Generalization: A statement or claim referring to an entire group or population as opposed to referring to some specific individual.

Incommensurable: Having nothing in common. For Kuhn, the strong claim that two paradigms have nothing in common.

Induction: Reasoning to the probable truth of some claim or explanation. A limited usage involves drawing probable generalizations from particular claims or observations.

Law of nature: A highly generalized description of a uniformity in nature which holds universally. Thus, Isaac Newton's law of universal gravitation accounted for both celestial mechanics and terrestrial mechanics.

Normal science: For Thomas Kuhn, that period in the life of a paradigm where the majority of scientific activity is focused on working out the details of the paradigm.

Paradigm: A theory with much explanatory power that solves a certain set of problems or anomalies and becomes the model for future scientific work. Darwin's theory of evolution or Copernicus's heliocentric theory of the solar system are examples of paradigms.

Pure reason: Thought, speculation without the use of the senses.

Scientific revolution: A period in the history of Western civilization, dated at the end of the Renaissance, in which critical thought about the world was naturalized, and many astronomical and biological insights gained. As used by Thomas Kuhn, a period of transition when one paradigm replaces some other paradigm. Thus an example of this latter concept occurred when the heliocentric theory of the solar system replaced the geocentric theory of the solar system.

SELF-TEST

Multiple Choice

1. Francis Bacon advocated a method of science
   a. requiring scientific hypotheses to be falsifiable
   b. requiring scientific hypotheses to be based upon accepted authority
   c. requiring scientific hypotheses to be inductively inferred from a collection of facts
   d. in which paradigms serve to define acceptable methodology

2. An inductivist model of scientific method places a strong emphasis upon
   a. initial observation or collection of facts
   b. attempting to disprove or refute a hypothesis
   c. guaranteeing that one's work is in line with the overall scientific community's work
   d. the mathematical description of a hypothesis

3. The inductivist model seems to make the role of the scientist too
   a. active
   b. passive
   c. lucky
   d. secular

4. According to Immanuel Kant, a scientist should approach nature as a
   a. pupil
   b. neophyte
   c. tape recorder
   d. judge

5. Karl Popper advocated a method of science
   a. requiring scientific hypotheses to be falsifiable
   b. requiring scientific hypotheses to be based upon accepted authority
   c. requiring scientific hypotheses to be inductively inferred from a collection of facts
   d. in which paradigms serve to define acceptable methodology

6. Thomas Kuhn advocated a method of science
   a. requiring scientific hypotheses to be falsifiable
   b. requiring scientific hypotheses to be based upon accepted authority
   c. requiring scientific hypotheses to be inductively inferred from a collection of facts
   d. in which paradigms serve to define acceptable methodology

Identify the events below as:

a. paradigm shifts
b. not paradigm shifts

_____ 7. Copernicus's heliocentric theory of the solar system versus the geocentric theory.

_____ 8. Darwin's theory of evolution versus the theory of creationism.

_____ 9. The discovery of a gene for Alzheimer's disease.

_____ 10. The discovery that the universe is closer to 15 billion than 12 billion years old.

11. According to Thomas Kuhn, normal science occurs when scientists
    a. are not having to deal with erratic funding sources
    b. are not having to deal with theories like astrology or phrenology
    c. work out the various details of the dominant paradigm
    d. go about their business setting up reputable experiments and controlling all of the pertinent variables

12. If scientific paradigms are genuinely incommensurable then
    a. progress in science may be an illusion
    b. progress in science is real
    c. the insights of a scientific paradigm constitute insight into the ultimate nature of reality
    d. only the social sciences mark progress

True or False

These questions are only from the reading assignment in Velasquez, Section 5.5. Specific page references are given in the answer key.

13. Francis Bacon and John Stuart Mill claimed that induction is the primary tool of the scientific method.

14. The way that Gregor Mendel developed his laws of heredity is a good example of inductionism.

15. William Whewell, an opponent of Mill, claimed that great scientific advances occur when scientists make a creative guess or hypothesis.

16. According to Kant, the mark of science is that it tries to disprove or falsify proposed theories.

17. Kuhn claims that scientists often continue to hold on to a theory even if some observations show up that do not fit into the theory.

PARADOXICAL PURSUITS

If you take an inductivist view of scientific method, which observations of species actually evolving did Charles Darwin observe in formulating his general claim regarding the evolution of species? Does Darwin's theory of evolution count against the inductivist's method? How about Stephen Hawking's work on event horizons around black holes?

❧

As a student taking a lab science, do/did most of your labs turn out to be consistent or inconsistent with what was predicted by your lab manuals? If your results were inconsistent with what the lab manual predicts, is this proof that: a) the manual is wrong, or b) you made a mistake? What if most of your fellow students got results inconsistent with

what the manual predicts? What might Popper say about such results?

❧

Some have argued that creationism should be taught alongside the theory of evolution since after all, the theory of evolution is just that, a theory. Does the theory of evolution differ from the theory of creationism in terms of falsifiability or any of the other criteria proposed in this episode?

APPLIED PHILOSOPHY

As a student taking a lab science, if your lab does not turn out consistent with what your lab manual has predicted, what does your instructor suggest you do? If your instructor suggests you redo the experiment so that you get the "correct" results—i.e. the results predicted by your lab manual—is your instructor taking a view of science more in line with Kuhn or with Popper? Would Kuhn and Popper agree or disagree with your instructor?

❧

Describe the methods of research used in a chemistry class, an anatomy class, an economics class, and a psychology class. Did you find a single method or varieties of methods?

❧

According to recent speculation concerning the extinction of the dinosaurs, there is a growing consensus in the scientific community that a large comet hit the earth just east of the Mexican peninsula and caused an ecological catastrophe. The result of this catastrophe was the extinction of the dinosaurs, with smaller, warm-blooded animals, the mammals, surviving and then becoming dominant. How does such a theory fit Bacon's, Popper's, and Kuhn's view of scientific methodology?

NET LINKS

Check out these Internet websites for additional relevant philosophical information. Remember the Internet is a web. Each of these listed sites is linked to other sites.

Philosophy Resources:

— http://www.earlham.edu/ ~ peters/phil-inks.htm

— http://www.epistemelinks.com

— http://www.refdesk.com/philos.html

— http://www.erraticimpact.com

Encyclopedia of Philosophy:

— http://www.iep.utm.edu

Philosophy Papers:

— http://philosophy.hku.hk/paper/info.php

— http://cogprints.org/view/subjects/phil.html

Philosophy of Science:

— http://philsci-archive.pitt.edu

— http://www.friesian.com/science.htm

Evolution:

— http://evolution.berkeley.edu

— http://www.pbs.org/wgbh/evolution

Francis Bacon:

— http://www.iep.utm.edu/bacon

Thomas Kuhn:

— http://plato.stanford.edu/entries/thomas-kuhn

Karl Popper:

— http://www.blupete.com/Literature/Biographies/Philosophy/Popper.htm

— http://www.eeng.dcu.ie/ ~ tkpw

Arthur Fine:

— http://phil.washington.edu/people_fine.html

Susan Haack:

— http://www.as.miami.edu/phi/haack

Ian Hacking:

— http://www.en.wikipedia.org/wiki/Ian_Hacking

W.V. Quine:

— http://www.wvquine.org

Stephen Toulmin:

— http://en.wikipedia.org/wiki/Stephen_Toulmin

— http://www.willamette.edu/cla/Rhetoric/courses/argumentation/Toulmin.htm

Lesson Sixteen

Does Science Give Us Truth?

LEARNING OBJECTIVES

Upon completing this lesson, you should be familiar with the concepts contained in the lesson and be able to critically discuss:

- the correspondence theory of truth and scientific realism.

- the coherence theory of truth and conceptual relativism (consensus theories).

- the pragmatic theory of truth and instrumentalism.

- quantum mechanics' challenge to theories of truth.

- Einstein's realism versus Bohr's instrumentalism.

- capital "T"—Truth; or small "t"—truth?

OVERVIEW

As man-made satellites now leave our solar system, and other satellites map in detail the surfaces of the moon and Mars, science appears to be generating an avalanche of truth or truths. Never in the history of civilization has our apparent knowledge of the universe, our solar system, the ecology of our planet, or the cures for and elimination of so many diseases and illnesses been so apparently sophisticated and effective. The very question, "Does science give us truth?" seems a question asked by someone either extremely gullible or perhaps a smart but silly person. However, the question is actually rather complex, and can be understood to be asking a number of quite different questions.

Does science give us all truths? Most philosophers, and probably most scientists as well, would agree that the methods of science are limited and are not appropriate in discovering truths within mathematics, logic, and morality. Perhaps the more significant limitation of science is that scientific methods cannot be used to give a rational or theoretical account of themselves and the concepts they rely upon. Science cannot tell us why its claims, which appear to be true, are indeed true. While scientific methods constitute powerful procedures for allowing us to seemingly know some truths, any theory or account of the nature of truth itself, has traditionally fallen within the domain of philosophy.

Questions about the nature of truth, or how the concept of truth functions, are not directed at doubting that some statement or belief is actually true or false, but are instead directed at attempting to give a rational account of what occurs when a belief is true. So the question, "What is truth?" or "What is it for a belief to be true?" should not be confused with questions as to whether or not someone *knows* that a belief is true. For example, knowing that Barack Obama is presently fishing is something you could come to *know* in a variety of ways. You could see him out fishing, watch live news footage of his fishing, or perhaps his neighbor—a chronic truth teller—calls you, reporting it to you. Thus, coming to know that a belief or statement is true is quite different from giving an account of what it is for a belief or statement to be true.

In this episode, John Searle claims that there are certain opinions which everyone starts from and finally goes back to before they ever start doing philosophy. Such opinions, Searle calls default opinions. One such default opinion concerns the intuitive notion of what makes a belief or statement true. For Searle, this default opinion is the claim that if a statement is true, then that statement is true because it accurately reports the way the world actually is. For example, if I claim that Santa Claus lives at the North Pole, then that statement should pick out a particular large elf, wearing a red suit with white fur trim, who lives in the far snowy reaches of planet earth. However, in this world, on this planet, there is no such elf living anywhere near the North Pole. Statements of this sort about Santa Claus are false because they do not correspond to or accurately report anything in reality.

Children may think such beliefs about Santa Claus are true, but though the child may genuinely believe it to be true, the belief is actually false. Such a belief remains false regardless of the child's enthusiasm for it, or any other psychologically interesting aspects of holding onto such a false belief. This view of the nature of truth, which Searle has put forth, is known as the correspondence theory of truth.

According to the correspondence theory of truth, statements are true if they correspond to or accurately report an actual state of affairs in the world. So again, the correspondence theory of truth can give an account of why a statement, such as Zeus lives in a palace on Mount Olympus, is false. Such a statement simply does not correspond to reality.

If science does give us truth, do scientific truths rely upon a correspondence theory of truth? According to scientific realism, scientific theories are true when they describe reality accurately. Scientific realism thus utilizes a version of the correspondence theory of truth. A question that arises is whether such a theory can give us the whole story about truth. Professor Hilary Putnam makes the point that the correspondence theory of truth (and realism in general) is not appropriate to "mathematics, logic, and morality." Alternatively, a theory of truth which, others have argued, can account for this diversity of statements or beliefs that we ascribe

truth and falsehood to, is the coherence theory of truth.

According to the coherence theory of truth, an idea or statement is true when it coheres or fits in with other ideas or statements. For some coherence theorists, Euclidean geometry and various systems of mathematics provide the most perfect examples of coherence. What a scientist actually does is work to find a theory which coheres with beliefs which he or she has already accepted as settled. Science does not compare a theory with a reality which is independent of all experience, as correspondence theorists seem to claim. Rather, scientists search for the "tightest" fit between some theory and those beliefs which we acquire as the final outcome of an incredibly complex process and which are only indirectly related to the world.

The holding of a coherent theory or set of theories within science has been described by Thomas Kuhn as a paradigm. Einstein's theories of relativity serve as a contemporary paradigm in physics. They account for much of the relevant data and serve as models that define present day understanding and research. Truth, in a coherence theory sense, is essentially a human-centered activity and as such is very much in conflict with realists' views of truth. Again, realists claim that our theories get closer and closer to capturing reality. Among philosophers of science, those who have taken a coherence view of truth have come to be described as consensus theorists or, sometimes, conceptual relativists. For all claims, beliefs, and theories about the world arise from some point of view or perspective. Thus there are no facts which are independent or neutral of some point of view or perspective.

Within the history of philosophical theories of truth, a third theory is that of pragmatism. Pragmatism claims that beliefs which are useful or have some practical application are true. Within the study of scientific methods, pragmatism is most closely associated with the view of science known as instrumentalism. According to instrumentalism, scientific theories are tools or instruments, and a true theory is one that yields successful predictions. Thus scientific theories do not aim to give us truth about some independently existing reality, as a realist claims, but rather aim at having some utility or reliability.

The twentieth century has seen the emergence of a number of profound scientific theories, or paradigms, as some would describe them. The theory of quantum mechanics is such a paradigm. Its subject matter concerns very small atomic and subatomic particles. The success of quantum mechanics has brought lasers, breakthroughs in our understanding and use of electricity and atomic energy. At the same time, the theory of quantum mechanics seems to generate some significant, perhaps problematic, implications for all of these various theories of truth.

One of the fathers of quantum mechanics, Neils Bohr took an instrumentalist view of truth regarding quantum theory. Bohr argued that not only did Newton's laws not apply at the level of quantum objects, but that our categories of space, time, and causality do not apply at this level either. Despite the fact that the theories of quantum mechanics yield very accurate predictions, they nonetheless defy traditional assumptions in Newtonian or classical mechanics in that we cannot, at the same time, know both the position and velocity of a quantum object. For Bohr, the physics of quantum objects may be stranger than we can even imagine or conceptualize. Thus, while the theories of quantum mechanics yield accurate predictions, we seem not to know what might really exist at this level. According to Bohr, quantum mechanics is a calculating tool and not a picture or representation of the inner secrets or workings of nature.

As a realist, Albert Einstein found Bohr's views unacceptable. Bohr's instrumentalism or pragmatism had a negative, if not degenerative, effect upon scientific knowledge. If our present concepts of space, time, and causality—or position and momentum—do not seem to work at the level of quantum objects, then according to Einstein, we need to discover new concepts that will allow us to penetrate the deeply hidden features of the universe. Einstein maintained that science could penetrate to the underlying structure of reality and as a result of this commitment he spent the last twenty years of his life unsuccessfully attempting to develop a unified field theory that would show that Bohr, in particular, was mistaken. Recent developments in quantum mechanics, some claim, vindicate at least a part of what Einstein was claiming against Bohr.

Like the apparently dubious notion that there is only one method of science, so it may also be with theories of truth. Perhaps our search for Truth, capital T, or for Reality, capital R, and the like is a mistake. Perhaps our search for such truth or theories is more of a reflection of our human psychology than the way things actually are. Perhaps "small letter" concepts like truth, reality, and knowledge are closer to the truth. But if that is so, then what is truth?

TEXT LINKS

⇜ Turn to Velasquez, *Philosophy: A Text with Reading*, eleventh edition, and read Section 6.1, "Knowledge, Truth, and Justification" for an introduction to these important epistemological concepts. Read Section 6.2, "What is Truth?" for a rich overview of the major philosophical theories of truth: correspondence, coherence, and pragmatism. Included at the end of this section is a provocative discussion on the value of truth in "Does Truth Matter?"

⇜ Velasquez Section 6.3, "Does Science Give Us Truth?" provides a more in-depth view of all of the main issue presented in this segment of *The Examined Life*. Notice Velasquez uses "conceptual relativism" for what this episode calls "consensus theories."

KEY TERMS

Anomaly: A deviation from what is normal or expected. In this episode, an anomaly is a fact which is not consistent with accepted theory.

Conceptual framework: Refers to the integrated structure of concepts and beliefs that give identity to the understanding of an individual or community.

Confirmation: Finding a state of affairs or a fact which supports or verifies some claim.

Correspondence theory of truth: The philosophical theory of truth which argues that a statement is true if, and only if, it corresponds to or correctly reports some state of affairs or fact(s) in reality.

Coherence theory of truth: The philosophical theory of truth which argues that a statement is true if, and only if, it "fits" or coheres within a consistent system or set of other statements.

Consensus theory: The view that scientific theories are true if they cohere with the accepted views of scientists. Sometimes called "conceptual relativism."

Default opinions: According to John Searle these are the sorts of opinions (seemingly philosophical in nature) which everyone starts with and ends with after philosophizing.

Falsification (to falsify, falsifiable): As used by Karl Popper, a criterion for testing the warrant of a scientific claim. A scientist tests a hypothesis by trying to prove it false rather than trying to confirm or verify.

Induction: Reasoning to the probable truth of some claim or explanation. A limited usage involves drawing probable generalizations from particular claims or observations.

Instrumentalism: The view that a true scientific theory is one that enables scientists to make accurate predictions.

Pragmatic theory of truth: The philosophical view that a statement is true if it works or has predictive value in science and everyday life.

Quantum mechanics: An area of theoretical physics that studies the structure and dynamics of atoms and sub-atomic particles.

Scientific realism: The view that a true scientific theory is one that correctly describes an objective reality that exists independent of human consciousness.

SELF-TEST

Multiple Choice

1. Two theories of truth discussed in this episode were
   a. empiricism and rationalism
   b. empiricism and transcendental idealism
   c. correspondence and coherence
   d. conceptual and categorical

2. According to the correspondence theory of truth, a true belief or statement
   a. accurately reports some aspect of reality
   b. fits in with other beliefs or statements
   c. has some usefulness or reliability
   d. is indubitable

3. According to the coherence theory of truth, a true belief or statement
   a. accurately reports some aspect of reality
   b. fits in with other beliefs or statements
   c. has some usefulness or reliability
   d. is indubitable

4. According to the pragmatic theory of truth, a true belief or statement
   a. accurately reports some aspect of reality
   b. fits in with other beliefs or statements
   c. has some usefulness or reliability
   d. is indubitable

5. The realist view of science tends to adopt the
   a. correspondence theory of truth
   b. coherence theory of truth
   c. pragmatic theory of truth

6. Conceptual relativism is a version of
   a. correspondence theory of truth
   b. coherence theory of truth
   c. pragmatic theory of truth

7. The instrumentalist view of science is a version of
   a. correspondence theory of truth
   b. coherence theory of truth
   c. pragmatic theory of truth

8. Albert Einstein took a/an
   a. realist's view of the truth in science
   b. consensus theorist's view of truth in science
   c. instrumentalist's view of truth in science

9. Neils Bohr took a/an
   a. realist's view of the truth in science
   b. consensus theorist's view of truth in science
   c. instrumentalist's view of truth in science

10. Karl Popper took a/an
    a. realist's view of the truth in science
    b. consensus theorist's view of truth in science
    c. instrumentalist's view of truth in science

11. Thomas Kuhn took a/an
    a. realist's view of the truth in science
    b. consensus theorist's view of truth in science
    c. instrumentalist's view of truth in science

12. Quantum mechanics is the study of
    a. galaxies and black holes
    b. gravitation as it is effected by huge bodies like our sun
    c. effects upon space and time as one approximates the speed of light
    d. the very small such as the structure of atoms and subatomic particles

True or False

These questions are only from the reading assignment in Velasquez, Sections 6.2 and 6.3. Specific page references are given in the answer key.

13. Modern philosopher Bertrand Russell held that a statement is true if it corresponds to reality.

14. The correspondence theory has problems explaining what a fact is.

15. According to the coherence theory of truth, a statement is true if it is consistent with other statements that we regard as true.

16. The instrumentalist view of scientific truth is based on the correspondence theory of truth.

17. The realist view of scientific truth holds that true scientific theories correspond to the way the world is.

PARADOXICAL PURSUITS

According to the correspondence theory of truth, a belief or statement is true if it corresponds to reality. Many find this a very persuasive, if not true account of truth. If this theory of truth is true, does it correspond to reality in the same manner as beliefs or statements about Santa Claus and who the president of the United States is supposedly correspond to reality? What do the statements describing the correspondence theory correspond to?

❧

Some paranoid schizophrenics are said to have extremely coherent, or consistent, belief systems, which are nonetheless accepted as being false. Can coherence theories of truth ever be intellectually acceptable if they only fit our beliefs or statements?

❧

Some philosophers have argued that pragmatists have confused a belief's or statement's usefulness or pragmatic value with a possible criterion of truth versus the actual meaning of truth. In other words, if a belief is useful or can be used to make predictions, do you think that is enough to know the belief is true? Or does truth actually mean something else altogether?

❧

If Bohr is correct in that quantum objects may be beyond our capacity to conceptualize, then is it possible that both he and Einstein are correct, though they disagree? What do the limits of conceptualization or logic have to do with reality?

APPLIED PHILOSOPHY

What are you, a correspondence theorist, a coherence theorist, or a pragmatist? If you are some combination, what theory do you use to prove the truth of your theory of truth?

❧

Ask science and math instructors what theory of truth they accept and why. Do you find more correspondence theorists amongst the scientists and more coherence theorists among mathematicians?

❧

Organize a showing of this episode of *The Examined Life* and invite faculty and students from a variety of departments for a discussion of the different views taken on truth and a scientific theory's relationship to reality.

❧

Do religious beliefs or statements primarily assume, in terms of their truth, a correspondence, a coherence, or a pragmatic theory of truth?

NET LINKS

Check out these Internet websites for additional relevant philosophical information. Remember the Internet is a web. Each of these listed sites is linked to other sites.

Philosophy Resources:

— http://www.earlham.edu/ ~ peters/phil-inks.htm

— http://www.epistemelinks.com

— http://www.refdesk.com/philos.html

— http://www.erraticimpact.com

Encyclopedia of Philosophy:

— http://www.iep.utm.edu

Philosophy Papers:

— http://philosophy.hku.hk/paper/info.php

— http://cogprints.org/view/subjects/phil.html

Philosophy of Science:

— http://philsci-archive.pitt.edu

— http://www.friesian.com/science.htm

Thomas Kuhn:

— http://plato.stanford.edu/entries/thomas-kuhn

Karl Popper:

— http://www.blupete.com/Literature/Biographies/Philosophy/Popper.htm

— http://www.eeng.dcu.ie/ ~ tkpw

Arthur Fine:

— http://phil.washington.edu/people_fine.htm

Susan Haack:

— http://www.as.miami.edu/phi/haack

Ian Hacking:

— http://www.en.wikipedia.org/wiki/Ian_Hacking

W.V. Quine:

— http://www.wvquine.org

Stephen Toulmin:

— http://en.wikipedia.org/wiki/Stephen_Toulmin

— http://www.willamette.edu/cla/Rhetoric/courses/argumentation/Toulmin.htm

Lesson Seventeen

Are Interpretations True?

LEARNING OBJECTIVES

Upon completing this lesson, you should be familiar with the concepts contained in the lesson and be able to critically discuss:

◆ hermeneutics and its historical context.

◆ Friedrich Schleiermacher and the outline of hermeneutics.

◆ Wilhelm Dilthey re-enactment and understanding versus explaining.

◆ Hans-Georg Gadamer hermeneutics and subjectivity.

◆ ideal languages: Georg Frederick Hegel & the early Wittgenstein.

◆ Ludwig Wittgenstein's language games.

OVERVIEW

In a recent edition of the journal *Nature*, speech pathologists Roger J. Ingham and Janis Ingham, faculty members and researches at the University of California at Santa Barbara, discovered that "stuttering is associated with unusual hemispheric (brain) processing of speech and aberrant auditory monitoring of speech." Some of history's more well known stutterers include Moses, Demosthenes, and Virgil, with Winston Churchill and Marilyn Monroe bringing us into the twentieth century.

Of those listed, Moses stands out because he received the Ten Commandments from God. If Moses was a stutterer and stuttering is associated with "unusual (brain) processing and aberrant auditory monitoring of speech," is it possible that Moses misinterpreted God's commands? Is it possible that the Ten Commandments contain "nots" where there were no "nots" or vice versa?

According to the ancient Greeks, interpreting the words of the gods (the Greeks were polytheists) was a most delicate undertaking strewn with potential error. Hermes, the messenger god in ancient Greek mythology, was responsible for bringing the words of the gods to humans. There were also the Oracles, most often young girls who, under the influence of hallucinatory drugs, had the gods speak through them. Why someone on hallucinatory drugs would be a good interpreter or mouthpiece for the gods is not explained.

The attempt to formulate a way of interpreting words that will avoid misunderstandings, is the branch of philosophy known as hermeneutics. Originally, hermeneutics was concerned with interpreting the words of the gods. Named after the messenger god, Hermes, hermeneutics recognizes both the complexity and significance of achieving true interpretations.

In the Middle Ages allegorical interpretation became one of the accepted standard activities of biblical interpretation. Allegorical interpretation did

99

not treat the Bible as a literal, sequential history but rather as wisdom literature in which the divine message lies hidden within metaphors and allegories. Thus the story of the fall of man is not necessarily a literal description of the early days of human existence on Earth, but possibly an allegory that depicts God's judgment of human impertinence.

Allegorical interpretation of the Bible ran into difficulties in the sixteenth century leading to the Reformation. When Martin Luther turned from the Catholic church's allegorical interpretations of the Bible and read the Bible for himself, he found he disagreed with many of the officially sanctioned interpretations. Luther also disagreed with the Church's practice of selling indulgences. For Luther, anyone could gain salvation through faith alone. He felt that the Church bureaucracy, protected by its official interpretations of the Bible, had become corrupt and was an impediment to knowing God's real will.

Luther provided his own translation of the Bible printed in German, the language of the common people in Luther's Germany, as opposed to Latin, the language of the educated and the Church. What considerations would support Luther or the Church in their differing interpretations of the Bible? How do we arrive at the correct interpretation of the Bible or any significant text for that matter? Can we arrive at a correct or true interpretation?

The nineteenth century philosopher Friedrich Schleiermacher appears to have been the first scholar to attempt to systematically formulate general rules for interpretation. For Schleiermacher a text must first be understood within its historical context. This historical context includes understanding the author's language and intentions for writing a particular text.

Wilhelm Dilthey extended Schleiermacher's method to interpret many human activities including art, suggesting that to understand a painting you needed to "relive" the painter's life in your imagination. By reliving or re-enacting, we can understand the writer's or artist's intentions and thereby correctly understand or interpret what they produce. This activity of re-enactment differs, according to Dilthey, from what a scientist does in giving an explanation. Dilthey additionally claimed that if a historian used his method of re-enactment, the historian could give an objective picture of the past. However, can anyone actually know the intentions of a historical figure?

The father of twentieth century hermeneutics, Hans-Georg Gadamer argued that we must abandon the idea of objective knowledge. Anyone who interprets a text must use his or her own subjective experiences. In contrast to Dilthey, Gadamer asserts that readers shouldn't distance themselves from their prejudices but rather should use their prejudices when interpreting a text. The subjective context everyone brings to an interpretation cannot be overcome so we cannot attain some objective view point.

For Gadamer not only are the methods of interpretation different from those methods used in the natural or hard sciences, but his methods of research in hermeneutics, he claimed, are the basic methods in the "soft" sciences. Gadamer recognized the overwhelming importance of language itself and thus the importance of hermeneutics for everyone. Every language speaker must interpret. Hermeneutics makes clear that this complex process is in part unconscious and subliminal.

Some philosophers have argued that ambiguity, vagueness, and other pitfalls that plague accurate interpretation could be avoided if there were an ideal language—a language in which "anything that can be said, can be said clearly," to quote Ludwig Wittgenstein, a twentieth century philosopher. In the seventeenth century, Gottfried Wilhelm Leibniz attempted to develop such a formal, almost mathematical language into which ordinary language could be translated to avoid misunderstandings. While Leibniz never finished the construction of his ideal language, further studies of language during the nineteenth century allowed Wittgenstein to take a deeper look at language and its relationship to reality.

According to the early work of Wittgenstein, language becomes meaningful through its ability to picture reality. Wittgenstein's early view of language has been characterized as a representational view. Propositions are pictures or representations of reality. And since reality is intimately related to experience, there are limits to what one could legitimately or meaningfully talk about. Questions about ultimate reality or a supernatural reality that is beyond ordinary experience—the reality that so much of traditional metaphysics and religion had been concerned with—are questions that we cannot meaningfully discuss. Thus Wittgenstein directed, "Whereof one cannot speak, thereof one must be silent." Believing he had shown that many of the traditional problems of philosophy and religion were the result of misunderstanding language, and that he had outlined what an ideal language was—namely one which pictured or represented the facts— Wittgenstein left philosophy. His work was done.

A decade later, Wittgenstein returned to Cambridge, convinced that he could still make some genuine contribution to philosophy, but now believing that his earlier view of language was in error. Still concerned with issues of meaning and language, Wittgenstein now argued that linguistic meaning is not determined by a word or sentence representing something beyond language. Thus, words are not fixed labels for objects, and do not acquire meaning as a result of labeling ideas or picturing facts. Rather meaning is more complex.

If one considers the word "game" one will see that it does not pick out some type of activity that all games, and only games, share in common. Rather, the concept of game works to pick out a spectrum of activities which, at either end of the spectrum, may not share anything in common. It is only when one looks at the whole spectrum one that sees how they are all related. For Wittgenstein, language is like a game, functioning or being used in a tremendous variety of complex but related ways. Thus, to understand meaning in language one must understand the language game of the word or expression that is being used. Representing is, perhaps, one way—but not the only way— for language to be meaningful.

If Wittgenstein is correct about meaning being a function of use, then the meaning of a text will be reflected in its use. Since there are many possible, and thus legitimate uses of a text, there are many possible legitimate interpretations. So how do the various language games relate? Are misunderstandings in interpretation, or translation between language games possible? According to thinkers like Jean-Francois Lyotard and Paul Ricoeur there is room for skepticism regarding the adequacy of such translations and interpretations. However, as Ricoeur remarks, "Make sure people can rely on your words . . . that's the basis of all interaction. It's the basis of the promise."

TEXT LINKS

⬄ Turn to Velasquez, *Philosophy: A Text with Readings*, eleventh edition, and read Section 6.4, "Can Interpretations Be True?" Included in the section are more extended discussions and examples of problems with issues of interpretation being raised regarding specific Biblical quotes, Blake's poetry, as well as United States Constitutional issues. A more detailed discussion of the important views of Ludwig Wittgenstein on language is also provided as well as discussions of Schleiermacher, Dilthey, and Gadamer.

KEY TERMS

Allegory: From the Greek *allegoreuo*, meaning literally, saying something different from what's actually said.

Genre: A style or method and typically used to describe types of stories, plays, and films.

Hermeneutics: The branch of philosophy that deals with the interpretation of words and actions by providing correct rules for interpretation. Its original focus was upon the meaning of texts.

Ideal language: A language free of the ambiguity and vagueness of ordinary language.

Indulgences: As used in this episode in referring to practices of the Catholic church, indulgences were sold by the church for the purpose of getting the souls of departed loved ones out of purgatory.

Intention: Ordinarily understood as the conscious motivating factor behind some action.

Language game: As used by Wittgenstein, it is the practice or use that gives meaning to a word or expression.

Subjective: Uniquely personal, such as your feelings or thoughts.

SELF-TEST

Multiple Choice

1. Hermeneutics is the branch of philosophy which focuses upon
   a. ultimate nature of reality
   b. theories of knowledge
   c. the study of the interpretation of words and actions
   d. issues and problems regarding the distribution of social goods

2. Hermeneutics gets its name from
   a. Hermits who wrote the Dead Sea Scrolls
   b. Hermes, the messenger god
   c. Hermenes, the ancient poet of Zybos
   d. the research method of hermeneology

3. Historically, an alternative method of interpretation as opposed to a literal interpretation of the Bible was
   a. divine interpretation
   b. secular interpretation
   c. antithetical interpretation
   d. allegorical interpretation

4. The story of Persephone is told here to illustrate
   a. divine interpretation
   b. secular interpretation
   c. antithetical interpretation
   d. allegorical interpretation

5. Martin Luther's conflict with the Catholic church was in part the result of
   a. Martin Luther's low pay as a parish priest
   b. the Church's lack of support for Luther's planned cathedral in Wittenberg
   c. disagreements over interpretations of the Bible
   d. an apparently rigged election, which kept Luther from becoming Pope

6. Friedrich Schleiermacher claimed that to correctly interpret a text, one must
   a. know the text's historical context
   b. simply find some personal meaning in the work
   c. look to the theme of the work
   d. understand how informed, educated people react to the work

7. Wilhelm Dilthey's work is most closely associate with that of
   a. Aristotle
   b. Hans-George Gadamer
   c. Paul Ricoeur
   d. Friedrich Schleiermacher

8. To know an artist's intention, Dilthey claimed you must
   a. almost relive or re-enact the artist's life
   b. actually give up the idea of being able to know an artist's actual intention
   c. study the work of art itself very closely
   d. find the allegorical meaning in a work of art

9. Hans-George Gadamer emphasized the
   a. need for objective interpretations
   b. need to find an artist's true intentions
   c. ever present subjectivity in all interpretations
   d. lack of intention in speaking a language

10. Historically, one method attempted for avoiding misunderstanding in interpretation was
    a. the creation of an ideal language
    b. universal literacy
    c. requiring people to speak more than one language
    d. having every educated person learn Latin

11. Wittgenstein's early work claimed that the ideal language
    a. would clearly or exactly represent reality
    b. would be formal and mathematical
    c. would be essentially religious
    d. was a fiction since language is much too complex

12. Wittgenstein's later view of language is most clearly capture in the notion of language
    a. as a picture
    b. as emotional expression
    c. labeling ideas
    d. as a game

True or False

These questions are only from the reading assignment in Velasquez, Section 6.4. Specific page references are given in the answer key.

13. The question of whether interpretations are true is important when trying to find out what the Constitution requires.

14. Thomas Aquinas claimed that biblical texts have only a literal meaning.

15. Schleiermacher and Dilthey embraced the correspondence theory of truth.

16. Wittgenstein's early theory of an ideal language accepted the coherence theory of truth.

17. According to Gadamer, the true interpretation of a text is the one that best coheres with both the prejudices of our own culture and what we believe the text meant in its own culture.

PARADOXICAL PURSUITS

If Gadamer is correct that subjectivity cannot be overcome in interpretation, can he be understood or can his writing understood? What is the purpose of his writing?

❧

Is it possible to create a work of art which "says" something greater, more powerful, more insightful than what the artist or even historian may have intended? Can you give an example? If this is possible, what is the value of Dilthey's claim of knowing the intention of the artist so as to interpret the work?

❧

The popular view of language and meaning is that words are meaningful when they label our ideas. If you believe this, aren't you taking a representative view of language—meaning similar to Wittgenstein's early view? Isn't such a view of the meaning of language erroneous and doesn't it face all of the problems that led Wittgenstein to abandon such a view?

APPLIED PHILOSOPHY

Watch ordinary situation comedies from the 1950s and early 1960s like "Leave it to Beaver," "The Donna Reed Show," "The Dick VanDyke Show," or "Father Knows Best." Do these shows and the life they portray seem stilted, strange, alien? Did the 1950s constitute a different culture from the 1990s? Since 40 years separate these eras, how different was life in the nineteenth century, the Middle Ages, or ancient Greece? Can someone today even begin to imagine what life was actually like in such distant and different eras? If not, what is the value of Schleiermacher's and Dilthey's work?

❧

Go to a movie with a group of friends then gather afterward to discuss the film. How many different interpretations are there? Do some accounts simply describe the story line providing no allegorical interpretation? Are the allegorical interpretations provided dependent upon knowing the intentions of the writer or director, or are they simply based upon the film?

❧

Wittgenstein claimed that the word "game" does not have an exact definition. Rather, if one looks at those things or activities which the word picks out or makes reference to, one would find a spectrum of examples that share some features in common but not others. Thus, the meaning of a concept should not be understood as rigidly standing for or labeling some single idea, as is popularly believed. Is this true of all concepts? Is this true of the concept of a triangle? How about chair or cup?

NET LINKS

Check out these Internet websites for additional relevant philosophical information. Remember the Internet is a web. Each of these listed sites is linked to other sites.

Philosophy Resources:

— http://www.earlham.edu/ ~ peters/phil-inks.htm

— http://www.epistemelinks.com

— http://www.refdesk.com/philos.html

— http://www.erraticimpact.com

Encyclopedia of Philosophy:

— http://www.iep.utm.edu

Philosophy Papers:

— http://philosophy.hku.hk/paper/info.php

— http://cogprints.org/view/subjects/phil.html

Hermeneutics:

— http://www.endtimes.org/hermeneutics.html

— http://www.friesian.com/hermenut.htm

Wilhelm Dilthey:

— http://www.marxists.org/reference/subject/philosophy/works/ge/dilthey.htm

Hans-Georg Gadamer:

— http://www.philosophyprofessor.com/philosophers/hans-georg-gadamer.php

Friedrich Schleiermacher:

— http://plato.stanford.edu/entries/schleiermacher

— http://people.bu.edu/WeirdWildWeb/courses/
mwt/dictionary/
mwt_themes_470_schleiermacher.htm

Ludwig Wittgenstein:

— http://www.iep.utm.edu/w/wittgens.htm

— http://plato.stanford.edu/entries/wittgenstein

Samuel Ijsseling:

— http://www.uta.edu/english/rcct/E5311/
notes6.html

Paul Ricoeur:

— http://en.wikipedia.org/wiki/Paul_Ricoeur

Stephen Toulmin:

— http://en.wikipedia.org/wiki/Stephen_Toulmin

— http://www.willamette.edu/cla/Rhetoric/
courses/argumentation/Toulmin.htm

Lesson Eighteen

Is Morality Relative?

LEARNING OBJECTIVES

Upon completing this lesson, you should be familiar with the concepts contained in the lesson and be able to critically discuss:

≈ examples of varying moral practices among different cultures, historical periods, and among individuals.

≈ moral relativism and the apparent paradox of tolerance.

≈ moral relativism and the giving of "good reasons."

≈ emotivism and moral language versus scientific language.

≈ judging a complex situation morally versus taking specific moral action.

OVERVIEW

Values and beliefs seemingly vary from person to person and culture to culture, even over time. At one time, for example, slavery was a legally sanctioned institution in the United States. While no longer tolerated in the United States, slavery is still practiced in some cultures. California and the south of France have nude beaches but such beaches are not tolerated in the southern United States nor in the Arab world. Perhaps one of the most popular beliefs about the nature of morality in our culture is that morality is relative.

As a result of this relativistic view of morality, some have gone on to argue that the reasonable position to take toward other cultures or another person's moral values is that of tolerance. Such a view of tolerance is expressed by the popular saying, "When in Rome, do as the Romans do." However, both Gilbert Harman and Ronald Dworkin point out, in this episode, that such a principle or rule seems absolute. It applies to everyone's actions regardless of culture, and thus appears to be in contradiction with a position of relativity.

Depending upon the type of relativism one claims to accept, the genuine relativist does whatever he or she takes the source of his or her values to be. Suppose he or she is a cultural relativist who subscribes to the values of a culture with no principle of tolerance for the values of other cultures. Then he or she would be morally justified in adopting a range of possible practices ranging from indifference to genocide, depending upon the culture. In principle, practices such as slavery or acts such as rape or stealing cannot be morally condemned cross culturally; they can only be described as being different. Thus slavery is not wrong nor was it wrong during an earlier era in United States history. The culture of the times and the economic arrangement was simply different than what we have now in the United States. But can or does morality stop at cultural boundaries? Does morality depend on one's culture?

In September 1994 the Dutchman Johannes van Damme was sentenced to death in Singapore for smuggling drugs. In Holland, Johannes's native country, the whole idea of the death penalty is strange, even alien. The Dutch population reacted with amazement and anger over his sentence. In Singapore, the death penalty is automatically applied if someone is convicted of drug smuggling. As the Dutch foreign minister issued a formal protest, the foreign minister of Singapore replied that his government respects the standpoint of other countries, who are opposed to the death penalty. But Singapore doesn't share that view and expects that other countries, whatever their particular views, show comparable respect to Singapore. Can more be said or are such views similar to differences in taste that are fundamentally irreconcilable?

Does the foreign minister of Singapore's position ring of, "When in Rome, do as the Romans do," and thus face an apparent contradiction? Is there any inconsistency between asking that countries show respect for one another's laws and the possibility that the death penalty is an excessive form of punishment for a particular crime, thus failing to show respect for human life? Can one consistently demand that respect be shown if he or she does not show respect?

To other thinkers, such cases demonstrate that difference of viewpoint is not enough to justify holding a position of moral relativity. Moral principles do not stop at culture's borders but apply to acts and practices no matter where or when they occur. Some acts are universally wrong from the moral point of view. James Rachels points out that it is not enough to know that someone or some culture has a different view from your own or your culture's. There must also be "good reason(s)" for taking a particular point of view. As Rachels argues, there are good reasons to believe that slavery is wrong no matter where or when it occurs. But what about the belief some groups hold that homosexuals are sinister people? If there are no good reasons, then it is simply a cultural product. In recognizing some cultural practices as lacking good reason(s) do we then have an account of what is bigoted or prejudiced?

Some philosophers have argued that the core of morality consists of promoting the interests or well being of those people who are affected by your actions; where everyone's interests are weighed equally. Does such a view only postpone the issue of relativism, since we may have no way of deciding what is in someone's interest or how to reconcile conflicts in interests when they arise? In the field of science, the international respect and global dependence upon the work of the Center for Disease Control when deadly bacteria are rampant illustrates that cross cultural solutions can be found. But why haven't moral methods been developed or discovered that produce similar agreement?

Emotivism suggests that such a moral consensus has not and probably cannot be reached since moral judgments are expressions of our personal feelings and emotions. Scientific judgments are descriptions of facts. While moral language and scientific language share some superficial similarities, moral language is expressive and directive whereas scientific language is factual and descriptive, and thus has a truth value. If your language is not descriptive in the right way, then it lacks truth value and hence you cannot develop methods for arriving at a consensus.

Given this distinction, one can see that unlike moral disagreements, a disagreement over facts can in principle, though perhaps not in practice, be reconciled. Take the issue of whether or not O.J. Simpson killed his wife versus the appropriate degree of punishment, if any, a killer should receive. Whether Simpson killed his wife is a factual issue. But questions regarding punishment take one into the moral domain and for the emotivists, since these are ultimately reflections of emotion or feeling, they lack truth value.

But how do "good reasons" fit into the emotivists' account? Some philosophers argue that because some moral positions are more reasonable, emotivism is only a part of the story about morality. So how does one determine the "true" moral judgment? When do reasons become "good reasons" in a case so that an issue can be morally resolved?

Presently there are over 250 million children who do not receive an education or spend time playing, as children in the industrialized world often do. Many of these children work, sometimes under very dangerous conditions, for long periods of time. Often their families depend upon their wages for the survival of the family. For some thinkers, such cases present perplexing moral quandaries. Should we act to abolish child labor, when a possible consequence may be the loss of income and harm to the families? It may be difficult to know what should be done in such complex cases but, according to Ronald Dworkin, we should not shrink from recognizing that the practices are immoral or morally wrong.

Action is an essential part of morality and the ambiguity which moral relativism presents may be something we simply need to accommodate ourselves to.

TEXT LINKS

➣ Turn to Velasquez, *Philosophy: A Text with Readings,* eleventh edition, and read Section 7.1, "What Is Ethics?" This selection opens with a series of provocative vignettes concerning the issue of abortion. The vignettes are intended not to discuss the abortion issue, but to illustrate how inescapable the moral dimension of our lives is. This section goes on to discuss in some detail the nature of morality.

➣ Velasquez Section 7.2. "Is Ethics Relative?" begins with a discussion of the crucial distinction between descriptive and normative studies of morality. This section goes on to raise significant questions about many of the issues surrounding the notion of ethical relativism as opposed to cultural relativism.

➣ Velasquez Section 7.8, "Historical Showcase," contains excerpts from Frederich Nietzsche and Mary Wollstonecraft. Nietzsche is skeptical of morality and considers it to a large extent historically relative while Wollstonecraft opposes relativism and takes more of an absolutist position, seeing morality as grounded in reason.

KEY TERMS

Absolutism: In the context of morality, the view that at least some moral standards or principles apply universally and thus are not culturally, historically, nor personally relative.

Aesthetics: As used in this episode, judgments of values having to do with beauty as opposed to moral values.

Culture: The totality of socially transmitted behavior patterns, arts, beliefs, institutions, and all other products of human work characteristic of a community.

Emotivism: In philosophy, a school of thought which claims that the primary function of language is to express emotions or feelings

The melting pot: A somewhat dated metaphorical expression used originally by sociologists to describe a cultural dynamic whereby a dominant culture changed and was changed by other cultures entering its cultural sphere. The "melting pot" metaphor is sometimes contrasted with that of the "tossed salad" metaphor where cultures entering the sphere of a dominant culture retain their cultural identity unlike the loss of identity suggested by the melting pot metaphor.

Morality: According to some, simply the values we hold. According to others, a type of evaluation that is distinct from other types of values.

Relativity: In the context of morality, the view that moral standards or principles do not apply universally and are in some sense culturally, historically, or personally based

Unconditional: In the context of this episode, the view that some standards or principles hold without regard to or on condition of culture, time, or personal preference.

Values: Preferences, expressions of good and bad, right and wrong, and the like.

SELF-TEST

Multiple Choice

1. In the opening sequence of this episode, the fate of the following creatures is used to illustrate differences in ideas about morality
   a. alligators being raised for making handbags
   b. turkeys being raised for Thanksgiving dinners
   c. lobsters in a restaurant aquarium
   d. dolphins trapped and drowning in gill nets

2. According to some philosophers, to insist that one should show tolerance toward other cultures, since morality is culturally relative is to take a position
   a. supported by the world's major religions
   b. which is inconsistent
   c. of fact marked by the truth
   d. typical of Democrats

3. The case of the Dutchman, Johannes van Damme, raised the issue of
   a. distinguishing Holland from the Netherlands
   b. whether there are legitimate, international war crimes
   c. international monetary responsibility and punishment
   d. the cross cultural legitimacy of the death penalty

4. According to some philosophers in this episode, the issue of moral relativity must include not only variations or differences in moral belief but
   a. there being "good reasons" for holding a belief
   b. whether or not a person was raised to hold the belief
   c. whether or not a person's community unanimously accepts the belief
   d. does the belief have any real "cash" value

5. Emotivism is the view that moral language is essentially
   a. a description of subtle moral facts
   b. an expression of certain emotions and feelings
   c. a language with truth value similar to scientific language
   d. used by people when they are highly emotional

6. According to emotivism as discussed in this episode, language can be used both
   a. descriptively and expressively
   b. by psychologists and philosophers
   c. culturally and socially
   d. intentionally and unintentionally

7. For an emotivist, moral judgments are
   a. either true or false
   b. neither true nor false
   c. always true and never false
   d. sometimes false but never true

8. According to James Rachels, conducting his interview in the nude would be
   a. morally wrong in an absolutist sense
   b. morally neutral but aesthetically problematic
   c. morally obligatory but illegal
   d. grossly immoral but only in our culture

9. If someone argues against moral relativism, saying that the core of morality has to do with promoting human welfare, then according to this episode one must
   a. give a nonrelativistic account of human welfare
   b. face the issue of the immortality of the soul
   c. confront so much superstition in the world
   d. guarantee that this is a genuine expression of one's emotions

10. According to this episode, the problem of child labor affects
    a. approximately 800,000 children worldwide
    b. approximately 5.5 million children worldwide
    c. approximately 25 million children worldwide
    d. over 250 million children worldwide

True or False

These questions are only from the reading assignment in Velasquez, Section 7.2. Specific page references are given in the answer key.

11. Ethical absolutism states that one and only one correct morality exists.

12. Ethical relativism and cultural relativism are the same.

13. According to James Rachels, "the fact that different societies have different moral codes proves nothing."

14. The fact that all societies have to accept certain moral standards to survive shows that ethical relativism is true.

15. A fundamental point the theory of ethical relativism is trying to make is that we should be tolerant of the moral beliefs of others and not assume our own are the only correct ones.

PARADOXICAL PURSUITS

According to moral relativists there are no universal or absolute moral standards. Given this belief, some moral relativists will claim that tolerance should be shown to other cultures; that one culture should not impose its morality on another culture. Is such a view paradoxical in that it directs a person to adopt the universal or absolute standard to show respect since there are no universal or absolute standards?

❧

I like red cars but you like black cars; therefore morality is relative. Do you believe that our values regarding car colors are moral values? Do you believe that all value judgments are moral judgments? Can you think of a value judgment that is not a moral judgment? If so, what is morality?

❧

Can the problem of moral relativity be addressed without a detailed discussion of the question of "What is morality?"

❧

When women were given the right to vote in the United States in 1920, did this mark a greater alignment of our laws with justice and morality, or did it only mark a difference in law and moral judgment? Are there "good reasons" for women having the right to vote or for their not having the right to vote?

❧

What is the difference between the question: "What is morality?" versus "Why be moral?" Does an answer to one suggest or entail an answer to the other?

APPLIED PHILOSOPHY

Ask your family and friends if they believe morality is relative. Are they primarily cultural or historical relativists? Do they claim that morality is personally relative? If they believe morality is both personally and culturally relative, can they hold such a position consistently?

❧

Taking the "good reasons" approach to moral relativity, discuss the issue of homosexuality. For example, a popular argument supporting the wrongfulness of homosexuality is that it violates the function of sex, which is procreation. If most people do not have sex to procreate then what is the function of sex? If it serves other functions, then does the

argument from procreation not constitute a "good reasons" approach to this debate?

❧

Organize a panel discussion on your campus or in your neighborhood on the topic of "Is Morality Relative?" Include at least one representative from the fields of science, business, or economics and one from psychology, sociology, or anthropology, and a philosophy representative. Is there a pattern to the positions taken? Is there variation in the articulateness of the positions taken?

❧

As you read the newspaper or watch a news program, does the article or program take a completely neutral position on the issue under discussion? Can you take a neutral position? Should you take a neutral position?

❧

Do you find any substantial distinctions between your favoring a particular athletic team versus your favoring a particular position regarding honesty or abortion?

❧

Do you believe that morality is relative?

NET LINKS

Check out these Internet sites for additional relevant philosophical information. Remember the Internet is a web. Each of these listed sites is linked to other sites.

Philosophy Resources:

— http://www.earlham.edu/ ~ peters/phil-inks.htm

— http://www.epistemelinks.com

— http://www.refdesk.com/philos.html

— http://www.erraticimpact.com

Encyclopedia of Philosophy:

— http://www.iep.utm.edu

Philosophy Papers:

— http://philosophy.hku.hk/paper/info.php

— http://cogprints.org/view/subjects/phil.html

Moral Musings:

— http://www.bigbrownbat.org/moralmusings/
Select v.2 no.1 (May 1998)

Moral Realism:

— http://www.bu.edu/wcp/Papers/TEth/TEth-Chew.htm

Moral Relativism and Moral Objectivity:

— http://ethics.sandiego.edu/theories/relativism

The Philosopher:

— http://www.the-philosopher.co.uk

Ronald Dworkin:

— http://en.wikipedia.org/wiki/Ronald_Dworkin

John Finnis:

— http://www.law.ox.ac.uk/jurisprudence/finnis.shtml

— http://en.wikipedia.org/wiki/John_Finnis

Gilbert Harman:

— http://www.princeton.edu/ ~ harman

James Rachels:

— http://www.jamesrachels.org

— http://en.wikipedia.org/wiki/James_Rachels

Lesson Nineteen

Does the End Justify the Means?

LEARNING OBJECTIVES

Upon completing this lesson, you should be familiar with the concepts contained in this lesson and be able to critically discuss:

- the utilitarian principle of ethics.

- the difference between qualitative and quantitative evaluations of utility.

- how problems of prediction and measurement raise difficulties for utilitarianism.

- utilitarian theories that allow several kinds of intrinsic goods.

- whether nature has an intrinsic dignity or value.

- whether the effects of our actions on non-humans should count in ethics.

OVERVIEW

On the island of Borneo in Malaysia preparations are underway for building the huge Bakun dam. The dam will produce immense economic benefits for the region. It will provide electricity, control flooding, create jobs, and help bring industrialization to a struggling third world nation. But the dam will also impose large costs on many people. Thirty villages will be uprooted, 10,000 people will have to move, 70,000 acres of rainforest will disappear, countless natural habitats will be destroyed, and immense ecological damages will be inflicted on the area. The culture and way of life of many indigenous people will be destroyed. Should the dam be built? How should such decisions be made?

Utilitarian philosophers, such as Peter Singer, argue that the moral or ethical way to resolve such issues is by carefully weighing the good and bad consequences of the action—its "utility"—and choosing the option that is most likely to produce the greatest balance of good over bad. The benefits the dam will produce for present and future generations must be measured and balanced against the costs that the dam will impose on present and future generations. The utilitarian principle holds that the moral course of action is the one that will produce the greatest net benefits or the fewest net costs for everyone affected.

Utilitarianism was pioneered by the eighteenth century British lawyer and philosopher Jeremy Bentham. Like other Enlightenment philosophers, Bentham maintained that humanity should rely on its own reasoning powers and not on the dogmatic authorities of the past. If we examine the matter reasonably, he held, it is clear that pleasure is the ultimate good that people pursue and pain is the ultimate evil. In everything people do, he argued, they are either pursuing pleasure or avoiding pain. Consequently, when making moral decisions people should attend only to what they are ultimately pursuing in their actions: maximizing their pleasure and minimizing their pain. People should always, in short, choose whatever course of action will produce the greatest balance of pleasure over pain. Bentham's position is sometimes said to be a form of hedonism; the view that pleasure is the ultimate aim of life. Bentham, in fact, developed an elaborate method or calculus for estimating the quantity of one pleasure as compared to that of another. A social reformer, Bentham championed democracy, women's right to vote, and humane punishment since these policies, he felt, were most likely to produce the greatest good for the greatest number.

John Stuart Mill was introduced to the views of Bentham by his father, James Mill. James forced his son John to study Greek at the age of three and to learn Latin when he was eight. At the age of 20, not surprisingly, John Mill suffered a mental breakdown. After he recovered, however, Mill went on to become one of the period's most respected moral philosophers. Mill agreed with most of Bentham's utilitarian claims, but argued that there are qualitative differences among pleasures and pains. Some pleasures are qualitatively better than others—and so count for more—and these qualitative differences have to be taken into account when making moral decisions. The pleasures of the intellect, for example, are "higher" than the pleasures of the senses. Mill expressed this idea in a colorful statement: "It is better to be a human being dissatisfied than a pig satisfied; better to be Socrates dissatisfied than a fool satisfied." Mill claimed that we should always choose the course of action that will produce the greatest balance of pleasure over pain, taking into consideration both the quantity and the quality of pleasures and pains involved.

Utilitarianism may look simple. But trying to predict and measure the long-term consequences of our decisions and actions is very complex and difficult. Is it really possible, for example, to predict all the significant long-term consequences of building a dam in Malaysia? And even if we could accurately predict what will happen, how do we measure the value of a rainforest or a culture? Perhaps the most troubling difficulty utilitarianism raises is what is sometimes called the problem of interpersonal comparisons: How do we compare the amount of pleasure or value that one person derives from, say, living in a forest, with the amount of pleasure or value that another person will derive from, say, living in an industrialized city? How do we determine the extent to which one person's pleasure or pain is larger or smaller than another person's? The Canadian philosopher Charles Taylor claims that it is impossible for utilitarianism to measure and compare the value of living in one culture with the value of living in another culture.

Early in the twentieth century the British philosopher G. E. Moore developed a new version of utilitarianism. According to Moore, pleasure and pain are not the only things that are intrinsically good. Other goods such as knowledge, beauty and life, he claimed, also have intrinsic value. Through the Bloomsbury group—a group of British intellectuals with whom G. E. Moore regularly exchanged his ideas—Moore's views became well known. Although Moore did not discuss the issue, he may have been sympathetic to the idea that natural habitats or ecological systems such as the rainforests of Borneo have an intrinsic value that it is wrong to destroy.

Some contemporary philosophers such as the Norwegian environmental philosopher Arne Naess, have claimed that nature actually has a dignity or intrinsic value that cannot be measured in the way that utilitarianism requires. The value of the rainforest that the Bakun dam would destroy, for example, cannot be measured, and it is wrong to destroy it because its dignity gives it a certain inviolability.

Utilitarian philosophers such as Jonathan Glover, however, contend that all that matters in ethics is how humans will be affected by a decision. The rainforest in itself does not have any intrinsic value and so it does not matter what we do to it, except to the extent that our actions will produce benefits or harms for human beings. However, other utilitarians such as Peter Singer claim that the effects of our actions on sentient creatures other than humans also matter. As a utilitarian, Singer believes that pleasure and pain are the only values that ethics must consider, and since nonhuman animals also experience pleasure and pain, their pleasures and pains are as relevant to ethics as those of humans. While skeptical of the intrinsic value of nature, Singer maintains that in making a decision we must take into account the benefits and harms that our actions will produce on animals as well as humans. If we think that the benefits or harms that we inflict on members of other species do not matter, we display a moral narrowness that is similar to that of the racist who thinks that the benefits or harms we inflict on members of other races do not matter.

Perhaps in the end utilitarianism cannot provide a clear answer as to whether the building of the Bakun dam is morally justified. Nevertheless, utilitarianism helps us to clarify the issues involved in making this moral decision, and it points to where efforts need to be focused for collecting morally relevant information. As the philosopher Ross Harrison points out, utilitarianism at least faces up to the difficulties involved in making a moral decision, something that other moral theories often fail to do.

TEXT LINKS

Read Velasquez, *Philosophy: A Text with Readings,* eleventh edition, Section 7.3, "Do Consequences Make an Action Right?" Velasquez discusses utilitarianism in detail, relating it to egoism, and discusses the views of Bentham and Mill. Velasquez also discusses the implications of utilitarianism for the issue of sexual morality.

See Section 7.9 where Velasquez includes three provocative readings related to utilitarianism. In "The Ones Who Walk Away from Omelas," science fiction writer Ursula K. Le Guin provides a fascinating description of an imaginary utilitarian world; in "Famine, Affluence, and Morality," utilitarian philosopher Peter Singer discusses what utilitarianism implies about our duty to alleviate hunger in impoverished nations; and in "All Animals are Equal," Singer discusses what utilitarianism implies about our treatment of animals.

KEY TERMS

Consequences: In utilitarianism, the good or bad results produced by an action.

Consequentialism: In ethics, the view that morality of an action depends entirely on its consequences and not simply on the kind of action it is; the view that no actions are intrinsically immoral.

Enlightenment: The eighteenth century philosophical movement marked by rejection of traditional social, religious, and political authority, and an emphasis on using one's own reason.

Hedonic calculus: The methods developed by Jeremy Bentham to measure the quantity of various pleasures and pain according to, for example, their intensity, duration, and certainty.

Hedonism: The doctrine that pleasure is the primary good that life has to offer.

Interpersonal comparisons: The attempt to determine the extent to which the pleasure or pain felt by one person is greater or less than the pleasure or pain felt by another person.

Principle of utility: The view that actions are morally right to the extent that they produce utility or beneficial consequences, and morally wrong to the extent that they impose costs or disutility, the morally right action being the one that produces the greatest net utility in comparison to the utility produced by all other possible courses of action.

Qualitative distinctions amongst pleasures: In classical utilitarianism, any differences among pleasures that make one pleasure count for more or less than another but which is not a mere difference of quantity.

Utility: In classical utilitarianism, the quantity of pleasure or satisfaction produced by an action, from which the quantity of pain or dissatisfaction can be subtracted.

SELF-TEST

Multiple Choice

1. Utilitarianism was a product of the philosophy of which era?
   a. ancient Greece
   b. the Enlightenment
   c. the Industrial Revolution
   d. twentieth century Global Capitalism

2. Which two forces govern the actions of humans according to Bentham?
   a. good and evil
   b. right and wrong
   c. pain and pleasure
   d. crime and punishment

3. Bentham and his follower, John Stuart Mill, championed social reforms such as women's right to vote and humane punishment because
   a. they benefitted the rights of individuals
   b. they were likely to produce the greatest good for the greatest number
   c. they produced good results
   d. they increased the level of pleasure in society

4. John Stuart Mill added a new dimension to the utilitarian movement by
   a. asserting that there are qualitative differences among pleasures and pains
   b. his belief in the greatest happiness for the greatest number of people
   c. measuring the quantitative differences among pleasures and pains
   d. judging actions by their consequences only

5. Which utilitarian philosopher had himself preserved as an "auto-icon"?
   a. John Stuart Mill
   b. Jim Mill
   c. G. E. Moore
   d. Jeremy Bentham

6. Consequentialism holds that
   a. no actions are intrinsically immoral
   b. some actions are always immoral
   c. pleasure and pain determine an action's value
   d. the net costs of an action determine its value

7. The theory of *ideal utilitarianism* was proposed by
   a. James Mill
   b. Peter Singer
   c. G. E. Moore
   d. Jonathan Glover

8. Sentient creatures, natural habitats, and goods such as art and love, according to G. E. Moore, have
   a. qualitative value
   b. moral value
   c. intrinsic value
   d. qualitative value

9. Norwegian philosopher Arne Naess has argued that
   a. the value of the environment can be expressed quantitatively
   b. certain natural habitats are living entities and as such can claim equal moral status to that of human beings
   c. the sacrifice of natural habitats is justifiable if it promotes social justice
   d. it is impossible to measure and compare the values of different cultures

10. According to philosopher Jonathan Glover,
    a. natural habitats have intrinsic value
    b. it is impossible to make precise interpersonal comparisons
    c. the attempts to calculate the costs of large scale projects such as the Bakun dam are a "formula for catastrophe."
    d. in ethics, all that matters is how humans are affected by decisions.

11. Utilitarianism, according to Peter Singer, should consider only
    a. pleasure and pain
    b. intrinsic values
    c. the greatest benefit for the greatest number
    d. net costs

True or False

These questions are only from the reading assignment in Velasquez, Section 7.3. Specific page references are given in the answer key.

12. Egoism is the view that holds that only pleasure is worth having for its own sake.

13. Some ethicists think that the most serious weakness of ethical egoism is that it undermines the moral point of view.

14. John Stuart Mill developed a hedonistic calculus that determines how much pleasure an action produces based only on quantitative criteria.

15. Rule utilitarianism holds that as a rule in each particular act we should strive to produce the greatest happiness for the most people.

16. The members of the Ramsey Colloquium use act utilitarianism to argue that moral rules tolerant of homosexuality, adultery, and divorce have harmful effects on society and so should not be followed.

PARADOXICAL PURSUITS

Sentient things are those sorts of things that appear to experience pain and pleasure. What classes of things would you put in the category of sentient beings? Do you think that an event, for example, can experience pleasure or pain? How about plants? Bacteria? Insects? Reptiles? Dogs? Chimps? Whales? All humans?

❧

Suppose that you always seem to be more sensitive to temperature than I am, and you cry over sad movies while I remain unmoved. According to utilitarianism, does it follow that your pain and pleasure must be more intense than mine and hence your comfort and discomfort should count for more than mine?

❧

It is the twenty-second century and you see an advertisement: "The new Hedono-drome is now available guaranteeing the perfect life. Step in, lie down, turn it on, and you can live and feel any fantasy or sensation you want in all of its vivid, virtual reality. If you are wealthy enough, you can spend the rest of your life living your ideal virtual life, which will seem as real to you as your actual life, except that we unconditionally guarantee that it will be much more pleasant. In your virtual life you win every contest, if that's what you want, and have every pleasure you desire. If you should die while on an extended Hedono-drome stay, (a minimum of two years is required) we will see that you are buried according to your requests. Welcome to Hedono-drome Inc." Would you take up the offer? Would other people? Why or why not? What does your decision and/or theirs imply about the utilitarian view that pleasure and pain are the only things that matter?

❧

Think about those times that you have been startled by someone who, for example, jumps out from behind a door to scare you. Ask yourself: at the exact moment of your scream were you afraid? Wasn't there a slight delay between the moment that your body responded with a jump and a scream, and the moment that your mind reacted with the feeling of fear? If so, then the discomfort, the pain of fear, doesn't set in until after the initial scare and thus requires some understanding of what is taking place. But if painful feelings like fear require the ability to understand what is happening, then is it possible that most animals do not actually feel pain in the way that we experience pain, even when they display behavior that we humans associate with pain? If so, what does this imply for utilitarianism and the environment?

APPLIED PHILOSOPHY

Take a day out of your life, and try for the whole day to base every decision you make on the utilitarian principle. What does your experiment tell you about utilitarianism?

❧

Survey your family and friends asking what they believe to be the greatest pleasure in life or the worst pain. Is there a pattern to the responses you get? Why does each person make the judgment he or she makes? Do you find any patterns reflecting age, gender, ethnicity, or culture? If there are differences, how do different people react to each other's claims?

❧

Do you agree with John Stuart Mill that there are differences in the quality of pleasures? If not, then would you agree there is no difference between the satisfaction or pleasure you will experience upon successfully completing your education and receiving your diploma than that experienced by some adolescent boys over a practical joke? If you do agree with Mill, then can the case be made that opera, given its complexity and appeal on multiple levels is generally better than other varieties of popular music such as heavy metal, rap, punk, soft-rock, or new age?

NET LINKS

Check out these Internet websites for additional relevant philosophical information. Remember the Internet is a web. Each of these listed sites is linked to other sites. By surfing you will soon be linked to a seemingly vast resource.

Links to the main texts mentioned in this episode:

— http://ethics.sandiego.edu/resources/books/books.asp

Environmental Philosophy:

— http://www.erraticimpact.com/ ~ ecologic/

— http://www.cep.unt.edu

— http://en.wikipedia.org/wiki/Environmental_ethics

Ethics:

— http://www.scu.edu/Ethics/links/

— http://ethics.sandiego.edu/

Moral Musings:

— http://www.bigbrownbat.org/moralmusings/ Select v.2 no.1 (May 1998)

Utilitarianism:

— http://www.hedweb.com/hedabuti.html

— http://philtar.ucsm.ac.uk/moral_philosophy/utilitarianism.html

— http://www.bltc.net/ethics/utility.htm

Jeremy Bentham:

— http://www.blupete.com/Literature/Biographies/Philosophy/Bentham.htm

— http://www.class.uidaho.edu/mickelsen/Bentham.htm

John Stuart Mill:

— http://www.philosophypages.com/ph/mill.htm

— http://www.utilitarianism.com/jsmill.htm

— http://ethics.sandiego.edu/theories/utilitarianism/index.asp

—http://plato.stanford.edu/entries/mill

James Rachels:

— http://www.jamesrachels.org

— http://en.wikipedia.org/wiki/James_Rachels

Stephen Toulmin:

— http://en.wikipedia.org/wiki/Stephen_Toulmin

— http://www.willamette.edu/cla/Rhetoric/courses/argumentation/Toulmin.htm

Lesson Twenty

Can Rules Define Morality?

LEARNING OBJECTIVES

Upon completing this lesson, you should be familiar with the concepts contained in the lesson and be able to critically discuss:

- autonomous and non-autonomous ethics.

- maxim, universal law, and the categorical imperative.

- at least two versions of the categorical imperative.

- applying the categorical imperative.

- when duties conflict.

OVERVIEW

You are standing in line patiently waiting your turn to buy a ticket. Everyone around you is excited and talking about the show. The couple in front of you worries that tickets will be sold out before they get to the box office. Glancing at the long line ahead, you, too, start to fret over getting a ticket when you suddenly notice a half dozen, surly male bullies cut into line just ahead of you. No one says a thing to these bullies as they flash threatening glances and challenging sneers. Whispers of resentment flow through the line. "Someone should do something!"

you say silently to yourself. You want to say something to them but you feel cowardly. You don't even care about a ticket anymore. You just want these bullies to know how rude, how arrogant, how selfish they are. The line starts moving along and everyone finally gets a ticket, but you and others still feel resentment. As the bullies walk down the aisle to take their seats, you see people glancing at them, whispering and shaking their heads.

In this little story, you could expect one of the bullies to finally respond, "Hey, what's the big deal? You got in, didn't you?" The "big deal" is not simply in getting to see the show, but in how you were treated. In the case of line cutting, the line cutter gives priority to himself or herself over the others waiting in line. Lines are an attempt to reflect equality among people. One takes one's place and waits like everyone else. But a line cutter says, "No! I go first." Hence, when we are not treated as an equal, or with respect, we tend to feel resentment, anger. According to Immanuel Kant, it is through recognition of the dignity of a person as an equal, rational being worthy of respect, that we find the source of morality.

If line cutters were concerned about the moral worth of their actions, then Kant would have them ask if the maxim—that is, the principle or rule by which they are guiding their act—could be made a universal law. That is, could everyone act on the principle or rule they are acting on? As a universal law, the act would reflect the equal status that all rational beings share. Take, for example, the maxim of the line-cutters. Suppose the maxim of their action is

117

"Everyone should simply cut in line when they want to see a show." Now let us try to elevate this maxim to the status of a universal law by imagining what would happen if everyone followed the maxim. We quickly discover that it is inconceivable. If everyone became a line cutter, then lines would not be formed, would not even exist. When it is impossible to make your maxim a universal law, then you know it is an action that not all rational beings could perform and so it is morally wrong, according to Kant. As a moral agent, you should not perform such an act.

To determine, in part, the moral worth of one's actions, Kant provides a test of the categorical imperative. "Act only on that maxim that you can will to be a universal law." The bullies that cut in line failed the first test of the categorical imperative; it is inconceivable that their actions would be considered a universal law. For Kant, deceitful or false promises also fail the test. Thus, if one makes a promise with no intention of keeping it, the wrongfulness of such an act becomes apparent when one tries to make such a maxim a universal law. It undermines the very practice of promising. No one would make promises knowing they will not be kept. Since the maxims of deceitful or false promises cannot be considered universal laws, they are morally wrong.

According to Kant, rational beings have a capacity to act autonomously, and are self-directed. Animals are not autonomous, and are said to be other-directed in that animal behavior is determined solely by the forces of nature. The instinct or desire that is strongest is the one that will move the animal, be it a trained domestic pet or a wild, cunning predator. Rational beings, in contrast, are not simply moved by their strongest desires. Because they have wills, they can act according to laws which they choose.

For Kant, this capacity to act according to universal laws we choose is the foundation of morality. In so acting, we treat other autonomous beings with the respect their dignity demands; as ends and never simply as means to our own personal ends. Both the chair I sit in and the computer I type on, while of much value to me, are simply things used by me as a means to the end. You and I, however, are persons, and persons should not be used as things but respected as equal, autonomous beings.

Autonomous beings recognize this equality of autonomy among themselves. Morality becomes a way of reflecting their respect for this equality. Imperatives or statements guide their behavior, and typically include terms like "ought" or "should." These imperatives are considered moral, according

to Kant, if they can be applied universally or categorically to all autonomous beings.

Since morality is concerned with autonomous beings and their equal worth, Kant offers a second version of the categorical imperative. It does not focus so much upon universal law, but rather on respecting autonomous beings. In this second formulation Kant states, "Act in such a way that you treat humanity, whether in your own person or in that of another, in every case as an end and never as a means."

Consider the case of slavery. At one time in the history of the United States, slave owners used other human beings to advance their economic interests. Much of the literature that attempted to justify slavery claimed that the slave was not really a person—the autonomous being Kant described—but was instead a savage, a wild animal. As long as the slave was not considered equal in worth or dignity to free men, then slavery appeared acceptable. However, if the slave was recognized as an autonomous being, and skin pigment was no more significant than the presence or absence of freckles, then major moral problems arose.

Critics have charged Kant with not adequately addressing the issue of conflicting duties. What happens when two duties, both of which Kant recognizes, come into conflict. You have invited guests over for dinner and promised to cook chicken tandoori. On the way to buy your groceries, you come across a homeless family with very hungry children. You only have so much money and given your budget you cannot both help this family and fulfill your promise to cook this meal for your friends. Perhaps everyone could have some peanut butter and jelly, given your budget, but you did explicitly promise chicken tandoori for your friends. While this may not constitute a morally momentous case, the problem of conflicting duties can occur at more serious levels, as your own imagination makes clear to you.

Kant may have been overly optimistic in thinking that conflicting duties are so rare that an ethical theory need not address them. His theory emphasizes the view that morality does not involve the balancing of positive or negative consequences, but rather the possibility that all autonomous beings could act in the same way. Thus, for Kant to point out that all autonomous creatures would not choose to act according to some maxim in a particular case is irrelevant from the moral point of view. If every autonomous creature could follow such an act, then it would appear that a rule can be formulated. Hence rules or laws, for Kant, not only define morality, but they reflect our equal moral worth as autonomous beings.

TEXT LINKS

☞ Turn to Velasquez, *Philosophy: A Text with Readings*, eleventh edition, and read Section 7.4, "Do Rules Define Morality?" In this section you will find a more complete discussion of Kant's ethics with a much fuller exposition of his views on autonomy and the distinctions between perfect and imperfect duties to ourselves and others. There is also included a more complete discussion of the traditional criticisms of purported weaknesses in Kant's theory.

KEY TERMS

Autonomy: Self-directed actions taken as a result of an individual exercising both rationality and freedom of choice.

Categorical imperative: Kant's formula for determining whether an action can apply universally or to all rational beings.

Consequences: The series of events or effects that follow as a result of some act or event.

Consistency: Statements or beliefs which do not contradict one another.

Ethics: The philosophical study of morality.

Golden Rule ethics: A moral principle typically associated with Christianity and attributed to Jesus in which a person is directed to do unto others has he or she would have them do unto him or her.

Imperative: A rule or directive for action. An ought or should statement.

Maxim: A reason or rule according to which someone acts on a particular occasion.

Morality: For Kant a type of evaluation which reflects respect among persons as opposed, for example, to prudence (self-interest) which is a type of evaluation reflecting only the interests of an individual. More generically, morality is sometimes defined simply as value or as a culture's, society's, or individual's most important or fundamental values.

Persons as ends: According to Kant, the recognition of persons as things that cannot be used simply as a means to some other end.

Persons as means: According to Kant, the using of persons without their informed consent, and in so doing, failing to show the respect which persons as ends requires from the standpoint of morality.

Universal law: As used by Kant in his ethics, a part of the test of the categorical imperative in which a person tests an action by determining if its application as a possible action for all rational beings—that is, being applied universally—is conceivable or desirable.

SELF-TEST

Multiple Choice

1. According to Immanuel Kant, the source of morality is
   a. divine commands
   b. pleasure
   c. the laws of the state
   d. reason

2. The only thing that is good without qualification is, for Kant,
   a. a good will
   b. gifts of nature such as courage and resolution
   c. talents of the mind such as wit and intelligence
   d. gifts of fortune, such as health and power

3. Within the Kantian moral system, a maxim is
   a. the highest good
   b. laws enacted unjustly
   c. the rule or reason by which a person acts
   d. the act with the best consequences

4. The categorical imperative asks
   a. "Is the maxim of my action the most beneficial?"
   b. "Can the maxim of my action give the greatest pleasure?"
   c. "Can the maxim of my action be consistent with divine law?"
   d. "Can I will the maxim of my action to be a universal law?"

5. For Kant, if an action can be made a universal law then
   a. all autonomous beings will act according to it
   b. all autonomous beings could act according to it
   c. all autonomous beings have already acted according to it
   d. it is a part of science and not morality

6. Kant uses the following example to illustrate an application of the categorical imperative
   a. making a false promise
   b. peeping in someone's window
   c. joining the military
   d. returning lost money

7. According to a second formulation of the categorical imperative persons
   a. are only to be treated as ends, and never as means
   b. are to be treated as ends, and only as a means if that is beneficial overall
   c. can be treated as a means as long as no cruelty is involved
   d. are to be treated only as a means and never as an end

8. Kantian ethics is an attempt to describe a morality that
   a. guarantees eternal salvation
   b. allows one to live a happy life
   c. reflects the dignity of persons
   d. allows one to be envied for one's good works

9. A traditional problem with the Kantian system of morality is
   a. how to get people to do what is moral
   b. resolving apparent conflicts between competing duties
   c. teaching children how to act on such abstract thinking
   d. being able to prove that universal laws actually exist

True or False

These questions are only from the reading assignment in Velasquez, Section 7.4. Specific page references are given in the answer key.

10. Scriptural divine command theories hold that we should obey God's commands as these are embodied in a set of sacred scriptures.

11. The natural law ethics of Thomas Aquinas claims that we have a moral obligation to pursue those goods toward which we are naturally inclined.

12. In his *Groundwork of the Metaphysics of Morals*, Kant claims that ethics relies on a consideration of consequences.

13. Kant argues that every human being has a price and the trick is to calculate the exact value of each person.

14. For Kant, to respect a person as an end is to respect her capacity to freely and knowingly choose for herself what she will do.

PARADOXICAL PURSUITS

Your friend has a learning disorder in addition to having a low I.Q. He wants to know what you've been studying and you begin to tell him about Kant's ethics and the role of the categorical imperative in evaluating actions for their moral worth. While being polite and listening attentively, even nodding, he does not understand a word of this abstract theorizing. Can your friend act morally according to Kant?

❧

You are a very busy person with many responsibilities. You have an assistant who you authorize to help you with all of your appointments. While your assistant promises your favorite charity that indeed you will attend their banquet, you are at the same time promising not to miss your child's baseball game. Both events are scheduled at the same time but on opposites sides of town. What should you do once this conflict of promises is discovered? How would a Kantian resolve such a conflict? Is the categorical imperative alone enough?

❧

Would Kant be willing to accept the principle of utilitarianism to resolve a conflict in duties? If not, why not and do you agree?

APPLIED PHILOSOPHY

You are sitting in class ready to take an exam. You stayed up late partying but knew you could cheat, if necessary, off the student next to you. You don't regularly cheat, and you are doing fairly well in answering questions but you need to just check a few answers and so you cheat. How do you think a utilitarian would judge your case? What would Kant tell you? What do you honestly think is the correct answer from a moral point of view?

❧

Are you essentially a utilitarian or a Kantian? Ask your instructor if he or she is a utilitarian or a Kantian and why.

❧

Organize a panel discussion on your campus or in your neighborhood on the topic, "What is Morality?" Invite at least one faculty representative from a variety of academic departments including the philosophy department. Is there a pattern to the positions taken? Is there variation in the articulateness of the positions taken?

NET LINKS

Check out these Internet sites for additional relevant philosophical information. Remember the Internet is a web. Each of these listed sites is linked to other sites.

Philosophy Resources:

— http://www.earlham.edu/ ~ peters/phil-inks.htm

— http://www.epistemelinks.com

— http://www.refdesk.com/philos.html

— http://www.erraticimpact.com

Encyclopedia of Philosophy:

— http://www.iep.utm.edu

Philosophy Papers:

— http://philosophy.hku.hk/paper/info.php

— http://cogprints.org/view/subjects/phil.html

Ethics:

— http://www.scu.edu/Ethics/links

— http://ethics.acusd.edu

Immanuel Kant:

— http://www.friesian.com/kant.htm

— http://www.philosophypages.com/ph/kant.htm

— http://www.hkbu.edu.hk/ ~ ppp/Kant.html

James Rachels:

— http://www.jamesrachels.org

— http://en.wikipedia.org/wiki/James_Rachels

Rudiger Safranski:

— http://www.litrix.de/autoren/autor/rudigersafranski/portraet/enindix.htm

— http://en.wikipedia.org/wiki/Rudiger_Safranski

Lesson Twenty-one

Is Ethics Based on Virtue?

LEARNING OBJECTIVES

Upon completing this lesson, you should be familiar with the concepts contained in the lesson and be able to critically discuss:

✑ the distinction between ethical theories such as utilitarianism and kantianism versus virtue theories

✑ moral theories that are principle- or rule-based as opposed to those that are character-based.

✑ *eudaimonia* and its relationship to virtue.

✑ Aristotle's theory of virtues.

✑ the issue of relativity in regard to virtue theories and the weaknesses of such theories in evaluating or guiding actions.

OVERVIEW

If you are between 20 and 25 years of age, take today's date and add 70 years to it. If you are between 25 and 35, add 60 years to today's date. If you are between 35 and 45 add 50 years. Do you have an exact calculation? Imagine as vividly as you can what you might be doing at precisely this time but at that future date.

If you are fortunate to have had a long life, then at that particular time, your life as you've known it will be nearly over. There will come a moment when you fully realize your death is imminent. There will now be no more meals, no more entertainment, no more getting up each day, no more colors, no tastes. The sound of the wind in the trees and the warmth of the sun will never be heard nor felt again by you. Your long life, seeming endless as a child, is at its conclusion. If, at this final moment, you look back over the wholeness of your life and whisper, "Yes, it was indeed a good life," then your life was one that some philosophers have described as having *eudaimonia*.

Julia Annas suggests, ". . . the entry point for ethical reflection [is] thinking about your life as a whole." Martha Nussbaum talks of the "complete life," and Bernard Williams "a worthwhile life." This concern with the quality of life was the primary focus for the ancient Greek ethical theory. At the core of their ethics was the concept of *eudaimonia*. While *eudaimonia* is sometimes translated as happiness, it does not mean a life dominated by pleasure, joy, or some other feeling or emotion, though they are a part of it. Rather, *eudaimonia* is a quality of a whole, or completely worthwhile life.

Aristotle defined *eudaimonia* as, "that activity of the soul in accordance with virtue." A life of virtue was the key to a happy life, to a life of *eudaimonia* for the ancient Greeks. Their ethical theory has thus been characterized as one of virtue ethics. Unlike the more modern ethical theories of utilitarianism and Kantianism, both of which focus on discovering some rule(s) or principle(s) to evaluate specific actions, institutions, and practices, virtue ethics focuses primarily on the character of the person. (See Episode 19, "Does the End Justify the Means?" and Episode 20, "Can Rules Define Morality?") The goal, then is one of developing a virtuous character. The virtues or vices, vice being a lack of virtue, largely define a person's character. Most significantly, the virtues and vices are, to some degree, acquired. While they can be acquired in a variety of ways, once acquired, virtues allow a person to flourish in any area of life.

The ancient Greeks had one word for both virtue and excellence. Thus, virtues were regarded as excellence of character. According to Aristotle's theory of virtue, virtue is to be found in the "mean," or middle, and so his theory of virtue came to be known as the Theory of the Golden Mean. What Aristotle meant was that the exercise of virtue regarding both feelings and actions falls between two extremes. Courage is the middle ground between cowardice and foolhardiness or bravado. If you have too much fear, then you act cowardly. On the other hand, if you have too little fear, you rush in foolishly. Think of the virtue of generosity. Too little, you are stingy. Too much, you are profligate. Generosity is thus the mean between stinginess and profligacy.

Living a life according to virtue—that is, in accordance with the mean—may have intuitive appeal, but difficulties arise when we attempt to apply this doctrine to the specifics of our daily lives. As Aristotle described, ". . . the mark of virtue [is] to act or feel at the right time, on the right occasions, toward the right person, with the right object and in the right fashion." The successful application of virtue thus involves understanding and balancing a number of variables, all of which are dependent on the situation.

In virtue ethics there are no formal principles or formulas to follow, as there are in utilitarianism or Kantianism. One cannot learn what one ought to do by studying a text, or understanding a principle or rule, and then applying it to a specific situation. Kantians and utilitarians focus on formal procedures; what Bernard Williams describes as procedures that allow a person to precisely evaluate actions and determine a course of action which everyone similarly situated should follow. This approach is foreign to virtue ethics.

Acting virtuously is learned not so much through studying theories and finding formulas as through examples of people who act virtuously. Acquiring virtue and acting virtuously is more like learning a skill or craft than intellectually discovering some set of commandments or rules to follow.

An athlete or performer will practice conscientiously to perfect his or her activity but when the actual game or performance occurs, there are no rigid, fixed rules to follow. For the athlete, on the day of the game it may be raining or colder than expected; a crucial teammate may be sick. You did have some game plans but now what? The coach whispers, "Go in there and do your best!" For the performer, a highly honored dignitary may arrived unannounced for the performance, lights may not be working, and someone may have ripped your costume but the show must go on. You look to your director and he or she whispers, "Give it your all. Break a leg!" You perform excellently because you've acquired the traits or dispositions to rise to the level of excellence demanded by your art or craft. Anyone who displays such excellence has *phronesis*, practical wisdom or intelligence, according Aristotle. To have *phronesis* is to have mastered a number of different virtues.

A further contrast between virtue ethics and the principled views of utilitarianism or Kantianism involves the role of the emotions and feelings in ethical action. For Kant, to act in such a way that one feels good about it, seems to dilute its moral worth. For utilitarians, an individual person's feelings are nothing special from the moral point of view. The principle of utility applies, in its social context, regardless of an individual's feelings.

According to Aristotle, acting virtuously is essential to the happy life or the life of *eudaimonia*. The person who acts virtuously, who has mastered a number of virtues, who has *phronesis*, feels good about his or her life. A unique sense of satisfaction is derived from the fulfillment of this rational activity of the soul. Having such a feeling demonstrates, for Aristotle, the authenticity of the virtue.

And again, in contrast to ethical theories concerned with principles or rules, the traditional virtue approach to ethics sees the human being as essentially a social animal. We are not isolated individuals making isolated, momentary choices. Joel Kupperman describes these rule-governed views of decision making as the "snapshot view of ethical choice." To virtue theorists, an evaluation of character brings with it a rich background or history. If there is a failure or a success, it must be understood against a history that includes a pattern of choices as well as personality or character.

For virtue ethics, problems arise when individuals or communities adopt competing virtues or sets of virtues. In such cases, a principle or rule beyond the set of virtues appears to be required to resolve the conflict. Related to this problem is Kant's criticism that virtues such as honesty, courage, temperance, patience, and perseverance can all be used inappropriately, for goals that are apparently immoral. Analogously, what does one tell a woman agonizing over an abortion decision, or a family torn by an emotionally wrenching case of euthanasia? To advise simply, "Be courageous!" "Be honest!" "Act justly!" is not morally helpful since a person can be all of these things yet not know what he or she should do.

Perhaps virtue is essential to a life of *eudaimonia* and we should all attempt to acquire *phronesis*. And perhaps, as Martha Nussbaum remarks, ". . . there is no incompatibility between virtue ethics and an emphasis on a universal account that also has a large room for principle." Perhaps we should view these diverse moral theories like a variety of lenses, as Manuel Velasquez suggests, looking at a moral situation from a number of theoretical vantage points. If so, "then we can ask questions about that moral situation that are not brought out by the other moral theories."

TEXT LINKS

🔖 Turn to Velasquez, *Philosophy: A Text with Readings*, eleventh edition, and read Section 7.5, "Is Ethics Based on Character?" In this section you will find a discussion of the strengths and weaknesses of virtue-based ethics. There are extended passages from Aristotle's "Nichomachean Ethics" included. Following the section on Aristotle's ethics is a presentation of the contemporary discussion of possible distinctions between male and female moral views. While the work of Carol Gilligan is emphasized, the work of Lawrence Kohlberg is introduced to provide a contrast.

KEY TERMS

Care Ethics: The point of view of giving value priority to particular relationships in which one is both caring and cared for and; as opposed to focusing upon broad social issues of justice and rights.

Character: A global concept referring to the unique combination of needs, desires, emotions, feelings, moods, beliefs, talents, and skills, which together make up who an individual's uniqueness.

Decision procedure: A description of how a person should and does decide or choose according to some clearly articulated rule(s) or principle(s).

Eudaimonia: Often translated as happiness, but it is not a synonym for joy, as is so often the case with happiness in ordinary language. For the Greeks, *eudaimonia* was an overall condition of life which includes many of the emotions—like joy—but it is not simply joy nor is it to be tied to a specific emotion or feeling, like pleasure.

Kantianism: In this episode, refers to Immanuel Kant's ethical theory, specifically Kant's view that the categorical imperative is part of the test for the moral worth of an action. (See Episode 20: "Can Rules Define Morality?")

The mean (golden mean): An average. That which falls in the middle. For Aristotle, virtuous action always fell within the mean or middle between two extremes.

Phronesis: Practical wisdom which, for Aristotle, comes after a number of virtues have been mastered.

Utilitarianism: The ethical theory which claims that actions are to be evaluated by how well they maximize the overall consequences of non-moral goodness or minimize the consequences of non-moral badness.

Virtue: For the ancient Greeks, virtue and excellence were the same word. For Aristotle, virtue was found in the mean between too much and too little.

SELF-TEST

Multiple Choice

1. Virtue ethics tends to focus on
   a. actions
   b. institutions
   c. rituals
   d. character

2. In ancient Greece, virtue was synonymous with
   a. duty
   b. excellence
   c. obligation
   d. natural right

3. A core concept to the ancient Greek ethical theory was
   a. *eudaimonia*
   b. euphoria
   c. euthanasia
   d. europa

4. In ancient Greece, if you mastered a number of virtues, then you were said to possess
   a. power
   b. knowledge
   c. *phronesis*
   d. pleasure

5. Virtue ethics, as opposed to utilitarianism or Kantianism, does not attempt to provide a
   a. formula or decision procedure for evaluating all actions
   b. any consideration of what a person should do
   c. any method for attaining happiness
   d. any role for an individual's history or emotions

6. The modern ethical theories of utilitarianism and Kantianism attempt to provide primarily a
   a. formula or decision procedure for evaluating all actions
   b. some consideration for the person's character
   c. a method for individuals to attain happiness
   d. role for an individual's history and/or emotional sensitivity

7. According to Aristotle, virtue is to be found in the
   a. commands of the gods
   b. maxim which can be consistently applied to all rational beings
   c. mean between deficiency and excess
   d. the greatest good for the greatest number

8. Generosity has been described as that virtue which falls between
   a. spitefulness and beneficence
   b. impulsiveness and inexorableness
   c. stinginess and profligacy
   d. cowardice and bravado

9. According to this episode, a strength of virtue ethics over ethical theories such as Kantianism is
   a. the inclusion of the emotions and personal history
   b. the emphasis upon the significance of intention
   c. the conceptual distinction between actions and behaviors
   d. an emphasis upon the consequences of an action

10. According to this episode, a weakness of virtue ethics may be found in the fact that
    a. it's an old, even ancient, theory for dealing with life
    b. it emphasized having an overall good life
    c. conflicts between virtues or sets of virtues held by different people or communities cannot be resolved by appealing to a virtue
    d. a society such as ours is not really concerned with living virtuously, but rather in acquiring wealth so that a person can do whatever makes him or her feel good

True or False

These questions are only from the reading assignment in Velasquez, Section 7.5. Specific page references are given in the answer key.

11. Contemporary philosopher Alasdair MacIntryre argues that modern ethics has forgotten moral virtue.

12. Aristotle rejects the idea that a virtue is the ability to be reasonable in our actions, desires, and emotions.

13. According to Aristotle, virtue is never easy and pleasant.

14. Carol Gilligan argues that men and women approach ethics in exactly the same way.

15. For philosopher Nel Noddings, the "feminine" virtue of caring is more fundamental than the "masculine" focus on principles.

PARADOXICAL PURSUITS

Can you think of a clear example of your happiness conflicting with morality? If you can come up with a case, what should you do? What would you do? Does it make a difference if the conflict involves a significant contribution to your happiness versus a rather minor breach of morality? What if it were morally very significant but of minor importance regarding your happiness? Can you imagine or have you faced a variety of cases ranging along such a spectrum?

✎

What is temptation? Does every case of temptation involve a conflict between values? Can you be tempted without having a free will or any sense of virtue?

✎

Immanuel Kant characterizes the virtues as gifts of character that have no inherent or unconditional moral worth. If ethics is the philosophical study of morality, but virtues have no inherent moral worth, how could one have virtue ethics?

APPLIED PHILOSOPHY

List the virtues you find most important and give a brief justification as to why you believe those are the most important. Do the virtues on your list relate to one another? For example, if you listed the virtues of honesty and kindness, we can all think of cases where honesty can be very unkind and kindness can lead to dishonesty. Thus how do or should such virtues relate to one another? How do those on your list relate?

✎

What are the primary virtues of being a good student? A good son or daughter? A good teacher? A good parent? Rank your list of virtues in terms of each virtue's importance and describe their relationships to each other.

✎

What is your strongest virtue? Your strongest vice? How about your weakest virtue and your weakest vice? Why do these virtues and vices have these strengths and weaknesses in your character? Make a similar list for your family and friends. Are there correlations?

✎

Would you describe your life as one possessing *eudaimonia*? If you think you'll be happy once you acquire some *thing*, like a car, a degree, a job, a house, a group of friends, do you think you have a mistaken understanding of genuine happiness?

NET LINKS

Check out these Internet websites for additional relevant philosophical information. Remember the Internet is a web. Each of these listed sites is linked to other sites.

Philosophy Resources:

— http://www.earlham.edu/~peters/phil-inks.htm

— http://www.epistemelinks.com

— http://www.refdesk.com/philos.html

— http://www.erraticimpact.com

Encyclopedia of Philosophy:

— http://www.iep.utm.edu

Philosophy Papers:

— http://philosophy.hku.hk/paper/info.php

— http://cogprints.org/view/subjects/phil.html

The Philosopher:

— http://www.the-philosopher.co.uk

Ethics Update:

— http://ethics.sandiego.edu

Greek Philosophy:

— http://www.iep.utm.edu/greekphi

— http://www.friesan.com/greek.htm

Moral Musings:

— http://bigbrownbat.org/moralmusings/

Select v.2 no.1 (May 1998)

Aristotle:

— http://www.ucmp.berkeley.edu/history/aristotle.html

— http://www.philosophypages.com/ph/aris.htm

Socrates:

— http://socrates.clarke.edu

— http://www.philosophypages.com/ph/socr.htm

Julia Annas:

— http://www.u.arizona.edu/ ~ jannas

Gilbert Harman:

— http://www.princeton.edu/ ~ harman

Martha Nussbaum:

— http://www.law.uchicago.edu/faculty/nussbaum

James Rachels:

— http://www.jamesrachels.org

— http://en.wikipedia.org/wiki/James_Rachels

Nicholas Smith:

— http://www.phil.mq.edu.au/staff/smith.htm

Stephen Toulmin:

— http://en.wikipedia.org/wiki/Stephen_Toulmin

— http://www.willamette.edu/cla/Rhetoric/courses/argumentation/Toulmin.htm

Bernard Williams:

— http://plato.stanford.edu/entries/williams-bernard/

Lesson Twenty-two

Moral Dilemmas . . . Can Ethics Help?

LEARNING OBJECTIVES

Upon completing this lesson, you should be familiar with the concepts contained in the lesson and be able to critically discuss:

- what a moral dilemma is.

- Kantian considerations for resolving a moral dilemma.

- utilitarian considerations for resolving a moral dilemma.

- virtue ethics considerations for resolving a moral dilemma.

- decidability and the resolution of moral dilemmas.

OVERVIEW

Moral dilemmas mark the gray areas of our understanding. They are cases where clear decisions seem impossible. Often such dilemmas are surrounded by black and white cases. Consider the simple case of being bald, a condition which seems to be without dilemma. But baldness may, if there is an event in which bald people get in for free, present a dilemma for those who have to decide who is bald and who isn't. In dealing with our practical lives, sometimes the most fundamental values by which we guide our lives give rise to moral dilemmas.

Suppose you are a young lady, 21 years old, about to graduate from an excellent university a year ahead of schedule. You are celebrating your graduation along with your acceptance to your first-choice medical school. A young man, two years older than you and in graduate school where you are, has been your boyfriend for almost two years. He's smart, seems to have fallen in love with you, has a great family, and your family seems to love him. You know now that with your moving away to go to medical school, he's going to ask you to marry him or at least to become engaged. When you first met you really liked him. But in your heart, you feel you just don't love him enough for such a step. "You're just being silly," your mother tells you. "You have some sort of unrealistic, Hollywood sense of romantic love. Life is about compromise. You'll never meet anyone who will love you more," she warns. You have a dilemma. In this case, some philosophers would debate whether or not this is a moral dilemma as opposed to a problem of self-interest. After all, it is

129

about your happiness; the worth of your life. However, consider the following additional twist of fate.

While you are struggling with these issues, you discover that you are pregnant. You've conscientiously practiced birth control, but it's never 100 percent. Your family has very conservative religious views about abortion and that is how you were raised, though you no longer actively practice their religion. The news of your pregnancy, you realize, would make your boyfriend ecstatic. Your family would heartily support you in postponing medical school a couple of years, and even then help you and your "husband" raise your baby. However, you don't want to have a baby now, not at this time in your life. You have so many plans, so many dreams, so many expectations. Now do you have a moral dilemma?

If you don't think this case presents a dilemma, let alone a moral dilemma, then use your imagination to find an area that does qualify. What if the young lady or the fetus has a heart or kidney condition, and carrying the pregnancy to term will negatively impact her entire life or the baby's life? Adjust the severity of the negative impact until you find the dilemma.

In this episode of *The Examined Life*, the moral dilemma faced arises out of the very sensitive issue of keeping premature infants alive. If a fetus makes it to approximately the 26th week, then it has a 50/50 chance of survival. If it survives, it has an 85 percent chance of leading a normal life, a 6 to 7 percent chance of a slight, but "manageable," handicap, and a 6 to 8 percent chance of a more severe handicap. The largest percentage of the cases seem to present no difficulty. Our moral system, whatever ethical theory you accept, directs us to save lives. However, when a handicap is involved, other issues urgently present themselves. As is often the case with moral dilemmas, they seem, fortunately, to constitute a small percentage of the total number of cases.

In this episode, one of the premature twins not only has significantly underdeveloped lungs, raising the issue of an adequate oxygen supply to a developing brain, but has also had brain hemorrhaging. How would a Kantian, a utilitarian and a person who espouses virtue-based ethics deal with this case? Do they come to differing or similar conclusions or do they each make a different but compatible contribution?

If one examines such a case according to the ethical theory advanced by Immanuel Kant, then issues regarding dignity and respect for the infant immediately arise. If a life threatening medical case were to arise concerning an adult, then for the Kan-

tian, the decision must remain with the adult who is capable of making an informed choice. As an autonomous being, the adult must be respected as an end in him or herself. However, the case of a child is different since a child is not autonomous and thus cannot choose.

For the child, one must evaluate the prospects of the child developing into an autonomous being. Would the child have the possibility of living a life autonomously, with dignity and respect? If so, Kant would direct parents and medical personnel concerned with the child's welfare to choose as if their own lives were involved. Could the type of action you are contemplating become a universal law, as Kant directed in the first formulation of the categorical imperative? If the child will live a short, painful existence severally retarded and only occasionally conscious, keeping it alive may not be right for a Kantian.

For a utilitarian, one acts so as to maximize overall utility for the greatest number of people. Hence, the principle of utility may arrive at a completely different conclusion since now one must also consider the consequences of the action on a large number of people. Contrary to Kant's view, a utilitarian primarily focuses on the consequences of an action. If one understands utility as pleasure, then at first glance at least, a life of some pleasure appears to outweigh no life at all, with dignity not being a central issue.

However, a serious application of the principle of utility requires many variables to be included in the calculation of the greatest good for the greatest number. It is not the child's potential good alone that counts. Once must consider the family of the child, the medical practitioners involved in the case, the medical support system, the community, even society as a whole, if indeed there are potential societal consequences. So, while the child may not have a life of dignity that is free of pain, the child's condition may galvanize society to commit resources for research. Now thousands of other infants will benefit. In this case, it is not obvious that despite the child's suffering, and the family's suffering, the child should be kept alive for these greater social purposes. While such an outcome might prove consistent with the principle of utility, it seems to violate Kant's second formulation of the categorical imperative to treat others only as an end and never as a means. Utilitarians and Kantians seem to face a moral dilemma.

In virtue ethics, the primary consideration is how this decision will affect the rest of one's life or the wholeness of one's life; one's character. Similar to the Kantian concern for the quality of the life that will develop, the virtue-based approach avoids the use of a specific principle or formula, as Kant offered with his categorical imperative. Since virtues are acquired partly through how we act, and then by acting a certain way we exercise and reinforce certain virtues, it becomes essential to these sorts of cases that we ask ourselves what sorts of virtues or vices this case would require in our decision making. We should not decide such cases in ways that foster immoral action by the family or medical staff. Rather, decisions should reflect virtuous actions.

Additionally, some philosophers claim that a virtue-based approach more readily recognizes the inherent conflict among the competing goods in our lives. As an approach, it is more willing to live with a degree of uncertainty, that there may be no formula whereby all rational beings come to an agreement. Instead, there is recognition that good arguments can be given supporting conflicting moral claims.

Moral dilemmas may be an essential feature of our lives. They may actually be an essential feature of our larger practical lives. A wise doctor knows that there are no cut and dried recipes for dealing with diseases and illnesses, as do engineers when designing space vehicles and teachers when transferring knowledge. Thus dilemmas are not just peculiar to morality. They are found in all areas of our practical life. As such, they force us to reflect, to clarify our understanding as we pursue wisdom in living our daily lives and becoming the characters we choose to be.

TEXT LINKS

Turn to Velasquez, *Philosophy: A Text with Readings*, eleventh edition, and read Section 7.6, "Can Ethics Resolve Moral Quandaries?" This section will provide you with a deeper understanding of the presence and significance of moral dilemmas in ethical theorizing. Important is the clarification of the notion that dilemmas do not render moral choices arbitrary. To further illustrate the role of dilemma and the significance of informed, reflective evaluation, this section includes an extended overview of some of the most important philosophical issues raised in the abortion debate and the debate regarding euthanasia. Given the conceptual refinement fostered by these debates, ask yourself if the issues of abortion and euthanasia will go the way of history in the twenty-first century, the way the issue of slavery and women's suffrage went in the twentieth century. In short, those are no longer significant moral debates as they have been solved.

KEY TERMS

Autonomous being: According to Immanuel Kant, a self-directed, rational being.

Consequentialism: A type of ethical theory that evaluates moral worth according to the nature of the consequences, which result from some action, policy, or practice.

Dilemma: A perplexity that seemingly confounds the understanding. Cases that do not seem to be clearly covered by available concepts or theories.

Ethics: The philosophical study of morality.

Kantianism: In this episode, refers to Immanuel Kant's ethical theory, which applies the categorical imperative as the moral test of action.

Moral dilemma: See definition of dilemma below.

Utilitarianism: Ethical theory which defines rightness as the maximization of non-moral good.

Virtue ethics: A non-formula-based ethical theory, which emphasizes character traits as excellences. For the ancient Greeks, it was through a life of virtue that *eudaimonia* (happiness) was possible.

SELF-TEST

Multiple Choice

1. The moral dilemma discussed in this case concerns saving
   a. starving children
   b. premature infants
   c. innocent victims in war
   d. dolphins from slaughter

2. According to the doctor in this episode, if an infant makes it to twenty-six weeks and is then born prematurely
   a. there is an extended medical discussion about saving the infant
   b. the parents are immediately consulted as to how the medical response should proceed regarding saving the life of the infant
   c. the parents and medical staff consult extensively about saving the infant
   d. they are always treated

3. To take a Kantian moral point of view in this sort of situation would be to place first priority on
   a. the dignity of and respect for the infant
   b. the best overall consequences of any course of action
   c. the character and whole life of the infant and those involved with it
   d. what seems the most natural course

4. To take a utilitarian moral point of view in this sort of situation would be to place first priority on
   a. the dignity of and respect for the infant
   b. the best overall consequences of any course of action
   c. the character and whole life of the infant and those involved with it
   d. what seems the most natural course

5. To take a virtues-based moral point of view in this sort of situation would be to place first priority on
   a. the dignity of and respect for the infant
   b. the best overall consequences of any course of action
   c. the character and whole life of the infant and those involved with it
   d. what seems the most natural course

6. Which of the following is Kant's categorical imperative?
   a. act so as to maximize the good for the greatest number
   b. act so as to maximize the good for yourself
   c. act so that the maxim of your action could be a universal law of nature
   d. act so that the maxim of your action exemplifies a virtue

7. Kant seemed to believe that good will and good intentions would automatically lead to
   a. the greatest good for the greatest number
   b. morally good actions
   c. wealth and prosperity
   d. happiness

8. Both Kantian and utilitarian ethical theories have been described as
   a. principle or rule-based theories
   b. virtue-based theories
   c. divinely-based theories
   d. overly concerned with character and emotion

9. Virtue ethics are sometimes contrasted to Kantian or utilitarian ethical theories in that they do not
   a. tell the individual what he or she ought to do
   b. do rely upon a fixed set of rules or principles
   c. do concern themselves with individuals but first with institutions
   d. deal with issues of happiness

10. Of the three ethical theories studied here, which one offers a clear-cut answer to the moral dilemmas faced in this episode?
    a. Kantian theories
    b. utilitarian theories
    c. virtue theories
    d. all offer critical considerations, but none offer an irrefutable answer.

True or False

These questions are only from the reading assignment in Velasquez, Section 7.6. Specific page references are given in the answer key.

11. The imperfect state of ethical theories demonstrates the importance of rejecting them.

12. Richard Hare adopts a utilitarian approach to ethics to prove that abortion is always morally right.

13. Jane English shows that abortion is always wrong by using a Kantian approach to ethics.

14. The natural law position on euthanasia argues that life is a fundamental good that should not be destroyed.

15. James Rachels uses both a utilitarian and a Kantian approach to ethics to show that active euthanasia is sometimes morally acceptable.

PARADOXICAL PURSUITS

You are the doctor heading up the medical team dealing with the troubled infant in this episode. What would you do? Do you agree with the doctor that every infant at 26 weeks should be saved? What if the baby was born retarded? What role would you allow the parents to play? Should you first approach the parents and ask them what role they wish you and your staff to play?

Still using the same case, consider the following scenario. The medical staff follows the virtues of conscientiousness, perseverance, and effectiveness. The parents follow sympathy and generosity, particularly concerning their other children. These virtues are in conflict in this case. How do you resolve such a conflict?

What is the most perplexing dilemma you can imagine? How would each of the three theories presented here resolve your problem? Which do you think is the most reasonable?

APPLIED PHILOSOPHY

Ask your family and friends what their most difficult moral dilemma is, then discuss possible solutions. Do they tend to follow one of the three theoretical approaches discussed in this episode? Do you find that males differ in their responses from females?

What moral dilemmas appear in today's newspaper? Are they genuine dilemmas or only apparent quandaries? How does the article tend to treat it? Check the editorial page and see what dilemmas are there and how the different writers treat them. Which ethical theories tend to dominate? Do male writers deal with moral issues in ways that are different from female writers?

Which of the three theories discussed do you think provides the most tangible, specific support for decisions? Do such decisions seem consistently moral?

What is, has been, or could be your most difficult personal moral dilemma? How would you attempt to resolve it? Which sort of ethical theory do you tend to intuitively adopt?

NET LINKS

Check out these Internet websites for additional relevant philosophical information. Remember the Internet is a web. Each of these listed sites is linked to other sites.

Philosophy Resources:

— http://www.earlham.edu/ ~ peters/phil-inks.htm

— http://www.epistemelinks.com

— http://www.refdesk.com/philos.html

— http://www.erraticimpact.com

Encyclopedia of Philosophy:

— http://www.iep.utm.edu

Philosophy Papers:

— http://philosophy.hku.hk/paper/info.php

— http://cogprints.org/view/subjects/phil.html

The Philosopher:

— http://www.the-philosopher.co.uk

Ethics Update:

— http://ethics.sandiego.edu

Greek Philosophy:

— http://www.iep.utm.edu/greekphi

— http://www.friesan.com/greek.htm

Moral Musings:

— http://bigbrownbat.org/moralmusings/
Select v.2 no.1 (May 1998)

Utilitarianism:

— http://www.hedweb.com/hedabuti.html

— http://philtar.ucsm.ac.uk/moral_philosophy/
utilitarianism.html

— http://www.bltc.net/ethics/utility.htm

Aristotle:

— http://www.ucmp.berkeley.edu/history/aristo-
tle.html

— http://www.philosophypages.com/ph/aris.htm

Jeremy Bentham:

— http://www.blupete.com/Literature/Biogra-
phies/Philosophy/Bentham.htm

— http://www.class.uidaho.edu/mickelsen/
Bentham.htm

— http://www.friesian.com/kant.htm

Immanuel Kant:

— http://www.philosophypages.com/ph/kant.htm

— http://www.hkbu.edu.hk/ ~ ppp/Kant.html

John Stuart Mill:

— http://www.philosophypages.com/ph/mill.htm

— http://www.utilitarianism.com/jsmill.htm

— http://ethics.sandiego.edu/theories/utilitarian-
ism/index.asp

Julia Annas:

— http://www.u.arizona.edu/ ~ jannas

Martha Nussbaum:

— http://www.law.uchicago.edu/faculty/
nussbaum/

James Rachels:

— http://www.jamesrachels.org

— http://en.wikipedia.org/wiki/James_Rachels

Nicholas Smith:

— http://www.phil.mq.edu.au/staff/smith.htm

Stephen Toulmin:

— http://en.wikipedia.org/wiki/Stephen_Toulmin

— http://www.willamette.edu/cla/Rhetoric/
courses/argumentation/Toulmin.htm

Lesson Twenty-three

What Justifies the State?

LEARNING OBJECTIVES

Upon completing this lesson, you should be familiar with the concepts contained in this lesson and be able to critically discuss:

- the social contract theory of the state.

- Hobbes' argument for absolutism.

- Locke's view of the state of nature and the purpose of government.

- Hume's attack on social contract theory.

- Rawls' new social contract theory of government.

- communitarian theories of government.

OVERVIEW

Government and its institutions—which we collectively refer to as "the state"—exercise an enormous amount of power over us. Government takes away our money through taxes, it can declare wars on other nations and use the draft to force us to fight in these wars, it can judge and imprison us, it can confiscate our property, force us to comply with its laws, and in numerous other ways it can interfere with our lives. What justifies the power of the state?

Perhaps the most widely known attempt to show that the state's power is legitimate is provided by what is sometimes called the social contract theory of the state. The social contract theory says that the state and its power are based on the consent of the people.

Social contract theory has a long history. It was discussed by Plato and Socrates, but it became prominent in seventeenth century England during the English Civil War when the legitimacy of government was hotly discussed. The seventeenth century British philosopher Thomas Hobbes argued that without government people live in a state of nature. In the state of nature people have none of the protections and advantages that government provides, and human life is "solitary, poor, nasty, brutish and short." To escape from this awful "war of all against all," people came together in the past and formed a government whose purpose was to protect us from harm. In particular, government is supposed to protect us from each other, since without government our greed would continually tempt us to use violence to steal from and attack each other. Hobbes felt that only an absolute government with unlimited power could succeed in keeping the peace, so he argued that government has absolute power over citizens. In the great debates that gave rise to the Civil War, Hobbes sided with those who supported an absolute monarchy.

John Locke, an eighteenth century British philosopher, agreed with Hobbes' view that the state is

135

the result of a compact that people make with each other when they band together in a state of nature and agree to form a government. However, Locke felt that people were not as aggressive in the state of nature as Hobbes said. In the state of nature, Locke argued, people have a natural moral sense that restrains them. Nevertheless, Locke claimed, in "the state of nature . . . the enjoyment of the property [man] has . . . is very unsafe, very insecure." Government is needed because in the state of nature even morally good people would have disagreements over their property and would need government to set the law, to arbitrate and interpret the law, and to enforce the law. Locke also disagreed with Hobbes' view that the power of government is absolute. On the contrary, Locke argues, the power of government is limited. Government has the power to do what it must to protect our "life, liberty, and estates, which I call by the general name 'property' " but it has no legitimate power beyond that. If a tyrannical government begins to exercise its power beyond these limits, Locke argued, then it has broken the original compact that brought it into existence, and the people then have a right to rebel and overthrow the government.

Locke's version of social contract theory influenced the founders of the American Republic, particularly Thomas Jefferson who wrote the Declaration of Independence. However, critics of the social contract theory, such as the eighteenth century philosopher David Hume, have argued that the theory is deeply flawed. In particular, he argued that governments are based on conquest and virtually none have been created by a contract. If we look back in our history, then, we will not find any evidence that people ever gathered in some state of nature to form government in the way that social contract theory claims. The social contract is a historical fiction.

Although the social contract tradition fell out of favor by the late eighteenth century, it was revived during the twentieth century in the work of the American philosopher John Rawls. In his major work, *A Theory of Justice*, Rawls agrees with Hume that the social contract is a historical fiction and that governments were never actually formed in this way. Nevertheless, he argues, social contract is a useful fiction because it shows us what governments ought to be like. Rawls invites us to see the social contract theory as an imaginary thought experiment. Imagine, he suggests, that the people of a society could all gather together to decide the rules they will live by in the future. Suppose, however, that none of them knows exactly what their situation in this future society will be like. No one knows, for example, whether they will be rich or poor, male or female, black or white, talented or untalented, young or old. In this original position where a veil of ignorance prevents them from knowing what they will be like in their future society, people will be forced to choose rules that are just to everyone no matter what they turn out to be like. The rules they choose, for example, will require that government not favor the rich over the poor, nor males over females, nor blacks over whites, since no one knows to which of these groups they will belong in the future.

The people in this original position behind the veil of ignorance, Rawls argues, will choose two principles by which any government must abide: "The first requires equality in the assignment of basic rights and duties, while the second holds that social and economic inequalities, for example inequalities of wealth and authority, are just only if they result in compensating benefits for everyone, and in particular for the least advantaged members of society."

Critics of the social contract tradition, however, have argued that it is not possible to know what people in the original position might choose. In fact, some have argued, if the people in the original position know nothing about themselves, they will be incapable of knowing what kind of rules they would choose to live by.

The most important critics of the social contract tradition in general and of Rawls in particular have been a group of philosophers characterized as communitarians. Communitarians such as Aristotle and Hegel have held that humans are social animals by nature, and that the state is a natural outgrowth of their social nature. Modern communitarians argue that the social contract tradition wrongly sees the state as a "necessary evil" needed to protect people from each others' antisocial tendencies. Georg Hegel argued, however, that humans can develop their abilities and potential only by living and growing within a state and absorbing its cultural values. The social contract theory, particularly as Rawls has developed it, ignores the vital importance of the community's cultural values and traditions. Rawls tells us that people are to choose their rules without knowing what groups they belong to. This means they must set aside the cultural values and traditions that they have absorbed. And it means that government must not support and nurture the values and traditions of any particular group. Communitarians argue that this is wrong. The state, through government, has a responsibility to nurture and protect the cultural values and traditions of the community. Without becoming immersed in the cultural values and traditions of their community, people could not develop their full humanity nor could they develop a full human character.

Modern communitarians like Michael Sandel claim that "to be flourishing human beings with the full range of capacities unfolded, requires that we engage in public life." In particular, he claims, as they mature, people must learn to rule themselves and their community. They must, in short, participate in the political life of their community. Only in this way will the individual acquire the full range of human abilities and capacities and thus be fully free. Both Aristotle and Hegel have made similar claims. Aristotle argues that a person who lives outside of society would have to be "either a beast or a god." Hegel claimed that "All the value a man has, all spiritual reality, he has only through the State." For the individual to develop fully, therefore, he must live in a state that has a flourishing political and cultural life. It is for this reason that the state must support the cultural values and traditions of the community.

It is on this point—that government must protect the cultural values of the members of the community—that communitarianism conflicts most deeply with the kind of liberalism supported by the social contract tradition. Liberals like Rawls claim that when individual rights conflict with community values, the rights of the individual take priority over the values of the community. Communitarians argue that the values of the community and of cultural groups should sometimes, at least, take priority over individual rights.

Critics claim that communitarianism raises a host of difficult questions. Should the government support the individual's right to free speech even when her speech is destroying the traditional cultural values of the nation? When the cultural values of one individual conflict with those of another individual, whose values should the government protect? Should government stop individuals from adopting lifestyles that the community's traditional cultural values condemn (for example, should government prohibit homosexual lifestyles in Christian communities)? Should government support only one group's cultural traditions and prohibit multiculturalism? In protecting traditional cultural values and ways of life, won't government often end up supporting cultural practices that are racist, sexist, or otherwise unjust?

Many modern communitarians, such as Michael Sandel, believe these issues can be solved through reasoned public debate. But what principles should we appeal to in such a debate: liberal principles of justice, which protect individuals, or communitarian principles, which support the community's cultural values and traditions? Perhaps Ronald Dworkin is right when he claims that at this time the need is for philosophy to find a way of reconciling the essential role of community values with the rights of the individual.

TEXT LINKS

- Read Velasquez, Philosophy: *A Text with Readings*, eleventh edition, read Chapter 8, Section 8.2, "What Justifies the State?" Velasquez provides discussions of the social contract tradition, including the views of Hobbes, Locke, and Rawls, and the criticisms of Hume and the communitarians Aristotle, Hegel, and Sandel. Section 8.2 also includes a discussion of feminist criticisms of social contract theory and a discussion of the social contract theory of Rousseau.

- Velasquez Section 8.1, "What Is Social and Political Philosophy?" provides an overview of the issues.

- Velasquez Section 8.5, "Historical Showcase: Marx and Rawls" includes discussions of the life and philosophy of Karl Marx and John Rawls with many excerpts from their original writings.

KEY TERMS

Communitarians: A group of philosophers who believe in the importance of belonging to a community of people who share a culture and a common set of values. Communitarians believe that the state must support and nurture the traditions the community values.

Egalitarianism: The belief that each citizen is an equal partner in the collective enterprise of self-government.

Original position: Corresponds to the state of nature in the traditional theory of the social contract. A hypothetical situation used by John Rawls to develop his concepts of justice.

Political obligation: The problem of why people should obey the state by agreeing to such commitments as paying taxes; and the question of the limits of such obligations.

Republicanism: People's ability to rule themselves; an idea that Aristotle valued.

Social contract theory: Justification for government's existence based on the idea that people agree to form a government simply to protect themselves from each other.

State of nature: In social contract theory, the situation of people who have no government.

Veil of ignorance: In *A Theory of Justice*, John Rawls refers to this as the situation that exists when a society must decide the rules of justice that will govern their future society without knowing what positions its members will hold in this new society.

SELF-TEST

Multiple Choice

1. The social contract theory holds that the power of the state is based on
   a. the power of a conquering army
   b. religious customs and beliefs
   c. consent of the people
   d. a community's cultural values and traditions

2. Thomas Hobbes believed that the best form of government was one that
   a. exercised limited powers
   b. exercised absolute powers
   c. remained neutral
   d. allowed people to be in a state of nature

3. John Locke argued that in a state of nature,
   a. life was "solitary, poor, nasty, brutish, and short"
   b. people lived under a "veil of ignorance"
   c. people will "seek out and . . . join in society with others"
   d. the very idea of government is "far beyond the comprehension of savages"

4. Who said "The greatest and chief end of men uniting into commonwealths, and putting themselves under government, is the preservation of their property"?
   a. David Hume
   b. John Locke
   c. Thomas Hobbes
   d. Thomas Jefferson

5. In his book, *A Theory of Justice*, philosopher John Rawls describes an imaginary thought experiment "characterized so as to lead to a certain conception of justice." Which two principles of justice did Rawls think people would agree to?
   a. equality in the assignment of basic rights and duties
   b. equality in the assignment of rights according to an individual's merits
   c. social and economic inequalities are just only if they result in compensating benefits for everyone, and in particular for the least advantaged members of society
   d. both a and c

6. Many communitarians have criticized Rawls' social contract theory because it
   a. ignores the vital importance of a community's cultural traditions
   b. undervalues an individual's rights
   c. encourages governments to protect cultural values and traditions
   d. fosters social inequalities

7. The idea that a person becomes actualized by subjecting personal interests to the larger common good of the State, thereby obtaining true freedom, was articulated by
   a. Georg Hegel
   b. John Locke
   c. Thomas Jefferson
   d. Karl Marx

8. The challenge to communitarianism that "individuals have rights and these are trumps over the social good," was expressed by whom?
   a. John Rawls
   b. Charles Taylor
   c. Michael Sandel
   d. Ronald Dworkin

Identify each of the statements below as representing one of the following:

a. liberalism   b. communitarianism

_____9. when individuals rights conflict with community values, the rights of individuals take priority

_____10. a society should be engineered so that people are free to do what they want, even when the majority thinks the lives they are creating for themselves are bad lives

_____11. without a larger community, political and cultural life cannot flourish

_____12. the state must remain neutral and allow individuals to choose their own values and ends

_____13. individuals have no social context outside the State

_____14. a requirement of human flourishing is engagement in public life

True or False

These questions are only from the reading assignment in Velasquez, Section 8.2. Specific page references are given in the answer key.

15. In *Leviathan*, Hobbes portrays humans as selfish, unsocial creatures driven by two needs: survival and personal gain.

16. For Rousseau, a group of wills is general when each member of the group aims at their own particular interests.

17. For Rawls government is not justified when it is the kind of government that we would choose in the original position.

18. Both Aristotle and Hegel argue that humans cannot develop fully unless they live in the state and that the state is more important than the individual citizen.

19. Feminists object that Hobbes, Locke, and Rousseau do not apply to women the idea that authority requires consent and that they assume only males enter the social contract.

PARADOXICAL PURSUITS

Suppose that since your first class in biology, you have been struck by the individuality and beauty of the human body. You have made a photographic study of nudes as they seem to capture most purely our uniqueness and vulnerability. Your photos seem to generate a deep sense of humility. Wanting to share your work, you organize a show for your community. While some citizens are initially very appreciative and supportive, others mount a protest that they do not want to be members of a community which allows the presence of pornography. They claim it violates the cultural traditions of their community. You argue that your work is not pornographic. But a committee of citizens insists that this is simply not a community that values public displays of nudity. You claim that individuals have rights to freedom of expression and freedom of assembly. Perhaps so, the response comes, but not to exhibit or gather to look at nudity in this community. You must move to another community, if you wish to show your work. Which rights should take precedence? How would you support your views if you were part of the social contract tradition? How would a communitarian look at this dispute?

You oppose abortion, as it is murder according your religious beliefs. Can you live in a society or community that protects the right to freedom of religion along with a right to choose abortion?

APPLIED PHILOSOPHY

Have a discussion with your friends and/or family about the rights of the individual versus the rights of the community. Topics that prove particularly controversial are those regarding victimless crimes. Discuss, for example, the legalization of drugs, prostitution, pornography, or gambling. Be sure there is sufficient information regarding psycho-pharmacology and black market influences upon the respective issues so that you have an informed discussion.

⤺

Organize a campus debate between representatives of the Libertarian, Democratic, and Republican parties. What views along the spectrum of individual rights versus community values are presented?

NET LINKS

Check out these Internet websites for additional relevant philosophical information. Remember the Internet is a web. Each of these listed sites is linked to other sites. By surfing you will soon be linked to a seemingly vast resource.

Philosophy Resources:

— http://www.earlham.edu/ ~ peters/phil-inks.htm

— http://www.epistemelinks.com

— http://www.refdesk.com/philos.html

— http://www.erraticimpact.com

Encyclopedia of Philosophy:

— http://www.iep.utm.edu

Philosophy Papers:

— http://philosophy.hku.hk/paper/info.php

— http://cogprints.org/view/subjects/phil.html

Political Philosophy

— http://en.wikipedia.org/wiki/Political_Philosophy

— http://people.brandeis.edu/ ~ teuber/polphil.html

— http://www.bu.edu/wcp/MainPoli.htm

— http://bubl.ac.uk/link/p/politicalphilosophy.htm

— http://members.tripod.com/ ~ batesca/aristotle.html

Communitarian Philosophy:

— http://en.wikipedia.org/wiki/Communitarianism

— http://plato.stanford.edu/entries/communitarianism/

Thomas Hobbes:

— http://oregonstate.edu/instruct/phl302/philosophers/hobbes.html

John Locke:

— http://plato.stanford.edu/entries/locke

Karl Marx:

— http://www.trincoll.edu/depts/phil/philo/phils/marx.html

John Rawls:

— http://www.iep.utm.edu/rawls

— http://oak.cats.ohiou.edu/ ~ piccard/entropy/rawls.html

Julia Annas:

— http://www.u.arizona.edu/ ~ jannas

Ronald Dworkin:

— http://its.law.nyu.edu/facultyprofiles/profile.CFM?personID = 19891

— http://en.wikipedia.org/wiki/Ronald_Dworkin

John Finnis:

— http://www.law.ox.ac.uk/jurisprudence/finnis.shtml

— http://en.wikipedia.org/wiki/John_Finnis

James Rachels:

— http://www.jamesrachels.org

— http://en.wikipedia.org/wiki/James_Rachels

Lesson Twenty-four

What is Justice?

LEARNING OBJECTIVES

Upon completing this lesson, you should be familiar with the concepts contained in this lesson and be able to critically discuss:

➤ the difference between retributive and distributive justice.

➤ egalitarian theories of distributive justice.

➤ justice based on merit.

➤ the socialist form of justice.

➤ Rawls' views on justice and social welfare.

➤ Nozick's views on justice as liberty.

➤ the problem of international justice.

OVERVIEW

Some people are rich, others are poor. Some revel in luxuries, have mansions, yachts, and leisure, while others labor all their lives and are still impoverished and starving. Some are born into wealth and high social standing, while others are born into lives of poverty and misery. Is this fair? Is it just that some should have so much, while others have so little? What, exactly is justice?

Often, when we think of justice, we think first of what philosophers call retributive justice. Retributive justice is the kind of justice that should prevail when punishments are fair. An ancient biblical rule for retributive justice is expressed in the saying, "An eye for an eye, and a tooth for a tooth."

But justice refers to more than just retribution. Justice also refers to how fairly or unfairly society distributes the benefits and burdens it produces. For example, some philosophers have argued that distributive justice requires some kind of equality among the members of society. Just as a pie is fairly distributed among children when it is cut in equal pieces, so also society's benefits and burdens are fairly distributed among people when they are distributed equally. Some philosophers take the notion of equality literally and argue that justice means that we should try to arrange things so that everyone is equally happy, or has equal wealth or equal income. These views are sometimes called egalitarian views of justice. Egalitarianism, however, runs up against the objection that if we give everyone exactly the same benefits no matter what they do, then we fail to reward those who choose to work harder or to do more than others. Yet if justice does not require strict equality, what does it require?

The ancient Greek philosophers Plato and Aristotle were among the first philosophers to discuss the concept of justice. Both of them lived in the city-state of Athens, which was then a highly stratified society. At the top were the male aristocrats. Below them, in order, were free men, then women, then children, and then, at the bottom, slaves. Writing in such a society, with its wide extremes of status and wealth, Aristotle claimed that justice is "treating equals equally, and unequals unequally, according to the differences between them." Aristotle seems to have meant that in a just society, benefits should be distributed according to what people merit. Those whose merits are equal should receive the same, while those who merits are greater than others, should receive more than those others. Individual merit might be determined by a person's social status, or, as Plato suggested, by a person's abilities and intelligence. The idea that justice depends on merit is still popular today, when many people believe that jobs, promotions, and awards should be distributed on the basis of individual merit.

But Aristotle's statement can be understood in a more general sense. Aristotle can be understood as saying that people should be treated the same when they are the same in all relevant respects, and treated differently when they differ in the relevant respect. When deciding how much to pay workers, for example, we might hold that they should be paid the same when they are the same in all relevant respects, but should be paid more when they work longer or work harder or work better than others.

Although Aristotle thought it was obvious that some should get more than others, he also felt that there was a minimum that all male citizens in a society should get. All male citizens should receive what they need to live a full human life, including an education and other material resources. Nevertheless, Aristotle did not feel that slaves—or women, for that matter—should receive what male citizens should receive.

Aristotle's notions of justice were transformed in the mid-nineteenth century by the German philosophers Karl Marx and Friedreich Engels. Society at that time was going through the throes of the Industrial Revolution. Capitalism rose and spread, and created tremendous inequalities of wealth. While workers labored in dirty noisy factories for long hours at miserable pay doing dehumanizing work, the capitalist owners of these factories grew extraordinarily wealthy and lived opulent, luxurious lives.

Marx adopted Aristotle's notion that people should have what they need to flourish and live fully human lives. However, Marx claimed that in every society workers failed to flourish. Throughout history every society has been divided into unequal economic classes in which those at the bottom were exploited by those at the top: slaves by masters, serfs by lords, and now wage workers by capitalist own-

ers. Justice would not prevail until workers took over the factories and other means of production, and did away with all social classes. In this new classless society, Marx wrote, everyone would receive what they needed to live fully human lives, and everyone would willingly contribute what they were able to contribute to society. In short, society would embody a new socialist form of justice: "From each according to his ability, to each according to his need."

In the early twentieth century, several countries, such as Russia, transformed themselves into communist nations modeled, they said, on the ideas of Marx. Some nations, while not becoming communist, nevertheless adopted many of the socialist ideas Marx had proposed, particularly the idea that society should respond to people's "need." The United States and other nations remained capitalist but developed social welfare programs to deal with poor people's need. In the 1960s American President Lyndon Johnson expanded welfare programs when he tried to eliminate poverty in what he called the Great Society.

In the 1970s, the American philosopher John Rawls developed a theory of justice that defended the new welfare state. Rawls' views on justice are based on an imaginary mental exercise. Imagine that the people of a society could all meet together. Imagine that none of them knew what kind of people they would be in their society. Nobody knows whether they will be rich or poor, male or female, black or white. Finally, imagine that they have to agree on the rules that will govern their society. Since nobody knows whether they will be rich or poor, they will want rules that are fair both to the rich and the poor; and since they do not know whether they will be male or female, black or white, they will choose rules that are fair to all these groups. In short, people in this imaginary situation are forced to be perfectly just. Justice, Rawls claims, is whatever people in this imaginary original position would choose.

What kind of rules would people in the imaginary original position choose? Rawls argued that they would allow the kind of inequalities that capitalism creates because these inequalities motivate people to produce more wealth. But they would want part of this wealth to be used to provide a minimum standard of living for the poor.

Rawls' ideas about justice—sometimes referred to as the liberal theory of justice—were immensely influential. But in many countries, such as England and the United States, a new conservativism emerged that was critical of welfare programs.

In this new conservative climate, the American philosopher Robert Nozick came forward and argued that Rawls' ideas on justice were mistaken. Justice, said Nozick, is really liberty: letting people keep what they make. Providing welfare for the poor like Rawls said, requires taking people's money through taxes to pay for government welfare programs. Such taxes are unjust because they take people's property against their will and so violate liberty. Nozick's views on justice—sometimes referred to as the libertarian theory of justice—also became highly influential.

For many philosophers, the views of Rawls and Nozick are the two most important modern views on distributive justice. Some argue that Nozick is right: taxing the rich to help the poor is unjustly stealing from the rich to give the poor what they have no right to. Others argue that Rawls is correct: justice requires that the rich help the poor.

If it is difficult to figure out what justice requires of the citizens of a single nation, it is even more difficult to figure out what justice requires among the many nations of the world. Some nations are rich, while others are poor. And within some nations the vast majority is impoverished and starving while a handful of elite live in luxury. Should rich nations provide the world's poor with resources that "empower" them to support themselves, such as job training or business loans? What, exactly, does justice require on a global level?

Perhaps justice on a global level means that the citizens of rich nations should provide aid to the impoverished citizens of poor nations. Rawls' views on justice seem to imply that such international aid is morally required and that governments should provide aid. Yet Nozick's views would oppose international government aid. For the citizens of rich nations would have to be taxed to pay for such aid, and those taxes would be a form of theft. Nozick's views imply that while citizens of rich countries can voluntarily contribute to international aid, governments should not force their citizens to pay for aid through taxes.

What, then, does justice mean on an international scale? Is Australian philosopher Peter Singer right when he claims that "we can't justify retaining luxuries for ourselves when others are starving"? If so, does justice demand that governments of rich countries tax their citizens to help the world's poor? Or is liberty such an important value that taxing the rich to help the poor is itself an injustice?

TEXT LINKS

🖎 Read Velasquez, *Philosophy: A Text with Readings*, eleventh edition, Section 8.3, "What Is Justice?" This section includes detailed discussions of the views of Aristotle, Marx, Rawls, and Nozick. Also included are discussions of the views of Plato and Mill on justice.

🖎 Velasquez, Section 8.5, "Historical Showcase: Marx and Rawls," provides an overview of the lives and philosophies of Karl Marx and John Rawls, with many selections from their writings.

🖎 Read Velasquez, Section 7.9, "Famine, Affluence, and Morality," where Peter Singer, in a classic article, discusses the obligations members of wealthy nations have toward members of poor nations.

KEY TERMS

Capitalism: An economic system based on profit, private ownership of the means of production, free markets, and wage labor.

Distributive justice: The justice that prevails when a society's benefits and burdens are fairly distributed.

Egalitarianism: The view that everyone should have the same benefits and burdens.

Inequality: A difference among people that results when some people have more or less of some good than others.

Liberal theory of justice: The view that justice requires equal civil rights, equal opportunity, and a minimum standard of living for all members of society.

Libertarian theory of justice: The view that justice requires leaving people free to do what they choose with what they have, so long as their activities do not directly harm others.

Merit: A quality that makes a person deserving of some benefit or advantage.

Retributive justice: The justice that prevails when wrongdoers are fairly punished.

Socialist justice: The view that justice should be based on the slogan: "From each according to his ability, to each according to his need."

SELF-TEST

Multiple Choice

1. According to Aristotle, justice is distributed in society
   a. equally
   b. to males only
   c. according to an individual's merit
   d. according to one's social status

2. Karl Marx's ideas of social justice drew on the ideas of
   a. Plato
   b. John Rawls
   c. Friedrich Engels
   d. Aristotle

3. Karl Marx based his analysis of capitalism on his study of
   a. Aristotle's *Ethics*
   b. governmental regulatory agencies
   c. labor unions
   d. economic growth

4. John Rawls' theory of social justice argues that all members of a society are equal based upon their
   a. moral status as individuals
   b. personal merits
   c. social status
   d. religious convictions

5. According to Rawls' theory of social justice, inequality can be reconciled with social justice by means of
   a. higher taxes
   b. a distribution of social resources through welfare programs
   c. elimination of taxes on private property
   d. voluntary charitable organizations

6. The ideas of Robert Nozick call for
   a. the redistribution of wealth through fair taxation policies
   b. the dismantlement of governments that tax citizens
   c. the elimination of taxation for the purposes of redistributing social resources
   d. social welfare programs to help the disadvantaged compete in capitalist economies

7. Empowerment is a type of economic aid that does NOT include
   a. direct monetary relief
   b. education programs
   c. small business loans
   d. job training programs

8. Large disparities in wealth can be harmful to societies that value a commonwealth, is a view held by
   a. Aristotle
   b. Karl Marx
   c. Michael Sandel
   d. none of the above
   e. all of the above

True or False

These questions are only from the reading assignment in Velasquez, Section 8.3. Specific page references are given in the answer key.

9. For Plato and Aristotle justice means that each should act and be treated according to his or her abilities, achievements, and social status.

10. Strict egalitarians reject the view that every person should be given exactly equal shares of society's benefits and burdens.

11. Mill argued that a just society is one that distributes benefits and burdens in whatever way will produce the greatest social benefits or the lowest social harms.

12. In *A Theory of Justice*, Rawls advocated "From each according to his ability, to each according to his need."

13. Robert Nozick argues that justice is respecting people's free choices.

PARADOXICAL PURSUITS

Jonathan Glover gives the example of three children and three pieces of cake and claims that if the pieces are distributed in anything but an equal manner, the children will be outraged. What if the child, whose birthday it is, asks for a larger piece? Is it obvious the others will be outraged? What if such an unequal distribution is part of this birthday culture? Is Glover inserting too much of his own "sentiments" or culture in this example, or do you agree with him, all things considered? If one child is large—that is, obese—and another quite small, would Marx claim that the larger child should get a larger piece of cake and the smaller child a smaller share, according to his principle, "From each according to his ability, to each according to his need"?

APPLIED PHILOSOPHY

Approximately every seven seconds someone dies of starvation on this planet. The funding sufficient to feed all of these starving people is currently being spent on pet food in the industrialized world. Is the having of a pet, when some people suffer so horrendously, immoral or unjust?

Organize a panel discussion on your campus or in your neighborhood, inviting experts in the fields of economics, business, philosophy, and religion to discuss the nature of the justice. Do opinions vary depending on the perspective of the panelist? How do the various views align with those theories presented in this episode?

NET LINKS

Check out these Internet websites for additional relevant philosophical information. Remember the Internet is a web. Each of these listed sites is linked to other sites. By surfing you will soon be linked to a seemingly vast resource.

Philosophy Resources:

— http://www.earlham.edu/~peters/phil-inks.htm

— http://www.epistemelinks.com

— http://www.refdesk.com/philos.html

— http://www.erraticimpact.com

Encyclopedia of Philosophy:

— http://www.iep.utm.edu

Philosophy Papers:

— http://philosophy.hku.hk/paper/info.php

— http://cogprints.org/view/subjects/phil.html

The Philosopher:

— http://www.the-philosopher.co.uk

Justice:

— http://plato.stanford.edu/entries/justice-distributive

Moral Musings:

— http://bigbrownbat.org/moralmusings/

Select v.2 no.1 (May 1998)

Moral Realism:

— http://www.bu.edu/wcp/Papers/TEth/TEthChew.htm

Poverty and Welfare:

— http://ethics.sandiego.edu/Applied/poverty/poverty.html

Retributive Justice:

— http://www.iep.utm.edu/punishme

World Hunger:

— http://ethics.sandiego.edu/Applied/worldHunger/

Ronald Dworkin:

— http://its.law.nyu.edu/facultyprofiles/profile.CFM?personID=19891

— http://en.wikipedia.org/wiki/Ronald_Dworkin

John Finnis:

— http://www.law.ox.ac.uk/jurisprudence/finnis.shtml

— http://en.wikipedia.org/wiki/John_Finnis

Gilbert Harman:

— http://www.princeton.edu/ ~ harman

James Rachels:

— http://www.jamesrachels.org

— http://en.wikipedia.org/wiki/James_Rachels

Lesson Twenty-five

What is Art?

LEARNING OBJECTIVES

Upon completing this lesson, you should be familiar with the concepts contained in this lesson and be able to critically discuss:

- the imitation or *mimesis* theory of art.

- Plato's criticism of art.

- the expressive theory of art.

- the formalist theory of art.

- Danto's "end of art" theory.

- the concept of an artworld and Dickie's theory of art.

OVERVIEW

From prehistoric times, when humans painted pictures of animals on the walls of caves, we have surrounded ourselves with art. We decorate our bodies with hand pretty clothes, neckties, jewelry, tattoos, piercings, hair dye, and cosmetics. We buy cars whose sleek looks attract us, hang up paintings that we feel are beautiful, and invest in furniture whose looks we enjoy. We play music and read literature that we find pleasing. We visit museums and art galleries, and go out to concerts and movies. Art seems

to be almost everywhere. But what is art? Some modern works of art seem ugly, shocking, even pornographic. Other works of art seem absurd, almost a joke. If you walk into a modern art museum you may see there, prominently displayed as a work of art, a urinal accompanied by the name of the artist Marcel Duchamp. What's the difference between Duchamp's urinal, and the urinal in the museum's restroom?

Early Greek philosophers claimed that art is essentially a form of imitation or *mimesis* (the Greek word for imitation). A work of art, they felt, is a copy or representation of some object. A good work of art presents us with a good imitation of reality, while poor art is art that does a poor job of imitating reality. From a good work of art a person could learn about reality. Poetry or drama that realistically portrayed human beings, for example, could give one insight into human nature and human character. This view of art prevailed for many centuries. During the middle ages, for example, many artists felt that in their art they were trying to represent a view of the real world around them or, perhaps symbolically, of some spiritual reality. As the centuries passed in Europe, artists gradually polished their techniques and became better at rendering lifelike imitations of the world around them.

But from the beginning, the view that art presents us with a copy or imitation of something was subjected to criticism. The ancient Greek philosopher Plato, for example, argued that art has little value precisely because it is merely an imitation. In Plato's view, the world around us is itself an imper-

147

fect imitation of the perfect ideas of goodness, truth, and beauty which exist in God's heaven. A work of art, then, is an imitation of an imitation. Instead of wasting our time contemplating the imitations that artists produce we should spend our time striving to contemplate reality itself. Plato's view is perhaps a precursor of the view heard often today that instead of wasting our time watching television or reading novels, we should live in the real world.

Almost all art up to the eighteenth century presented a more or less realistic imitation of reality. But a different kind of art emerged in the nineteenth and twentieth century. Much of the art of the nineteenth and twentieth century is more than a mere copy of reality: it seems intended to express feelings and emotions. Pablo Picasso's well-known painting "Guernica," for example, commemorates the Spanish civil war. The painting includes shapes that are recognizable representations of heads and limbs of animals, along with bodies and heads of people. But Picasso's painting seems to be an expression of the horror of war rather than an accurate picture of a war scene. Art here has become more an expression of feeling than an imitation of reality.

The expressive theory of art holds that art is essentially an expression of emotion, so that good art expresses emotion well, while bad art does so poorly. The expressive theory of art has its roots in the Romantic philosophers and artists of the eighteenth century who favored feelings over reason. They felt that through his feelings the artist can get in touch with the deeper significance of reality. In poetry and in painting, the aim of the artist was to capture and convey emotion: anger, horror, loneliness, sorrow, and joy. Much of the art of the late eighteenth and nineteenth centuries can be seen as prime examples of the expressive view of art.

Yet many twentieth century philosophers have not been satisfied by the expressive theory of art. As art became less and less representational during the late nineteenth and early twentieth centuries, it also often became less expressive. The work of the early twentieth century Dutch artist Piet Mondrian, for example, gradually became less representative and more abstract. Eventually, his paintings consisted entirely of grids of black lines on white with occasional rectangles of color.

A third theory of art emerged along with this new abstract art: the formalist theory of art. The formalist theory of art holds that art is nothing more than a form—an arrangement of lines, colors, and shapes—designed to please our artistic or aesthetic sense. The formalist theory holds that art should not be evaluated in terms of something outside of itself.

We should not evaluate art, for example, by its ability to imitate some other object, or by its ability to "express" some emotion. Art should be evaluated only in terms of its own parts and how these parts are arranged.

For many philosophers the three main theories of art—art as imitation, as expression, and as form—are mutually exclusive. But some philosophers feel that works of art from every age can be seen from all three perspectives. Even music can be appreciated as representational, as expressive, and as formal.

But twentieth century works of art have raised new questions about the nature of art. Early in his career, the French artist Marcel Duchamp produced art that could be understood as representational, expressive, and formalist. But in 1915 he declared that the artist has the right to choose any object whatsoever and turn it into an artwork by simply exhibiting it and calling it art. In museums and galleries Duchamp began to exhibit bottle racks, snow shovels, bicycle wheels, and even urinals as art. This "art" was not imitation, it did not express emotion, it was not an arrangement of elements into an aesthetic form, and it was certainly not beautiful. Was it even art? Duchamp's art seemed designed to teasingly raise the philosopher's question, "What is art?"

The American philosopher Arthur Danto has argued that art like Marcel Duchamp's indicates that art has now ended. The contemporary artist, Danto argues, no longer explores beauty, form, and feeling, but instead asks philosophical questions about art: What is art? Thus, the artist has become a philosopher, and his art is no longer art but a kind of philosophy. Art has ended and has been replaced by philosophy.

Not all philosophers agree with Danto. Recently the American philosopher George Dickie has suggested a new theory of art that can take into account the art of mavericks like Marcel Duchamp. Dickie points out that art is produced within an "artworld" that consists of artists, critics, audiences, museums, galleries, and patrons. Art, Dickie argues, is whatever an artworld accepts as art. Duchamp's urinals became art as soon as the artworld accepted them as art, in the same way that Andy Warhol's Brillo boxes, soup cans, and pictures of Marilyn Monroe became art when museums agreed to display them.

The French philosopher Jean-Francois Lyotard also disagrees with Danto. Lyotard claims that art has not ended because it can never be stopped. Lyotard believes that art is that which is sublime.

Art is what wakes you up, startles you, takes you by surprise. Art, in this sense, changes constantly with the times and is not fixed. It is perhaps a kind of game whose rules are continuously explored and criticized and thus subject to constant change.

TEXT LINKS

There is no assignment in Velasquez, *Philosophy: A Text with Readings*, eleventh edition, for this lesson.

KEY TERMS

Aesthetic: Related to the contemplation and evaluation of art.

Artworld: That group of artists, exhibitors, critics, audiences, patrons, and institutions that share an understanding and appreciation of what a particular kind of art is and how it should be evaluated. Different kinds of art (classical music, rock music, classical painting, pop art) may have different artworlds corresponding to them.

Expressive theory of art: The theory that a work of art is an expression of feeling or emotion.

Expressivism: The view that art is an expression of emotion.

Formalism: The view that a work of art must be appreciated solely in terms of its components and their arrangement, which may be called the "form" of the work of art.

Formalist theory of art: The theory that art must be defined and appreciated in terms of its own components and their arrangement, and not in terms of their relationship to something external such as emotions or objects in the world.

Imitation theory of art: The theory that a work of art is a representation or copy of some real or imaginary object in the world.

Representational: The quality of being a copy or reproduction of some object.

Mimesis: A Greek word meaning representation, or imitation.

SELF-TEST

Multiple Choice

1. Works of art concern philosophy because
   a. they challenge notions of reality
   b. they result from a search for deeper values
   c. they concern changing definitions of such values as beauty, form, and feeling
   d. all of the above
   e. none of the above

2. Which ancient philosopher did not think that art could teach us about reality?
   a. Aristotle
   b. Socrates
   c. Plato
   d. Heraclitus

3. The Greek word *mimesis* means
   a. formal
   b. conceptual
   c. representation
   d. reality

4. During which era did expression assume an important role in art?
   a. the Englightenment
   b. ancient Greece
   c. the Middle Ages
   d. the Romantic Era

5. Which modern artist is often cited as an example of a formalist painter?
   a. E. L. Kirchner
   b. Pablo Picasso
   c. Piet Mondrian
   d. Marcel Duchamp

6. Which of the following elements do not describe formalism?
   a. composition
   b. color
   c. arrangement
   d. representation

7. Which modern artist first introduced ordinary objects into a museum and called it art?
   a. Pablo Picasso
   b. Marcel Duchamp
   c. Andy Warhol
   d. Bruce Nauman

8. For the French artist Marcel Duchamp, when artists define what art is, art becomes
   a. formal
   b. realistic
   c. abstract
   d. conceptual

9. According to the American philosopher Arthur Danto, art ends when it becomes
   a. formalistic
   b. abstract
   c. a form of philosophy
   d. ugly

10. According to philosopher Marteen Doorman, art cannot end so long as it
    a. teaches us new ways of interpreting the world
    b. teaches us new ways of thinking about art itself
    c. continues to comment on other works of art
    d. all of the above
    e. none of the above

11. The American philosopher George Dickie argues that art
    a. has ended
    b. is essentially philosophy
    c. is whatever the artworld accepts as art
    d. should only be evaluated on formalist grounds

12. The French philosopher Jean-Francois Lyotard defines a type of art as "sublime." Which of the following works of art would qualify as an example of "sublime" art?
    a. the Cathedral of Chartres
    b. "Striped Concrete Posts" by Daniel Buren
    c. cave paintings in Lascaux, France
    d. all of the above
    e. none of the above

True or False

13. Aristotle claimed that art can imitate feelings and moral qualities.

14. The view that art is an expression of feeling was held by Plato.

15. The formalist theory claims that art should be judged by how its lines, shapes, and colors are arranged.

16. Danto held that "beauty is that which pleases when seen" and that a thing has beauty when its form has "integrity or perfection, due proportion or harmony, and brightness or clarity."

17. The philosopher George Dickie has argued that art is whatever the artworld says is art.

PARADOXICAL PURSUITS

Andy Warhol puts a picture of a soup can on the wall and it is viewed as not only art but significant art. You put a picture of a soup can on the wall, perhaps one that looks just like Mr. Warhol's. Is your picture art? What if you use a can of beans instead? Why is one art and the other not? Could soup can art also simply be in the cupboard? Must it be a photo?

What are the conceptual distinctions between noise, sound, and music?

APPLIED PHILOSOPHY

Visit the largest art gallery you have access to. Allow yourself enough time to start in the gallery with the oldest art in the collection then proceed, at an even pace, don't linger too long at one spot for this exercise, but walk slowly through all of the galleries until you reach the contemporary period. How has the subject or content of the works changed over time? Have the colors changed? Is there a marked difference in the framing of art works?

Visit the largest art gallery you have access to with a group of friends. Each of you take enough time to go your various ways and find that work which most appeals to you then regroup and visit each of your paintings and have each person explain why he or she chose the one they did. Do the explanations say more about the person or the chosen painting?

NET LINKS

Check out these Internet websites for additional relevant philosophical information. Remember the Internet is a web. Each of these listed sites is linked to other sites. By surfing you will soon be linked to a seemingly vast resource.

Philosophy Resources:

— http://www.earlham.edu/ ~ peters/phil-inks.htm

— http://www.epistemelinks.com

— http://www.refdesk.com/philos.html

— http://www.erraticimpact.com

Encyclopedia of Philosophy:

— http://www.iep.utm.edu

Philosophy Papers:

— http://philosophy.hku.hk/paper/info.php

— http://cogprints.org/view/subjects/phil.html

Aesthetics:

— http://en.wikipedia.org/wiki/Aesthetics

— http://aesthetics-online.org

Cognitive Science and the Arts:

— http://www.hfac.uh.edu/cogsci/index.html

Film and Philosophy:

— http://www.library.yale.edu/humanities/film/filmphi.htm

— http://plato.stanford.edu/entries/film

Lesson Twenty-six

What is the Meaning of Life?

LEARNING OBJECTIVES

Upon completing this lesson, you should be familiar with the concepts contained in this lesson and be able to critically discuss:

↝ mortality and the meaning of life.

↝ religion as a source of meaning.

↝ human progress as the source of meaning.

↝ Hegel and Marx, the systems builders.

↝ Kierkegaard, existentialism, and the three stages of life.

↝ Jean Paul Sartre and creating meaning.

↝ Simon de Beauvoir and the second sex.

OVERVIEW

For many people—including many philosophers—the most important philosophical question is this: Does human life have any meaning? The question presses in on us most urgently when we are confronted by our own death or the deaths of those we love. Our mortality raises the prospect that the end of human life is final and so puts an end to everything we are and were trying to be. If in the end it comes to nothing, what is the point of all our striving?

For many people it is clear that life has a meaning and that its meaning is defined by religion. Buddhism asserts, for example, that the purpose of human life is to experience liberation from the great wheel of death and rebirth by achieving enlightenment. The Judeo-Christian tradition holds that life has meaning because humans are part of a larger plan devised by God, and within this plan human life has a purpose.

But these religious responses to the meaning of life are of little help to the unbeliever. Some philosophers, for example, argue that Darwin's theory of evolution has shown that humans and human life have no purpose whatsoever. Others are unmoved by religious claims because they do not believe in God.

Although many people are unmoved by the idea that religion is the basis of meaning, they are often moved by another idea that has deep religious roots: the idea that human history is progressing toward a goal and that our lives acquire meaning by contributing to this progress of history. The German philosopher G.W.F. Hegel, for example, claimed that history is progressing toward an ever fuller achievement of human freedom and reason. Humans will achieve satisfaction and fulfillment to the extent that they are a part of this progress. Hegel's disciple, Karl Marx, agreed that history is moving toward a goal, but the goal is a society in which there are no economic classes and justice prevails for everyone. Early in the twentieth century Marx's vision gave many millions of people a sense of meaning and inspired them to establish communist economic and political systems.

But these systems have collapsed in most parts of the world. And for many people the idea of inevitable progress makes little sense in a world that is becoming increasingly polluted, and crowded and that has witnessed the atrocities of countless major wars. Disillusioned by the optimistic cosmic visions painted by religion and the philosophies of human progress, many people today seek meaning in the present moment. For many the meaning of life is focused on experiencing the pleasures and excitements of the moment.

But many philosophers argue that such attempts must end in disillusionment. The Canadian philosopher Charles Taylor, for example, argues that such a life will end in a "terrifying sense of meaninglessness, of emptiness, of nothing being really worthwhile."

Where, then, can the unbeliever and skeptic find meaning? If meaning cannot be found in an external vision, can it be found in ourselves and our inner choices? This is the view of existentialism.

Existentialist philosophy has its roots in the writings of the nineteenth century Danish philosopher, Soren Kierkegaard. Although a committed Christian, Kierkegaard was not a supporter of conventional Christianity. Kierkegaard, who died when he was only 42, felt deeply anguished throughout much of his life. His anguish, he felt, was the product of his realization that he alone was responsible for his life. He wrote: "Anguish reaches its full maturity when the child becomes aware that it will be able to choose what it wants to do with its life." Kierkegaard was convinced that each of us must choose for himself the truth by which he will live.

Kierkegaard described three lifestyles, which he called the aesthetic, the ethical, and the religious stages of life. The key to living authentically is to choose decisively among these, and to face up honestly to the shortcomings of each. The first stage, the aesthetic stage, is the lifestyle of a person who seeks meaning in the pursuit of enjoyment and satisfaction. The honest individual will eventually sense such a life is not enough and will freely commit himself to the second, the ethical, stage. In the ethical stage the individual finds meaning in trying to live morally. But eventually the individual will see that he is incapable of fully living up to all the demands of morality and may, in a "leap of faith," entrust himself to God, in "fear and trembling" because he

can never be sure that God will be there to save him. This leap is the choice of the third or religious stage of life.

A hundred years later, many of Kierkegaard's themes were taken up by the French philosopher Jean-Paul Sartre. Unlike Kierkegaard, Sartre was an atheist. But like Kierkegaard, Sartre argued that meaning is based on our free choices and commitments. Because there is no God, Sartre argued, there are no objective values and meanings that we must accept. Instead, humans have to create their own meaning by freely committing themselves to whatever actions or causes they choose. Sartre exhorted people to accept responsibility for whatever meaning they chose to give their lives, and to accept the anguish that goes along with it. To refuse to accept this responsibility is to live in bad faith.

Sartre's lifelong companion, the philosopher Simone de Beauvoir, accepted Sartre's view that meaning is created through our free choices. But in her book, *The Second Sex*, de Beauvoir argued that women did not have the same freedom to choose that men had: they were always relegated to being the sex that counts for less.

What can be learned from existentialism? Perhaps its most important insight is the idea that we ourselves are ultimately responsible for finding meaning in our lives. Although many philosophers reject Sartre's view that there are no objective values, most would agree that even objective values have to be chosen and passionately embraced if they are to be an authentic source of meaning for us. Even if I choose to commit myself to following some religious or ideological authority, I am responsible for my choice and cannot blame it on that authority.

TEXT LINKS

👉 Read Velasquez, *Philosophy: A Text with Readings*, eleventh edition, Chapter 9, "Postscript: The Meaning of Life." In this Chapter Velasquez discusses religious views on the meaning of life, the views of Hegel and Marx that meaning is based on the progress of history, the view that life has no meaning, and the views of Kierkegaard and Sartre that meaning is chosen.

👉 See Velasquez Section 8.5 for a detailed discussion of the life and philosophy of Karl Marx.

KEY TERMS

Aesthetic stage of life: In Kierkegaard's philosophy, a lifestyle characterized by the pursuit of his own satisfaction and enjoyment.

Ethical stage of life: In Kierkegaard's philosophy, a lifestyle characterized by a commitment to a life of moral duty that admits no exceptions in one's own favor.

Religious stage of life: In Kierkegaard's philosophy, a lifestyle characterized by a trust in God that is not based on reason but on a "leap of faith."

SELF-TEST

Multiple Choice

1. The idea that man has no purpose is central to the ideas of
   a. Karl Marx
   b. G.W.F. Hegel
   c. Soren Kierkegaard
   d. Charles Darwin

2. The idea that human history is progressing toward a goal of fuller achievement of human freedom and reason is central to the philosophy of
   a. Karl Marx
   b. G.W.F. Hegel
   c. Jean-Paul Sartre
   d. Charles Darwin

3. The ideas of Karl Marx are best described as
   a. Darwinian
   b. existentialist
   c. Hegelian
   d. Aristotelian

4. The view that meaning in life can be found in ourselves and our inner choices is associated with which philosopher?
   a. Jean-Paul Sartre
   b. G.W.F. Hegel
   c. Soren Kierkegaard
   d. Simone de Beauvoir

5. What state of mind did the philosopher Soren Kierkegaard regard as modern man's symptom of the awareness that the meaning of life cannot be found in external sources?
   a. misery
   b. apathy
   c. anguish
   d. happiness

6. Which existentialist philosopher describes three stages through which a seeker of meaning in life passes?
   a. Simone de Beauvoir
   b. Soren Kierkegaard
   c. Jean-Paul Sartre
   d. Martin Heidegger

7. Which statement best summarizes the stand taken by Danish philosopher Soren Kierkegaard on the existence of God and man's purpose in life?
   a. God has devised a plan within which man's purpose lies
   b. man must put his faith in God's purpose for man
   c. man must create God by his own choice in order to know the meaning and purpose of life.
   d. God does not exist and man has to find his own purpose in life

8. The French philosopher Jean-Paul Sartre shares with Soren Kierkegaard the idea that
   a. meaning in life is based upon our free choices and commitments
   b. we must entrust ourselves in a "leap of faith" to a higher power
   c. the seeker for meaning of life passes through aesthetic, ethical, and moral stages
   d. human beings are condemned to be free

9. According to Jean-Paul Sartre, to live in "bad faith" is to
   a. choose a conventional path in life
   b. choose a religious path in life
   c. refuse the anguish that goes along with meaning that one chooses in life
   d. accept the consequences of the choices one makes in life

10. The French philosopher Simone de Beauvoir focused her writings on which central idea of existentialism?
    a. that the individual has no essential nature
    b. that the individual must freely choose values and meanings in life
    c. that human beings are condemned to be free
    d. that human beings must accept the anguish that accompanies freedom

True or False

These questions are only from the reading assignment in Velasquez, Chapter 9. Specific page references are given in the answer key.

11. For Albert Camus, "the meaning of life is the most urgent of questions."

12. One theistic response to the meaning of life claims that human life has meaning because humans are part of a larger plan or order devised by God.

13. Karl Marx wrote that "the history of the world is none other than the progress of the consciousness of freedom."

14. According to the nihilist, the end of the world is nigh.

15. For Kierkegaard, the move to the religious stage is a commitment not to a rational principle, but to a relationship with a person.

PARADOXICAL PURSUITS

J. L. Austin claimed that the question, "What is the meaning of life?" commits the fallacy of Asking Nothing In Particular. Take, for example, the questions "Is shooting good?" or "What is the purpose of writing?" To ask such questions without a specific context does not allow for any genuine answer. Thus, regarding the meaning of life, if the question is made specific, such as what is the meaning of my typing this Paradoxical Pursuit right now, the question can be readily answered with a specific, true response. The meaning or purpose of this moment in my life would include such claims as, this is how I support my family, pay the mortgage, buy clothing, this is part of my profession and the like. So, do you agree with Austin that to simply ask, "What is the meaning of life?" appears to pose a profound intellectual problem only because the question is not a genuine question?

⫷

In a world with zealous Hindus, Moslems, Christians, Buddhists, and Jews, can religion give a genuine, non-arbitrary meaning to life? Among these world religions are monotheistic, polytheistic, and atheistic views regarding the existence of a god, some gods, and no god. Isn't someone wrong and thus some view ultimately misguided?

⫷

Does our mortality and inevitable death make life meaningless or meaningful? If there is life after death, how does the prolonging of life make this life, or even that future life, meaningful? How does length of life make a life meaningful or meaningless?

⫷

If, as Robert Solomon claims in this episode, the meaning of life is to be found in living according to the grandest of passions, then what is the role of reason and rationality as these are traditionally contrasted with the passions?

⫷

How is it possible for an individual to give his or her life meaning and that meaning not be, in some sense, arbitrary?

APPLIED PHILOSOPHY

Would you describe your life as meaningless, empty? If not, is this because of your age and, perhaps the fact that your youth has in a sense literally blinded you to your mortality? Or if age is not a relevant consideration, and your life is meaningful, what is the meaning of life for you?

⫷

Given Kierkegaard's distinctions between the aesthetic, ethical, and religious stages of life, which most typifies your life? Lennart Koskinen characterizes, as does Kierkegaard, the religious stage as the highest stage. What do you think this means and do you agree? Which would you characterize as the highest and why?

⌒

Organize a panel discussion in your neighborhood or on your campus, inviting experts in philosophy, business, physical education, administration, and religion for a colloquium on "The Meaning of Life." Do the various responses of participants follow Kierkegaard's distinctions among life's attitudes?

NET LINKS

Check out these Internet websites for additional relevant philosophical information. Remember the Internet is a web. Each of these listed sites is linked to other sites. By surfing you will soon be linked to a seemingly vast resource.

Philosophy Resources:

— http://www.earlham.edu/ ~ peters/phil-inks.htm

— http://www.epistemelinks.com

— http://www.refdesk.com/philos.html

— http://www.erraticimpact.com

Encyclopedia of Philosophy:

— http://www.iep.utm.edu

Philosophy Papers:

— http://philosophy.hku.hk/paper/info.php

— http://cogprints.org/view/subjects/phil.html

Metaphysics:

— http://plato.stanford.edu/entries/aristotle-meta-physics/

— http://en.wikipedia.org/wiki/Metaphysics

Appendix

Answer Key for the - Self Test

LESSON 1: WHAT IS PHILOSOPHY?

1. d (25–26)
2. b (4–6)
3. a (4–6)
4. d (synthesis)
5. b (26–28)
6. a (4–6)
7. d (24)
8. c (24–26)
9. c (6–8)
10. d (Video)
11. True (8)
12. False (22–24)
13. False (18–21)
14. True (24–26)
15. False (25–28)

LESSON 2: WHAT IS HUMAN NATURE?

1. b (52)
2. d (53–54)
3. b (54)
4. a (Video)
5. d (54, 62)
6. a (57)

LESSON 2: WHAT IS HUMAN NATURE?
(continued)

7. c (58–59)
8. a (59)
9. c (63)
10. b (62–63)
11. a (67)
12. False (53–54)
13. True (58)
14. False (63)
15. False (69)
16. True (67)

LESSON 3: IS MIND DISTINCT FROM BODY?

1. b (76)
2. b (79)
3. b (Video)
4. a (77)
5. a (Video)
6. a (79)
7. a (81–82)
8. a (82)
9. d (84)
10. c (85)

159

LESSON 3: IS MIND DISTINCT FROM BODY? (continued)

11. a (Video)
12. a (78)
13. True (76)
14. True (76)
15. True (80)
16. True (82)
17. True (82–83)

LESSON 4: IS THERE AN ENDURING SELF?

1. b (88)
2. a (89–90)
3. d (Video)
4. a (91–92)
5. c (92)
6. a (96)
7. d (96)
8. a (Video)
9. a (Video)
10. b (Video)
11. False (89)
12. True (89–90)
13. True (92)
14. False (92)
15. True (95)

LESSON 5: ARE WE SOCIAL BEINGS?

1. b (100)
2. c (102–103)
3. b (101–103)
4. a (99–101)
5. b (101–103)
6. a (99–101)
7. b (Video)
8. b (102)
9. b (Video)
10. a (100)

LESSON 5: ARE WE SOCIAL BEINGS? (continued)

11. False (100)
12. True (100–101)
13. False (101)
14. True (102)
15. False (100, 104)

LESSON 6: WHAT IS REAL?

1. c (136)
2. b (145)
3. a (153)
4. d (141–142)
5. d (139)
6. a (140)
7. d (146–147)
8. b (145)
9. d (153)
10. a (164)
11. True (136)
12. False (144–145)
13. True (148)
14. False (153–155)
15. True (160)

LESSON 7: HOW DO WE ENCOUNTER THE WORLD?

1. c (Video)
2. b (171)
3. a (171)
4. c (175)
5. b (Video)
6. a (174)
7. a (Video)
8. a (Video)
9. True (174)
10. True (179)
11. True (176)
12. False (181)
13. False (183)

LESSON 8: DO WE HAVE FREE WILL?

1. c (191–192)
2. b (193)
3. a (190)
4. a (189)
5. d (Video)
6. a (192–193)
7. c (191)
8. b (Video)
9. a (189–190)
10. a (189–190)
11. b (189–190)
12. b (189–190)
13. b (189–190)
14. a (189–190)
15. False (190)
16. False (190)
17. False (193)
18. False (193)
19. False (194)

LESSON 9: IS TIME REAL?

1. d (Video)
2. c (Video)
3. a (199)
4. a (199)
5. c (200)
6. a (198)
7. d (197–198)
8. a (Video)
9. a (Video)
10. False (197)
11. True (197–198)
12. False (200)
13. True (202)

14. True (202)

LESSON 10: DOES GOD EXIST?

1. d (228)
2. a (228–229)
3. a (Video)
4. c (233)
5. d (235)
6. a (248)
7. c (232)
8. b (236)
9. a (243–244)
10. True (226)
11. True (228)
12. False (236–237)
13. True (240)
14. False (247)

LESSON 11: CAN WE KNOW GOD THROUGH EXPERIENCE?

1. c (255)
2. d (Video)
3. a (Video)
4. a (255–256)
5. d (Video)
6. c (Video)
7. c (256–257)
8. b (Video)
9. d (Video)
10. b (252)
11. c (Video)
12. True (251)
13. True (256–257)
14. True (260)
15. True (261)
16. True (263)

Lesson 12: Is Reason the Source of Knowledge?

1. b (300)
2. a (300)
3. d (Video)
4. a (304–305)
5. d (307)
6. c (304–305)
7. a (308)
8. a (Video)
9. a (Video)
10. b (308)
11. c (309–310)
12. b (309–310)
13. c (311)
14. True (303–304)
15. True (306)
16. False (308)
17. True (309–310)
18. False (311)

Lesson 13: Does Knowledge Depend on Experience?

1. d (313)
2. b (Video)
3. c (Video)
4. b (318–319)
5. d (319–320)
6. d (321)
7. b (321–322)
8. a (354)
9. d (355–356)
10. b (325–326)
11. c (Video)
12. a (Video)
13. b (Video)
14. a (Video)
15. b (Video)

Lesson 13: Does Knowledge Depend on Experience? (continued)

16. a (Video)
17. True (313)
18. True (314)
19. False (317)
20. False (321)
21. True (325)

Lesson 14: Does the Mind Shape the World?

1. d (327)
2. a (327)
3. a (327)
4. b (328–329)
5. d (328–329)
6. a (331–334)
7. c (Video)
8. a (328)
9. d (336)
10. b (Video)
11. c (Video)
12. False (327)
13. False (327)
14. True (335)
15. False (335)
16. True (336)

Lesson 15: How Does Science Add to Knowledge?

1. c (339)
2. a (340)
3. b (339)
4. d (343)
5. a (343–344)
6. d (345)
7. a (345–346)
8. a (345–346)
9. b (345–346)

LESSON 15: HOW DOES SCIENCE ADD TO KNOWLEDGE? (continued)

10. b (345–346)
11. c (Video)
12. a (Video)
13. True (339–340)
14. True (340)
15. True (342)
16. False (343)
17. True (345)

LESSON 16: DOES SCIENCE GIVE US TRUTH?

1. c (378–389)
2. a (378)
3. b (385–386)
4. c (389)
5. a (400–401)
6. b (401)
7. c (399)
8. a (Video)
9. c (Video)
10. a (Video)
11. b (Video)
12. d (Video)
13. True (378–379)
14. True (381)
15. True (385–386)
16. False (399)
17. True (400–401)

LESSON 17: ARE INTERPRETATIONS TRUE?

1. c (406)
2. b (406)
3. d (406)
4. d (Video)
5. c (407)
6. a (407)
7. d (407)
8. a (407)

LESSON 17: ARE INTERPRETATIONS TRUE? (continued)

9. c (410)
10. a (408)
11. a (408)
12. d (409)
13. True (405–406)
14. False (406)
15. True (407)
16. False (409)
17. True (410)

LESSON 18: IS MORALITY RELATIVE?

1. c (Video)
2. b (Video, 435–436)
3. d (Video)
4. a (435–436)
5. b (Video)
6. a (Video)
7. b (Video)
8. b (Video)
9. a (435–436)
10. d (Video)
11. True (434)
12. False (434)
13. True (435)
14. False (435–436)
15. True (436)

LESSON 19: DOES THE END JUSTIFY THE MEANS?

1. b (Video)
2. c (441)
3. b (Video)
4. a (442)
5. d (Video)
6. a (437)
7. c (Video)
8. c (Video)

LESSON 19: DOES THE END JUSTIFY THE MEANS? (continued)

9. b (Video)
10. d (Video)
11. a (Video)
12. False (438)
13. True (440)
14. False (442)
15. False (443)
16. False (445)

LESSON 20: CAN RULES DEFINE MORALITY?

1. d (456)
2. a (456)
3. c (456)
4. d (457)
5. b (456)
6. a (457)
7. a (460)
8. c (459)
9. b (461)
10. True (447–448)
11. True (450)
12. False (456)
13. False (460)
14. True (460)

LESSON 21: IS ETHICS BASED ON VIRTUE?

1. d (469)
2. b (Video, 470)
3. a (Video)
4. c (Video)
5. a (Video, 468–469)
6. a (Video, 468–469)
7. c (Video, 470)
8. c (Video)
9. a (Video)
10. c (Video)
11. True (468–469)

LESSON 21: IS ETHICS BASED ON VIRTUE? (continued)

12. False (469–470)
13. False (471)
14. False (478)
15. True (479)

LESSON 22: MORAL DILEMMAS . . . CAN ETHICS HELP?

1. b (Video)
2. d (Video)
3. a (Video, 484)
4. b (Video, 484)
5. c (Video, 484)
6. c (Video)
7. b (Video)
8. a (468–469)
9. b (468–469)
10. d (489)
11. False (489)
12. False (487)
13. False (487–488)
14. True (490)
15. True (491–492)

LESSON 23: WHAT JUSTIFIES THE STATE?

1. c (520–521)
2. b (521–522)
3. c (523)
4. b (523–524)
5. d (Video)
6. a (530)
7. a (531–532)
8. d (Video)
9. a (Video)
10. a (Video)
11. b (Video)
12. a (Video)
13. b (Video)

LESSON 23: WHAT JUSTIFIES THE STATE? (continued)

14. b (Video)
15. True (521)
16. False (526)
17. False (529)
18. True (531–532)
19. True (534)

LESSON 24: WHAT IS JUSTICE?

1. c (Video)
2. d (Video)
3. d (Video)
4. a (Video)
5. b (550)
6. c (552)
7. a (Video)
8. e (Video)
9. True (542)
10. False (544)
11. True (546)
12. False (548)
13. True (552)

LESSON 25: WHAT IS ART?

1. d (Video)
2. c (Video)
3. c (Video)
4. d (Video)
5. c (Video)

LESSON 25: WHAT IS ART? (continued)

6. d (Video)
7. b (Video)
8. d (Video)
9. c (Video)
10. d (Video)
11. c (Video)
12. d (Video)
13. True (Video)
14. False (Video)
15. True (Video)
16. False (Video)
17. True (Video)

LESSON 26: WHAT IS THE MEANING OF LIFE?

1. d (Video)
2. b (603–604)
3. c (604)
4. c (607–608)
5. c (Video)
6. b (608)
7. c (608–609)
8. a (609)
9. c (Video)
10. a (Video)
11. True (598)
12. True (601)
13. False (604)
14. False (606)
15. True (609)